MW00948435

To My Family,

my backbone,

And for football fans everywhere

Chapter 1

Overlooking the area of the Blue Hills, from the top of his familiar trail, Chris viewed the rising mist. His face and shirt covered in perspiration, he had come to feel this beautiful area as a beginning of even bigger things to come. He bent down to put his hands through the thick browning grass, a cool morning breeze running through his hair. Each time he touched this grass he thought of the smell of fresh cut grass on Saturdays during warm-ups before each game. He would always gather a few blades from each field he played. This ritual had reminded him of Gladiators and soldiers before him who would do the same to feel a part of the world around them. Rubbing the grass into his hands always helped Chris turn on the football switch. Once he was able to feel the grass between his fingers, he was able to visualize himself crashing into opposing Quarterbacks and dislodging the ball for a forced fumble. He could imagine picking up the pig skin and returning it to the house for a winning touchdown!

Chris stood for a moment viewing the expanse of the landscape before him and thought about the daunting task before him, Training Camp! Just a few short months removed from his final collegiate game. A Bowl game in which he recorded two sacks, a forced fumble, and twenty tackles. For a middle linebacker, a game for the ages. Chris could not help but smile at the thought of bringing his skills to Sunday on the Gridiron. One never to shy away from a challenge, he had heard the doubters his whole life. He could not help but feel that fire in the pit of his stomach, "I will prove them all wrong!" From his third grade teacher who told him he would never amount to anything, to his Pop Warner coach who told him he was to slow and not mean enough to play football, he would show them all. His parents who should have supported him in these endeavors had yet to see him play a game, even though he would leave tickets for each game for them.

Chris had come to realize if he wanted to make it to the Show, he would have to go it alone! He had fought and scratched his way in each school to be an outstanding student and athlete. His parents had at least instilled this work ethic in their son. On the field he had an uncanny ability to channel all of his anger and aggression towards anyone who stood in his way, creating an explosive player. Always confident in his ability and love for the game, he did have some questions in the back of his mind. The most pressing of which, "will my weight ever catch up to my height?" By junior year in high school, Chris stood 6' 2". This was a great height for a middle linebacker, but at 170 pounds, he was not the most imposing figure on the field. However, with the help of a friend who was a wrestler, he learned how to bulk up without losing speed.

When two a days opened up during his senior year, his weight was up to 220 pounds. His football life began to soar from this point on, without loss of speed and now terrific size he became unstoppable. Even though he attended a small Massachusetts school, he had scouts at every game. The scouts always had the same reaction; they loved his size, strength, and speed. The only negative against Chris was the level of competition he was playing against compared to other candidates playing larger, stronger schools. Chris thought he had answered this during his senior year in his division's super bowl, in which he had a terrific game against a much larger school. The issue that arose during the game was one of leadership. Even with him playing well, his defense gave up over three hundred yards through the air. Being the quarterback of the defense meant people looked to him for answers, questioning his ability to make his teammates better.

The question of leadership was quickly put to rest during his college career. As a four year starter he quickly became known as, Sargent Slaughter, for his affinity for the former professional wrestler. Also, because he would lead his team and others would follow, destroying opponents in his wake! He was relentless and demanded his teammates follow his lead. As his college career came to a close and it became apparent that he would make it to the next level, he dared let himself dream of playing in his Massachusetts back yard, for the Massachusetts Bay Marauders. He would sit after workouts and think of his name being called to be drafted by the Marauders. He recalled college scouts sitting in the stands busily writing in their notebooks after each play he made.

During his college career he was under more scrutiny, each play dissected and results put into a computer. By his senior year you would have thought him more of a video game rather than a college ball player. In spite of being under a microscope Chris thrived, once the helmet went on and he stepped on that field, it was all business and he went to work! It was his work ethic and attention to detail that had put him over the top during team interviews as part of the predraft process. His leadership no longer in question, his skills and size were perfect for the league. He just had to assure teams he would be able to handle the rigors of the NAFL (North American Football League) season on and off the field. The interview process was grueling but one thing each person interviewing him learned is Chris had the most determination and he was one of the hardest workers they had ever seen. One final question remained, where he would go in the first round and to whom!

In the days leading up to the draft questions began swirling around where the quarterbacks would go in the draft, one prospect in particular, Ray Riley, had been projected to go as high as the number four pick. However, Ray did not do well during his Pro Day and his stock began to fall. Many teams who did not think they could get the franchise quarterback they needed were now jockeying for position, therefore opening up the draft board. By draft day, no one knew quite what was going to happen. Chris' agent had told him to stay home in spite of being invited to attend the draft because the Green Room was going to be such a mess. Chris followed the advice and waited to see what would take place.

On draft day teams scrambled to adjust their big boards as prospects were quickly taken. Chris sat at home in anticipation of that remarkable phone call that said, you had been selected. Toward the middle of the first round, however he began to get nervous. His agent had told him to expect to be a mid-round pick. Chris had been watching the draft since he was a young man and was quite aware of the uncertainty of the draft. Two quarterbacks, two defensive backs, offensive linemen, and defensive linemen, made up the picks so far, no linebackers. He had been projected behind a couple of outside linebackers because many teams needed pass rushers. As each name went off the board he thought he would end in the second round. His agent assured him this would not happen. When the call came, at the end of the first round by the Massachusetts Bay Marauders, Chris was beside himself. He had been a Marauders fan his whole life, being from the area this was a dream come true. When the coach got on the phone and welcomed him to the team, it still seemed like a dream. In later years, he couldn't even recall what he had said to the coach that day!

Ever since draft day Chris had been working with a fitness trainer to be prepared for Training Camp. Marauders Coach, Ray Ridel was known for his particularly brutal training camps. He wanted to be prepared for anything the coach might throw at him. The players association had purposefully changed many things as a result of many coaches no nonsense approach to training camp and practice. With that said, Coach demanded you be in excellent shape even before you arrived at camp. Chris, being a rookie, was not about to have his first training camp be his last. On draft day he was able to run the forty in 4.47 seconds and weighed in at 260 pounds. The coach had told him he wanted him to report to camp at 250 and not to lose any speed.

Chris and his trainer complied with the coaches wishes by working less with weights. He instead worked on a Cross training regimen to work on his explosiveness, speed, and strength. Chris had always been a workout freak and had been bulking up in anticipation of a hard camp. One in which he was sure to lose some weight and bulk due to adverse summer conditions. The Boston area for all it's beauty during the summer, could also be known for it's extremely hot and humid days during the dog days of summer. He would be ready for whatever coach threw at him in camp. As Chris turned from the top of the hill and ran back down, he began to think of how far he had come but reminded himself he had a lot further he wanted to go.

Chris grabbed his suitcase from the SUV and began to walk eagerly toward the dormitory he had been assigned. He reached his destination and opened the door; it felt to him that he was a freshman in college once again. The room, a mixture of simple furniture, was not very bright with a subdued feel to it. As soon as Chris entered the room he immediately felt the need for more space. He was to spend this camp with his mentor, Zack Johnson, an eleven year veteran whom Chris would be in competition for the position of middle linebacker. Zack had welcomed him to the team during OTA's and had been a little stand offish. Chris could easily understand that Zack viewed him as a threat to his lively hood. As a Professional football player this was going to be quite an adjustment for Chris, who knew he had that deer in the headlights look during OTA's. How could he not feel this way, he was playing on the field against many of the players he grew up watching.

During tackling drills, Zack welcomed the rookie to the league by planting him in the ground repeatedly. To Chris' credit he continued to get up and face off against his childhood idol. During every drill and every meeting it was easy for Chris to see why Zack was still a force to be reconded with. By watching the way Zack handled himself, Chris could tell he was going to have up his own game to compete. At the end of the OTA's, Zack had told him that he had looked good and that he liked Chris' aggressive play on the field. To Chris this was the equivalent of him receiving his acceptance letter to the school of his dreams. Acceptance was one thing Chris had been fighting for his whole life and here his idol had given him the time of day as a peer, not just another kid seeking an autograph.

While in conditioning drills, to Chris it became apparent there was a pecking order in relation to new players and veterans! The veterans paid very close attention to stretching and took a great deal of time to prepare their bodies for contact drills. The younger players on the other hand stretched and did their running rather quickly. The veterans would smile and remember that eagerness they once had to prove themselves in every aspect of Training Camp. They would also make the Noobs wait for them to arrive before Offensive and Defensive drills would begin. During his first OTA Chris had marveled at how fast all the players on his team where. There were many times during his college career where he would run down a wide receiver and keep a big play from becoming a huge play. Coach Ridel had spoken to his whole defense many times in meetings during OTA's about speed being a key element to an aggressive defense. There were signs around camp that said, "You can't teach Speed!", however the saying that Chris liked most was, "FINISH!" This saying was on each players T-shirt front and back. Finish, such a simple word but yet to a football player and a football team, the implications were far reaching and never ending. Each player in some shape or form during their career had it ingrained in their DNA that they had to finish. Finish the play, finish the tackle, finish the block, finish the run, or what coach would say, "Finish your job!"

Training camp was the very building blocks to the entire season. Coach Ridel knew and instilled in the players that each year is different and each team was different. Each year Coach Ridel spent a great deal of time using various trust building and team building activities to build comradery and team chemistry. Chris was reminded of his college team where there was quite a bit of turn over from year to year. Coach Ridel made a point of telling the team that it did not matter what happened last year, this was a new squad and a new year. The coach called camp, "Ground Zero." He wanted his players new and old to compete for every position on the field. He wanted to mold them into a team and not just have expectations from previous years or glory. Team chemistry an important ingredient to a winning team was constantly scoffed at by the media, but anyone who had ever played a team sport understands the importance of a team and its chemistry.

Coach was constantly preaching that the mental aspect of the game was just as important as the physical side. Of course this was the most difficult part for Chris, being an ADHD kid growing up; he had plenty of trepidation when it came to being able to focus on his studies. Football had been a great outlet for all his energy. Linebacker could not have been a better position for him, he was constantly in motion and his extra energy served him well on the field. Film study was something totally new to Chris, however being a student of the history of the game; he came to appreciate the nuances of the game on film. Game film opened up a whole new aspect of Chris' game; his college coaches would show him a few plays and tell him he was out of position. Coach Ridel was another matter entirely, he would demand each play be broken down and each player understood their responsibility on each play. Coach was always quizzing players on the sidelines about what their jobs were on each play. He would continue with game situations, if a player did not know the answer for the situation they would find themselves running extra wind sprints. These quizzes were something Chris looked forward to as he was always looking to learn more about the game.

Chris held his own during his first training camp. He made typical Rookie mistakes but as a first rounder the coaches did not seem to mind teaching him to correct those mistakes. For Chris it was about attention to detail he was aware of all eyes on him and the media waiting for him to make mistakes. He really seemed to fit in well with the Coaches Defensive scheme. Excitement started to build during 7 on 7 drills when the defense stuffed the offense. Chris' squad did not allow a first down and forced two turnovers, a fumble, and an interception. This surprised many because the offense of the Marauders was always one of the league's best.

The Marauders quarterback, Joe Morton, had been league MVP and a World Champion. In spite of this there were quite a few headlines that sang the praises of the defense that day. To Chris, he had always been told Defense wins Championships. The team started to have a little attitude during week four of camp leading up to the first scrimmage. Although tempers would flare from time to time no one went over the edge. The veterans would not allow any nonsense and always kept everyone on point when it came to Coaches expectations for behavior from a professional team. The level of preseason game had given way to a glorified scrimmage. The fans loved it because these games were open to season ticket holders and a lottery of fantasy football players.

The Preseason was pretty uneventful and the injury count seemed to be extremely low in Chris' eyes! He always had been told by his agent to come in to camp in the best shape possible to avoid injury. This Chris took very serious; he was not going to let injuries derail his career before it began. He was amazed at how in shape his teammates were. In college many players used training camp to get into shape for the upcoming season. Chris had been warned that this would not be tolerated at the next level and had prepared accordingly. Still he watched the linemen hit each other for what seemed to be hours and look like they could go play another game. After going 2 and 2 during the preseason, Chris did not feel like his team was a 2 and 2 team, he felt confident that when the regular season it would be extremely difficult for any team to beat them.

As camp wound down Chris started to feel as though he a had a shot at a starting position. He found himself taking more and more repetitions with the one's, which seemed to be a bit more than he was used to a first. The coaches constantly wanted to see the same play over and over again until it was perfect. Of course he spent most of the time repeating these same plays, with the first unit. What he really enjoyed was seeing Zack in the line up next to him. When Zack was next to him on defense he was constantly telling Chris where to line up and what gap he should fill or when to blitz. Chris was amazed at Zack's knowledge of the game and when they were on the field together, Chris did not have to think he just reacted and made plays.

When Chris had to call defenses on his own is when he would feel the weight of the world on his shoulders. Having an entire defense depending on the right defensive call was a daunting responsibility. Coach had told Chris early on in training camp that being a first rounder came with great expectations. Chris had been used to having people put expectations of leadership upon him, so this came as no surprise. He also had come to understand that these expectations came with the position. Playing middle linebacker meant he was the quarterback of the defense and that the defensive calls would have to come from him. Coach also spent a lot of time teaching the defense; even though he was a head coach he spent a great deal of time with his defense. Chris could see that the coach wanted to put his own personal stamp on the defense. Each time he would meet with the defense he would preach, "Finish!"

Chapter 2

Ray Ridel, Coach/General Manager of the Massachusetts Bay Marauders walked out of the large glass doors of the Luxurious Hilton Hotel that crisp March afternoon five years earlier with a feeling on dread. The game he loved beyond everything but his children was in danger of becoming extinct due to overwhelming concerns regarding the health of players currently playing as well as retired players. He continued to walk to his car with a sick feeling in his stomach, "was this it?" As he closed the door on his SUV, he could not help but think about everything he had accomplished in football. Yet, he found that he had an insatiable feeling for doing more and turning the next crop of young men into Champions! Football, a simple game by definition did not really take into account advances in technology and medicine. One would look at these advances on the surface and expect the two would greatly enhance the game of football.

For many years this is exactly what happened, the sport continued to grow at what seemed to be light speed in the eyes of owners, many of whom had owned their team for much of their life or inherited the team from their family. The owners just kept signing the most lucrative Television deals in the history of mankind. Their sport was the pinnacle of Professional sports. They had everything, a great CBA for both owners and players, and their game had never been so popular. The owners just kept raking in the money. To everyone that watched, purchased, and enjoyed the game there seemed to be no end in sight to the untamed riches the game had secured.

That was before head injuries sought to derail the game everyone so dearly loved. Head injuries had always been an area of concern for fan and player alike. It wasn't until the technology and medical advances that helped grow the game actually caused the most harm to the game itself. Players that once had careers ended by injury were now making remarkable recoveries. Special helmets had been designed with a liquid gel in the helmet to the helmet absorb much of the shock of a blow to prevent head injuries. However, research continued to pour in linking head injuries to diseases such as, ALS, Alzheimer's, and especially CTE (Chronic Traumatic Encephalopathy). Concussions had always been viewed as part of the game. Growing up many players were told, you just got your bell rung, get back out there. As the game evolved the medical and technological advances, such as nutrition caused a great increase in the size and speed of the players now playing the game. With greater size and speed came greater collisions on the football field causing much more brain trauma than in the past.

The public of course, loved seeing these terrific athletes and their amazing hits over and over again on NAFL TV. Whole documentaries were put together glorifying the head hunters, the gladiators of the game. So much attention was given to glorifying the hit, from owners, to coaches, to players, to Monday morning quarterbacks, to the Pop Warner kids who were trying to take each other's head off during a game. The idea that there could be diseases and consequences caused by these hits were the furthest from anyone's mind.

The very same media who helped build the Goliath known as the NAFL now had its own huge issue to deal with. Technology had come to the point of instant information and instant trouble. If something happened in Football camp in Florida, all the General Managers as well as the fans knew within minutes of any injury or signing for that matter. Free agency had caused an uproar not allowing teams to create Dynasty's but yet promote parity in the league. However, with the advent of instant information over wireless devices teams and players were at the mercy of anyone with access to one of these devices. This information included the latest in medical breakthroughs. What caused such an uproar, however, was Football's direct link to CTE. This debilitating disease caused many issues for patients, including, loss of memory, aggressive behavior, mental illness, and an exceptionally high mortality rate.

A football player's life had been for generations defined for actions on the field; however, it is what happened off the field that began to concern people greatly. Once the bright lights of fame and fortune came and went for the football player what was left with his thoughts and memories. These thoughts and memories, a legacy of football greatness was taken away from many players as a direct result from too many blows to the head. Concussions that were not allowed to heal properly or multiple sustained head trauma were endured for the love of and the need of the game. As a result of such head trauma over extended periods of time, in the case of professional football players this meant most of his life measured in shortened years, concussions continued to take their toll.

A devastating toll on current and former players alike, one that has in some cases caused death! Armed with this knowledge media and fans alike were in an uproar about what to do and how to help both current and former players. Most players had grown up in a culture that glorified the horrific hit and they had been applauded for their toughness on the field. The more players became educated about the results of all these traumatic hits to the head, the more they became upset that not more had been done to protect their long term health. It came to the point where parents were no longer allowing their young people to participate in contact sports, especially football. Pop Warner suffered greatly, college recruiting became a mad scramble to find players, and the NAFL product on the field began to suffer because of rule changes intended to make the game safer.

Football began to notice for the first time since the inception of the league, a loss of viewers. People began to latch onto soccer, which already had a huge International following. Only when it started to hit the owners wallets did they sit up and take note. Something had to be done before their billion dollar industry was in serious Jeopardy. Safety committees spent most of their time reinventing the football uniform, with special emphasis on the helmet. In spite of a more safe uniform and equipment it seemed the rule changes had the most adverse effect and brought the sport to the brink of destruction. In pursuit of safety, the physical game everyone loved became a glorified flag football game. The game was on the brink, sponsors were pulling out, many teams were having trouble filling out rosters and then the coaches went back to basics.

The old adage, "keep it simple stupid, took over!" Coaches who knew the history of the league knew when there were no helmets there were not so many horrific head injuries. The only issue there was that today's player was much too big and fast to play without helmets. However, what happened was a return to playing the game right with technique and precision. Football being a game of strategy, of blocking, and tackling became that game once again. Blocking with hands and moving feet, form tackling with heads up was once again used and taught. Rules were put into place to balance both offense and defense. The game everyone loved seemed to be back.

Coach Ridel, being a traditionalist liked the return to fundamentals and a cleaner brand of football. Gone were the crushing head to head hits, however one could still tackle with just as much force the right way. Instead of launching one's self at another player, the tackling player had to wrap up and run through the player keeping their legs driving to tackle again. Defensive backs were allowed to play more bump and run coverage keeping the DB's closer to the receiver so they would not become a defenseless receiver. The coach kept thinking about this quite a bit as he reached the handle of his SUV to head home for the day. Tomorrow's meeting would be interesting, how does the league try and incorporate more soccer players into its scouting trips. Of course free agency was always on the table, he needed to fill out his rooster with excellent football players. Yes, tomorrow was another day.

Chapter 3

Chris sat in the Doctor's office awaiting his physical, so he could sign his first professional contract. The doctor's office looked more like a sports shrine rather than a medical facility. The walls were lined with shelves recessed into the walls with the sanitary white walls were covered with sports paraphernalia. Chris could not help but stand in awe of the history before him, especially the game balls. The one that intrigued him the most was a somewhat deflated, dried, cracked ball from the 1963 Championship, the team's first! Growing up in the Boston area Chris was well aware of the teams glorious beginning. The Marauders had become the only expansion team to actually win the Championship in its first year of existence. Quite a feat considering there were still original teams that have not won a Championship.

However, the team became a victim of its own success. Immediately coaches and players were plucked by other teams because the fledgling team did not have the financial resources to keep everyone at that time. This caused a downward spiral that saw the team go into a prolonged slump of forty years. It was not until the 2000's that the team began to show life again and built a Championship team. This was followed up by several decades of dominance; the team once again had a great blend of talent and coaching. That is what Chris remembered most as a child growing up watching his team pound others into submission each Sunday. Chris's father on the other hand would always remind him to enjoy it while it was here because it could go away anytime. His father had lamented with his brother's and friends the hardships of the franchise had endured for all those years.

The one thing Chris really gained from those many conversations through the years was a fierce sense of loyalty. Chris had asked his Dad many years ago why he remained a fan during those lean years; he had been quite surprised by the response. At first, his Dad looked like he was going to back hand him, but his expression softened when he saw his son tense up. His Dad went on to simply state, "that is my team and will always be my team, what kind of fan would I be if I only supported them when they are winning!" He further elaborated, "I am not a bandwagon fan, I have seen players and coaches come and go but even in the lean years this team has always had grit, a workman like feel to it! I have always identified with hard work and loyalty!"

Chris remembered that last statement most because Coach Ridel during his first press conference after having signed on as the Marauders head coach had basically repeated the words his Dad had told him about hard work and loyalty. Chris was once again reminded of this as he continued his viewing of the artifacts on the shelves, when he came to a picture of Coach Ridel holding his first of four Championship trophies with the Marauders. Chris thought about wanting to be an important part of the Coaches next Championship team.

Chris was in an almost trancelike state, dreaming of football glory, when he heard someone calling his name. He came to his senses and realized it was one of the medical assistants telling him he was next. He was taken into an examining room, where he had to disrobe and put on a johnny. As he waited for the doctor, he could not help but smile, he was in a state of euphoria about beginning his career. He was thinking about how long the exam would take because he wanted to see the rest of the facility, when he heard the door of his room open. He knew someone would be in shortly but still was a little startled until he looked up.

Chris found himself looking into the most striking blue eyes he had ever seen. The eyes were of perfect roundness, but it was the color that took his breath away. Chris' eyes were also blue, so seeing and knowing about blue eyes were nothing new to him. However, what he was looking into at this moment did not seem real, these eyes were such a beautiful blue that one would have to question whether or not they were contacts. Chris looked more closely, while the eyes seemed to be drawing him in as if they almost had their own light and power behind them. He did not even hear the young lady say hello and tell him she was a nurse who would be taking his vitals. He shook his head and said, "I am sorry what did you say?"

She looked at him and laughed, "My name is April Jones, and I am going to be your nurse for your physical. I am going to take your vitals and answer any questions I can before the Doctor goes through the entire physical with you." As she took his temperature, Chris felt warm as though his temperature was rising. He found it increasingly difficult to avoid those eyes, so he tried to look elsewhere, big mistake. With her standing right in front him, he was her captive. He noticed her luminous beautiful blond hair, her soft feminine features, and her luxious full lips. She had just a hint of strawberry in her hair and he felt himself starring mesmerized by April. He tried to look down but was struck by April's stunning figure with full breasts at eye level. Even through the Lab coat one could see that the woman standing before him was devastatingly beautiful. He could feel his face start to redden but he had nowhere to run.

As if April sensed his turmoil, she gave him a disarming smile and took his blood pressure. Chris looked her smiling face and immediately felt better but yet as she took his blood pressure he felt as though his heart was going to pop out of his chest! Chris had several girlfriends growing up and knew what it was like to be around pretty women, especially in college. While in college playing ball, he had his share of women throwing themselves at his feet. He had definitely enjoyed the attention and the company of a pretty lady now and then but this was something altogether different! He felt as though he had been hit by a bolt of lightning. By the time she had checked his height and weight, he felt as if he was going to sweat bullets. When she finally left, he sat exhausted like he had just gone through a two a day practice. He just kept shaking his head as if he needed to wake himself from a dream.

When Doctor Henry Chase came into his room he walked straight to Chris and introduced himself while shaking his hand. He assured Chris that the physical should not take very long and he knew how anxious Chris was to see the rest of the stadium. The physical itself was nothing earth shattering, a typical physical that Chris had gone through countless times. When Doctor Chase finished he told Chris everything looked great. He did inform Chris that they had to run a few tests, take an MRI of his knees, do a chest X-Ray, and do a brain scan to make sure they had not missed anything along the way.

Dr. Chase called April to return and assist. Chris immediately began to feel his cheeks flush and feel that warm feeling once again. The Dr. asked April to take him to Radiology while waiting for him to finish and return him safely when finished. April turned to him, "Nothing to worry about, Chris these tests and scans are just routine. The team needs all of these as records to show how healthy you are when you sign your contract." Chris found himself thinking of the deal his Agent had negotiated for him. Even though there was a Rookie pay scale, there was nothing to say that little perks could not be negotiated into the deal. Chris, as a first rounder, had perks galore, including a trip with his family to the Championship for life. This was something Chris had asked for himself and being a fan of the game he thought it would be awesome to go to the Championship each year. Although Chris planned to be there a lot as a player, he knew at some point his career would end and he wanted to stay connected to the game.

After Radiology, Doctor Chase asked April to take Chris down to the lab. April looked at Chris playfully and smiled, "Do you need me to hold your hand while they take blood?" Even before he knew he said it Chris blurted out, "you can hold my hand anytime you want!" Immediately he felt himself wince and get red with embarrassment. "Sorry," he said, "I guess I am more nervous than I thought!" April looked at him with those piercing eyes, "Chris, I can tell you are going to be nothing but trouble." She looked at him slyly and walked out of the lab. The lab looked like any other lab with chairs with extended arms for the patients so they would be comfortable during the blood drawing process. Just as in any other Doctor's office, the environment was sterile but yet comfortable. There was soft music playing in the background. The lab tech came in and drew his blood which was nothing special about that except for the amount.

Usually during a physical a couple of vials were taken. During this session the lab tech took five vials! Also the lab tech took several strands of hair and the oddest of all he was asked to open his mouth and he had a big cotton swab put into his mouth several times. Chris knew that they would be very thorough but he really did not understand all of the blood and extra tests. Chris had to ask, "Why all the blood and hair?" The lab tech answered, "now that you are a member of the team, medically we are responsible for everything that happens to you. The team is not only investing substantial funds into your career they would like to see you remain healthy and help the team for many years to come."

Chris could not argue with that logic, the team had invested heavily in him and they had to be sure he would be around during that investment. Something about the blood, hair, and swab kept eating at him as he was waiting in the waiting room. April came in laughed and said, "I see you didn't pass out!" Chris looked at her, "I thought I would for a minute. It felt like they took all my blood! Thanks for the warning!" April looked at him; "They have to do a lot of tests to make sure they do not miss anything" The way she looked at Chris he could tell she was genuine in her response. This put Chris at ease and he went with her to the front desk. April turned to him and told him, "security will take you on a tour of the facilities, and the stadium is huge so we don't want you to get lost before you play!" She laughed, "They will bring you back after lunch and the Doctor will go over all your tests with you." She warmly put her hand on his shoulder and told him it was a pleasure to have met him!

As April had told him the stadium was huge and he definitely would have gotten lost. The stadium was more like a small city rather than a place for gridiron greatness. Growing up Chris played in small stadiums where the kids ran around and played under the bleachers while parents tried to watch the game and hope their kids did not get into any trouble. Even in college the stadiums were larger and more elaborate but nothing this grandiose. Chris remembered little after the locker room and the training room. His mind kept going back to those eyes, eyes of blue ocean on its bluest day. April's eyes and smile seemed to be imprinted on him even when he closed his eyes. The security guard brought him back to the doctor's office after a lunch fit for a king. Doctor Chase brought him into his office and closed the door. Dr. Chase had a tablet in front of him, he looked up and started by saying, "you my friend are an interesting case, and your physical is absolutely perfect everything looks great!" The doctor continued to look at Chris, put his chin like he was pondering what to say next. "Chris," he said, "Do you dream a lot?" Chris did not even think of the question, he just responded, "Yes, I dream a great deal and they are very real and detailed. Sometimes in the morning I could swear these things actually happened to me!"

The doctor continued to look at Chris with his eyebrows raised. He continued looking at his tablet and then glanced up at Chris saying, "Your brain scan is absolutely amazing, everything looks great but I can see the neurons firing in the dream center of your brain. It is as though you are always dreaming!" Chris looked at the doctor and responded, "I have always dreamed, early on it got me in trouble in school until my mom went to the school and explained that I was not being disrespectful. It was this dreaming that allowed me to put my ideas into artwork and really helped me focus on the rest of my schoolwork. Even today when not getting ready for football I am always creating artwork, especially sports pictures." Doctor Chase looked genuinely impressed, "Chris that is awesome, it sounds as though I know what you will be doing after your playing days are over."

Chris sat straight up with a bright smile on his face, "Yes, I cannot begin to tell you how many ideas I have for artwork to be done. It surely will keep me busy." The doctor typed a few notes in his tablet, when finished he stood and beckoned Chris to come with him. Chris followed him through a set of double doors into another training room. This was much smaller than the one next to the downstairs locker room. In the room were standard things such as an ice bath, training table, and first aid supplies. What was different however was the triangular shaped box along the wall. The box looked not all that different than the old fashioned steam boxes in which a person would sit inside and let the steam cleanse their pores.

The doctor brought Chris to the front of the box and typed in a code on the keypad on the front. The box seemed to split in half; the inside looked much like the inside of a tent with a flat screen TV on the wall. "This is a Hyperbaric Chamber Chris; you may have even used something like this in college." Chris had seen similar chambers and had even used one that was like a bubble once, so he just nodded his head in agreement. The doctor continued, "This chamber is quite a bit more advanced than any you have seen of used. The idea of the Hyperbaric Chamber is to increase the Oxygen in ones body through total immersion. The oxygen in ones body is a key element to recovery and staying healthy. As you are aware as a highly trained athlete your body needs all the help it can get in order to recover from the brutal onslaught the gridiron throws at it. We have found this chamber to be a remarkable way to help the recovery process, especially in light of having only a few days to prepare for another game.

We have negotiated into the CBA the use of these chambers and the use of special proteins to help our athletes maintain the highest level of performance. Every team is allowed this but I would like to think we are perfecting it's use. These methods are completely natural and will not harm or have any ill affects down the road. We have standardized these treatments and do it here for everyone, so as to not have any issues arise about our athletes using PED's. We continue to find ways to help our athletes recover naturally faster. Why don't you step inside for a minute." Chris did just that, when he first sat down he did not think there would be enough room. Yet when the doors closed and the TV came on he had plenty of room. It felt as though he were in a small man cave watching a game. He began watching the video of the Marauders last Championship four years ago. The players seemed to pop out of the screen at him.

He had seen the new TV's that could do just that, the images could be a 3D holographic image in front of you but he did not have the money yet to purchase one. He tried to touch the wispy image only to see the image or light on his own hands. He relaxed, sat back and enjoyed the game. Chris could feel the air conditioning on his back which felt good and it smelled like fresh air inside the chamber, not musty and cramped as one might expect. Chris inhaled deeply and felt so relaxed he almost wanted to take a nap. He then heard the doctor come over the speaker and ask how he was doing. He told the doctor, he felt amazing. Doctor Chase told Chris that was great but he did have to give him his protein supplements and let him get home.

The doors slowly opened revealing the bright fluorescent lights; it took a moment for Chris's eyes to adjust. When his eyes were able to see everything, the doctor was standing before him smiling. "You did terrific for your first time,

I have to check everyone and make sure they are not claustrophobic. At the beginning of each game and the end every player will spend time in the chamber to recover and get ready for the next game." He gave Chris three bottles of different amino acids and told him when to take them. He was quite surprised when the doctor told him that sleep is one of the most important things he can do to help himself recover and remain healthy. His mom used to preach to him the same thing but here was a doctor of a major sports team telling him to get proper rest.

Chapter 4

With the season fast approaching Coach Ridel was looking at the huge white board with names of players all over it when Chris arrived. The secretary had told Chris to go in that the coach had been expecting him. He knocked on the door to the coach's office and was told to enter. Chris felt extremely anxious because this was the final cut down day before getting ready for the season opener. Not that he had really all that much to worry about because first rounder's never got cut but he did not want to get demoted. Chris had felt during training camp that he had a great grasp of the defensive calls now. He was also sure that he was making fewer mistakes and was in the right position most of the time. By the time he stood in front of Coach Ridel, he really was confused about what the coach might want him for.

Coach continued to look at his big board for a moment and then turned in his chair to take Chris in for a moment. Chris could tell by the gaze that the coach was trying to make a big decision. The coach gestured to him to have a seat. Chris pulled the chair out and sat in front of the coach's expansive desk. Coach Ridel looked straight at Chris and began with, "Okay Rookie, what are you made of?" This question did not completely catch Chris off guard, he had spent months preparing for the Combine and difficult interview questions such as this. "Coach," he responded, "I am your man, whatever you need me to do to help this team win, I am all in!"

Having said that statement with such conviction made the coach sit up in his seat and just stare at Chris. The coach sat there for what seemed to be hours and then said, "You are my man. I have watched you for a long time, from high School, to College, and during training camp. You have an amazing ability to make everyone around you better! That is something that cannot be taught. Yes, you have great ability, speed, and size but it is the intangibles that are intriguing to me. You hear coaches all the time state they want winners on their team. Well, what is the definition of a winner, I am sure it is different for each person. However, I know football players, I know whether he can play or not. Once the players hit the field I have to rely on them as football players and people, it is out of my hands.

Sure we practice like crazy, teach as much as we can to try to put the player in the right situation but it is the player that has to make the plays. Plays are made not just with athleticism and talent, they are made with a certain feel and flare for the game. These are things that cannot be measured with numbers they have to be viewed first hand. Players who are around the ball and make plays all the time are extremely rare and when you find one you have to cultivate that player! You hear experts all the time say, he has a nose for the ball. You my friend have a nose, mind, and body for football."

Chris sat across from his coach stunned; this was the games most winning modern day coach giving him the ultimate compliment. "Coach, I will give to everything I have, it has been my lifelong dream to play for you and this team. I will not let you down!" Coach looked at Chris with a sly smile on his face and then spoke, "I have not even told you what I need yet, you may not be so sure when you hear what I have to say." "Chris," he began, "you are an amazing young man and I have no doubt you are a terrific football player." Coach paused and then continued, "Are you the leader I need for this defense? That remains to be seen."

"Zack is a special football player but his clock is ticking and unfortunately we all get replaced at some point by someone younger and hungrier. Zack is still one of the best linebackers in the league but as coach I have to look to the future." The coach's eyes pierced right through Chris, "you, Chris are the future as I see it before me, but can you lead this team?" Coach Ridel left that statement hanging in the air a moment and continued. "I have been playing you a lot with the first unit to see how you respond in game situations, and yes they have been Preseason, which is the reason for this conversation, this week the games are for real!" Chris looked at the coach and right away understood the gravity of the situation, the coach was asking for the ultimate commitment, Team Before Dream!

As far back as Chris could recall he wanted to play for Coach Ridel and the Marauders. Growing up playing in the backyard he dreamed of throwing the winning touchdown or intercepting a pass and bringing it to the house. His dream had become reality and the reality is the coach, the team, the Boston area was now counting on him to be a professional and lead this team. When in college Chris was no different from any other professional prospect, he dreamed of a big contract and buying a nice home for his parents. He had thought about taking luxurious vacations and buying cars. Sitting here now with the Coach brought those ideas to a screeching halt.

The coach was always talking about Team, a well-oiled machine each player focused and performing the job asked of them on each play. For the first time Chris began to understand how his job and leadership could make or break this coming season. Right now the coach was testing his meddle but in a few days during the season opener it would be a team full of eyes judging his character as a man and a football player. That thought to Chris was just a daunting as sitting before the man that was about to determine his future. Chris sat for what seemed to be hours letting this wash over him; his resolve hardened, he looks up at is coach and said, "Understood, what do you need me to do!"

The coach smiled at him, "just be you! I do not need a superstar this team needs a super football player, one they can count on, one they can look to for leadership. We use that term leadership in football all the time, the fact is leadership comes in many forms. When you are on the field you bring an intensity and energy to an already strong defense. In order to be a Championship defense we need what I have seen from you on the field, which is the ability to raise the game of others on your team! Your mixture of youth, energy, intelligence, and ability is rare to see in a rookie. Many players have a few of these traits but you have a great blend of all the traits. This Sunday, I just want you to play, don't think, play! You are ready and after sitting with you here today I feel confident that you are my man!"

As Chris left the coaches office he felt as though he had been interrogated by the FBI. His palms were sweaty and his throat was dry. He felt his heart still racing with the thought of the coach having such confidence in him. During training camp it had been hard to read how the coach felt about any player, he always seemed to be yelling at everyone to pick it up. He reached the locker room to pick up his things to return home for the day. He found a brilliantly clean uniform and helmet sitting in his locker. He sat in the chair in front of the locker holding up his game jersey just staring in disbelief. Here it was a few days away, his first professional football game. A million things started whizzing through his brain. He could see himself and Zack next to each other on the field, dirty and grass stains all over them, blood on their pads, this was football. They had just broken the huddle and had a full on blitz called.

The ball was snapped and all Chris could hear was the pounding of pads into one another, grunts, and the crash of helmets. To Chris everything was moving in slow motion, he saw the quarterback ball fake and turn to set up the play action, the back tried to chip him but Chris just put his blocker's head in the dirt. There was an open lane to the quarterback. Chris could see the quarterbacks eyes were down the field going through his progressions and when he came to his third read he noticed Chris a little too late! Chris could feel his shoulder pads hit and crush the quarterback's flak jacket into his ribs. He could hear all the air whoosh out of the lungs of the quarterback as he seemed to bend in half. It was such a perfect hit with his head up and driving through the tackle, he couldn't believe he did not feel more pain himself. Both players landed on the ground, Chris landing right on top of the other. He could hear and see the pain in the quarterback's eyes as Chris landed on top of him. How the quarterback managed to hold onto the ball was amazing to Chris. As Chris got up he realized how far back from the line of scrimmage they were. He looked up at the scoreboard to confirm his observations and found that he had caused a fifteen yard loss on the play. This put the other team out of field goal range and bringing up fourth down, a huge play in the game!

Chris blinked his eyes many times; once again he was sitting before his locker holding his jersey. He looked around to see if anyone else was there but he found himself alone. The feeling was very strange, he always had dreams but lately these dreams seemed to be so real that he was having a hard time getting to sleep. Of course the one thing Doctor Chase had told him was to make sure he got his rest.

Sunday morning Chris popped out of bed and stood before his window. He could just make out the first rays of sunlight trying to make it over the trees in the distance. What a beautiful day for football he thought and looked at his clock, 5:55. Chris had to be at the stadium for breakfast and team meetings at 8:00. He had a slight panic attack because he still had some studying of the game plan to do before arriving at the stadium. Of course this being his first game, as a rookie being in the starting unit he did not want to disappoint anyone.

He hardly remembered showering and dressing as he parked his car in the players lot and made his way to the conference room. The conference room was cavernous; it was large enough to hold a practice in, which is what the coach did often. The coach informed the players that he wanted to do a walkthrough of a few things before breakfast. Coach was a perfectionist and if he did not like something the team would run it until he was satisfied, this to the dismay of many players. The walkthrough was just that though, offense, defense, and special teams while the coach reviewed the game plan with his team.

Breakfast was interesting, the offense still sat with the offense and the defense with the defense, like training camp. Chris thought for sure everyone would sit anywhere and talk to anyone. He could see that all the Veterans already had their game faces on and were going over things in their heads. Many of the rookies had their play books in front of them as they were eating. Yes, it was time to go to work. After breakfast the Coach came in and went through the game plan one more time and then told everyone that home openers were special and let's make this one to remember. He also told everyone to get their time in the H-Chamber before the game.

Chris arrived in plenty of time to get in his time in the H-Chamber. The training room was abuzz with activity, people scrambling everywhere getting tape, making sure there was plenty of ice, it definitely was controlled chaos. Chris was walking to his assigned training table and H-Chamber when he saw April. He stopped dead in his tracks and immediately felt his cheeks redden; he could not take his eyes off her. Her long blond hair was in an up do and she wore a team polo with a skirt. More than what she wore it was how she wore these clothes that really made Chris's eyes seem to pop out of his head. Chris had not seen April that often since his physical. Sometimes he would see her briefly running different errands around the stadium but really had not much face to face contact. Today Chris just looked at her shirt and skirt and how they conformed to her body and he found himself just utterly taken in by this creature. He tried to prey his eyes away to no avail, April noticed him and gave him a warm smile. Every time he did see her and she smiled at him he immediately felt better.

He was in another world when he heard Doctor Chase greet him, "Well Chris, let me guess, you are ready for today's game!" Chris replied, "I have been waiting for this my whole life!" The doctor looked at him and began, "Chris, I have been here a long time and it is still awesome to hear people say that,

36

it is one of the reasons I am still here. I love this game and I would do anything to see it remain strong." As he said this Chris could almost sense a bit of sadness in his voice. This was very surprising to Chris, every interaction Chris had ever had with the doctor had been one of upbeat enthusiasm. Today the doctor was from what he could see somewhat subdued.

As Chris went into his H-Chamber the doctor put his hand on Chris's shoulder and wished him good luck in the game. He told him he would see him after the game during his recovery H-Chamber session. Chris could sense the doctor's nervousness but he chalked it up to this being the first game and everyone nervous hoping for a good showing. Yet, Chris could not help but be curious about the look he had given Chris as he shut the door to the H-Chamber. A look of I hope this works!

With the door to the chamber closed Chris relaxed as he knew the concentrated oxygen was flowing into the chamber. It was also very cool in the chamber which made Chris feel refreshed and being that is was September and still very warm he looked forward to hanging out in the nice climate controlled chamber. He also loved the nice flat screen TV, today's entertainment was this week's opponent, the New Jersey Sharks. The Sharks were a division rival of the Marauders which added to the significance of this home and season opener.

Offensive football was the Shark's M.O. and Chris felt very prepared to face the fire power. He would have his hands full stopping the run but it was his coverage that had him nervous. The Sharks ran a spread offense with a lot of five wide formations and a double quarterback set. This dual quarterback threat was an innovation that had been on the horizon for years. Quarterbacks had been becoming more and more mobile but the league had held firm to the idea that they needed a pocket passer. The Sharks changed all that, they had a traditional pocket passer who was terrific but they had drafted a kid in the fourth round that no one knew what to with because he was six foot three, 230 pounds and could run like a gazelle and throw like a howitzer.

The problem of what to do with the kid became apparent early on in OTA's. During training camp, it also became apparent that this kid needed to be on the field but how do you sit an already established great quarterback. The answer is, you don't, the coach incorporated the two into a brand new system that had not been seen before. The new system drove defenses nuts, they simply did not know how to prepare for it and never knew what was coming. Even though one was a runner, the runner was also an excellent passer. The red zone became increasingly difficult to defend because the playbook was still wide open. At first the coach had been ridiculed and laughed at because the league viewed this offense as a gimmick. The coach had gone on to prove it could work, so much so that the Sharks won the title last season with that system in full force.

Chris was viewing film on this offense and was intimidated at first; however Coach Ridel had told him not to over think it. He explained to Chris that the other team still had eleven men on their side and Chris did to, it was he told Chris, a chess match. Coach instructed his defense on the match ups, which was the fun part of the game the coach had told them. The coach was always stressing, do your job, don't worry about other positions, focus on your assignments and what you need to do. He had done just that during his preparations for the game and felt confident his defense was up to the challenge.

He was viewing the plays on the TV when he began to dream the plays happening to him rather than being on the screen. As had happened many times in the past because of the player having these types of dreams for years. Today, however, he felt every play. On one play in particular, he was blocked from the side and right now his side felt like it was on fire. These added sensations were frightening to Chris he had never had dreams this vivid before. He was still holding his side when the next play began. Even though Chris was a middle linebacker, Coach Ridel moved his defensive players around a lot to confuse the offense. Today's opponent demanded a lot movement to keep the two quarterbacks off guard.

On this particular play Chris was lined up as a defensive end and was faking a rush. Chris noticed the tight end was shading slightly toward the offensive line, which was usually a tip off that the team was running up the middle. Chris took a straight rush to the center of the backfield and met the running back as he received the hand off. Chris hit the running back with a perfect form tackle and felt himself and the runner going to the ground. As they both hit the ground the running back put his arm out to catch his fall. Chris continued to fall on top of him hearing a snap and feeling the backs elbow dislocate.

He could hear the running back as he screamed in agony, Chris felt as though he was going to get sick as he saw the player's arm just hanging there going the wrong way. It was that feeling that brought Chris to his senses, he felt groggy, as if he had just woken up from a deep slumber. He found himself still in the H-Chamber but everything was dark. He started to feel anxious. Although used to the H-Chamber he started to look around knowing something was not right. He knew the chamber had a computer locking mechanism but he started to slightly panic wondering if there had been an electrical issue and whether or not the door would open.

Chris sat for a moment and started to feel around the seam of the chamber where the doors were closed. His fingers found a little control box on the bottom of the door. He pushed buttons until the door snapped open; he took both doors and swung them open. As he stepped out of the chamber he was stunned to see all the lights out and the huge training room was completely empty.

Chapter 5

Down the hallway Doctor Chase sat at a computer screen watching the football game as it progressed. The doctor grimaced as he saw Chris hit the running back and watched the back's elbow bend back ninety degrees the wrong way. He had dealt with injuries of this nature many times during his career. It wasn't the surgery that bothered him. Even the recovery and the rehabilitation were a science of their own now. The doctor genuinely felt sympathetic for each player because of the mental toll these injuries took on the athlete trying to return to the field. A professional football player was a gladiator and many felt they were infallible. Not to mention that many of these players were still in their twenties and had the attitude on invincibility. As the trainer went out to attend to the downed player, Doctor Chase's phone rang. The doctor was being summoned to help attend to the fallen player. Being the host team, the doctor was responsible for the health and wellbeing of both teams. Doctor Chase turned and looked around at the huge control room full of computers and people bustling about and walked toward the door. He stopped to issue some orders to his assistant Susan, a young lady on the computer closest to the door and hastily left the room. The Doctor's work station was now left unattended and among the commotion no one noticed on the monitor that Chris was emerging from his H-Chamber much too early.

The game continued on without further major injury with the Marauders prevailing 34-31 in a shootout. The Doctor had just returned to congratulations and a very excited control room. This being the home opener and against a division rival as well as the reigning Champion had made for a ratings bonanza. The fact that they had won the game just increased the feeling of triumph in the room. To everyone in the control room, they felt a great sense of pride when the team performed well.

It was during this elation that Susan; the doctor's assistant had approached the doctor with a panic stricken look on her face. She grabbed the doctor by the arm and dragged him to the side. "Doctor Chase, you had better see this," she hustled the doctor over to his computer station. The doctor looked at the screen and at first was about to accost Susan for bothering his celebration. It was then he took a closer look at the H-Chamber on the screen, it was wide open and Chris was gone. The celebration immediately ended!

Chris still groggy stood in the training room in shock, "Where is everyone, did they forget me?" That is when he noticed the chamber next to him was still operating, this was Zack's chamber! He walked over to the chamber to take a closer look and almost lost his breath. He could see on the monitor that Zack was still in the chamber and looked to be asleep. Chris was dumbfounded, "what the hell is going on here!" He began to wonder if he himself was still dreaming. Out of the corner of his eye he saw movement and whipped around only to be confronted with the large TV monitor in the training room for injured players to watch the game.

As he watched the TV, he watched in horror as he saw a replay of the hit he had made on the running back and watched the player's elbow snap backwards. He just stood in front of the monitor as they continued to show highlights from the first half of the game. "Half-time, what is this!" and then he saw himself walking back into the stadium for the second half, while nearly doubling over. He found the nearest chair and sat, "I must be still dreaming, no that can't be it, wow, this is messed up! I have to find Doctor Chase!" Chris scrambled to large set of double doors at the far end of the training room, they were locked tight. Chris quickly scanned the room to see if there were any more exits. Then he remembered the small door off to the side that April had brought him through on the way to the training room to show him around month's before. He ran to the door and as he was about to open it he saw the knob start to turn.

Chris could feel a sense of relief, the door opened and he recognized one of Doctor Chase's, assistants, Rachel. She opened the door and saw Chris and immediately turned ghostly white. They both stood there for a moment and then she said, "What are you doing out of your chamber, it is not time for you to be out!" Chris was highly confused at this point. She continued, "Chris come over here and have a seat at the training table. I want to have a look at you." He thought it a bit puzzling that she could not examine him on any table but his own. "It's okay," she said nervously, "I just have to make sure you are okay. You made some amazing hits today but you took some shots as well."

At this point Chris did not know what to think, had he gotten his bell rung during the game. "That's it," he said under his breath. He began recalling a time in college where he had received a concussion and everything had gone black while he could not remember anything that had happened to him. It had taken a few weeks to clear out the cobwebs and return to normal functions on the field. He followed Rachel and sat down at his table. Rachel asked him, "Do you remember anything?"

He looked at her and recounted every event that had happened to him that day in stunning detail. Rachel just looked at him in a state of panic for a moment and then composed herself. "Okay, I am going to have Dr. Chase look at you. I think you got hit a bit harder than we thought."

She took out her phone and texted the doctor. Immediately came a response text and she did not look to sure about what she was supposed to do at this point. She turned back toward Chris and said, "Chris would you mind laying down on the table, the doctor asked me to give you something to calm you down. He does not want your heart racing while he examines you." To Chris this did not seem to out of the ordinary, he had seen things like this happen to guys that had come off the field in panic due to injury. He had begun to lie down as Rachel was preparing a needle. It was by total chance that he happened to be glancing up when he noticed Rachel's cell phone screen just a few feet from him. The screen read, "We have a situation, Chris is awake!" The response was, "Take care of it," from Doctor Chase, "Keep him there!"

Rachel turned to him with a large needle in her hand, "this may pinch a little," and she moved toward Chris. Sirens started to go off in Chris's head and he instinctively grabbed Rachel's arm wrestling the needle out of her hand. Throwing the needle against the wall, it shattered into a million pieces. His eyes seemed as if they would pop out of his head as he frantically scanned the room. His eyes came to rest on an escape route. He jumped off the table and ran to the small door dashing through it. He could hear Rachel telling him to stop that it was okay. Everything was not okay and every sense in his body was telling him something was seriously wrong!

Doctor Chase was running down the hallway full speed with his cell phone in hand. His phone had walkie talkie capability and he was frantically trying to contact Rachel. Suddenly Rachel's voice came over the phone, "Doctor, he has escaped!" "Escaped, what do you mean, he was there and you were sedating him!" Rachel's voice was shaky, "He just freaked out when he saw the needle and bolted!" Doctor Chase did not miss a stride, "Get security down here right now. I want the response team to meet me in the training room, now!" The Doctor raced down the hall and went around the corner and almost lost his footing and slid into the wall. As he righted himself he looked down the hall to see a swarm of bodies milling around in front of the training room.

He grabbed his Head of Security, Steve Johnson. He was a hard man to miss at six foot six and a hulking man. Steve was a former Army Ranger and had owned his own security firm before joining the Marauders organization. Steve always the professional was being apprised of the current situation by members of his response team. A team comprised of former military, law enforcement, and federal agents. Doctor Chase stood in front of Steve with a sheer look of panic, "What can we do to contain him. We are not dealing with a closed practice here; there are over a hundred thousand people here today!" Steve just turned and had a sly smile look on his face and stated, "I have been here for years and still end up having to pull up the maps on GPS to find my way sometimes. There is no way he can find his way out of this maze."

Doctor Chase stared at him, "That's not what I am worried about. We have staff all over this place and if any of them see Chris before the game is over, we are sunk!" Steve smirked, "Just tell them he took a blow to the head." "Great," the Doctor said, "How do we explain the fact that Chris is still playing in the game right now Genius!" Steve looked at him with a look of swift realization he turned to his team and started feverously talking and hand gesturing. Rachel rushed to the Doctor's side, "He ran out the small door on the side of the room that leads to the tunnels."

Marauder Stadium had literally been built as an underground city. The public viewed the stadium as just a place to go to enjoy a game or concert, but looks can be deceiving. If the public really had looked into the building and refitting of Stadiums around the league there would be many questions to answer. As it was many of the tunnels and underground structures were passed off as needed for irrigation, locker rooms, training rooms, and other facilities. When patrons arrived at the stadium they were so busy taking photos of themselves and admiring the façade of the stadium that they noticed little else. They were so engrossed in finding their seats and getting ready to view the game that they hardly noticed all the comings and goings by staff and security. Most people did not think twice about the inner workings of a huge stadium such as this.

Sure the teams were private and the public was told the stadiums were financed with private funding but that was not entirely true. The type of research being done at this facility required actual live subjects. Research that both the team and the government wanted to be kept secret. For decades researchers have been fighting public views on human research, especially where stem–cell research was involved. As the banter politically went back and forth research and technology marched on. Private industry and defense contractors were always financial well springs for those who knew how to follow the money.

Professional football, nearly a trillion dollar a year business was in perfect financial position to be a patron of research. Years before when professional football was at a crossroads with so many documented concussions and dealing with former players the league set up specific head trauma research funds to show the public they were dealing with the issue. The research they funded helped everyone understand concussions and treatment but it was prevention that proved most difficult to obtain. In the end stadiums were built as hospitals and research labs because their patients and subjects were right there and readily available. Rather than outsource the research keeping everything in house was efficient and cost effective.

Doctor Chase thought about his years of research as he looked at the maze of tunnels on his cell phone. He stated, "Where does he think he is going, he has no idea where he is in the stadium." This statement was solidly true; all players when allowed in the stadium were greeted and brought around to the common areas by security team members. Player's movements around the stadium were minimal. Mostly players were brought to the training room and the locker room by security.

Chapter 6

Chris raced around another corner; each corridor looked the same to him, just a white maze. He began to think of himself as a rat stuck in a maze, which would not be too far from the truth. The more surprising thing to Chris was he had not come into contact with another person since fleeing the training room. Beads of perspiration began to form on his brow as panic set in looking to him what seemed to be one endless hallway. He knew it was game day and there were thousands of staff members here at the stadium, "Where is everyone!" Out of the corner of his eye he detected movement, immediately he ran toward it and started shouting, "Wait, wait!" He rounded the corner only to see no one there, the only thing Chris could see was a computer monitor with all kinds of lights blinking.

He took a closer look at the monitor; it was a split screen with various video feeds from area cameras. The videos kept cycling to other areas of the stadium. One image in particular panicked Chris; he saw Doctor Chase very red and agitated barking orders to people. Chris could see the screen filled with security team members. He stood staring at the screen, he did not truly understand what was going on but he was sure his instinct to flee was the correct response. He could see team after team being told by Steve were to go; Chris knew he had to find a way out of the stadium.

He had met Steve on numerous occasions, he was not what you would call mister laughs, he was military all the way through. As he took off again he began to think about his situation, if he truly had a head injury this would not be happening. Why in the world would they be chasing after him this way, he had done nothing wrong. These thoughts were racing through his head as he came across a door that opened to a stairwell. He tested the door and was in luck the door opened easily. Thinking his best way to get out was to go up he started sprinting up the stairs two at a time. He continued to spiral up stair after stair he had lost count but was very surprised he had not reached the top of the stadium yet.

When entering the stadium the players were met by security and escorted to the locker room. Every locker room Chris had spent time in was underground or least under the stadium, so this was never something he questioned as they got into the elevator to go down to the locker room. Chris never even paid any attention to the number of floors down it took to reach his destination. After what seemed to Chris to be the twentieth floor he had passed he came to a door labeled nurses station. Standing with his hand held toward the knob he thought about what he would say if he met someone. "Does everyone but me know what's going on here?" he blurted aloud. He jumped back as the door opened, Chris did not know whether to run or knock the person out coming through the door, his adrenaline still coursing through him after his escape.

He decided to pounce when coming face to face with those eyes. The eyes that had put him into a trance every time he saw them staring at him. "Chris! "she screamed in horror. Chris then realized he had his fist in a position to strike and realized what he probably looked like to this statuesque beauty standing before him. Staring at her for a moment he just collapsed against the wall, the weight of the moment felt to crush him. Sitting on the stairs he put his head in his hands. The day that was to be a fulfillment of a dream had become a nightmare. If April was somehow involved, he could not even bring himself to face that thought. April kneeled beside him and come to the realization that something was very wrong. "Chris," she started, "Why are you not on the field and why you are not wearing a uniform?" Chris just stared at her, "I am on the field, don't you know that!" April's eyes raised, "What are you talking about, the last time I saw you, you were going into the H-Chamber to get ready for the game." April looked very confused.

Chris was livid but he looked at April and could tell by the look on her face that she was just as confused as he was with the situation at hand. "April, don't mess with me right now I am in no mood for lies right now. April starred at him, "What the hell are you talking about, you are looking and talking like a crazy person! I am still trying to figure out why you are here right now. I am going to call Doctor Chase." She went to leave and Chris grabbed her by the arm and pulled her close to him and growled, "You are not going anywhere until I find out what is going on!" She swatted his hand away, "Get your hands off me," and then she looked at him with pity and then sat down with him. She gently put her hand on his shoulder, "Alright Chris what happened?"

He looked into her beautiful eyes and felt he could tell her anything. He sighed, "I went to the locker room to get ready for the game and went into the H-Chamber." He paused, "I have gone into the H-Chamber probably a hundred times, I don't understand it. Anyway I was inside the Chamber watching video of our opponent when I started day dreaming. Of course this is nothing new for me, it has been happening my whole life. This was much different though much different, I physically felt the hits in my dream." He felt his side which still had a dull pain

50

to it. "Then I tackled one of the other players and he put his arm out to brake his fall and landed awkwardly and dislocated his elbow!" He winced as if reliving the hit. "I felt his elbow give out, I could sense his pain, how do you dream that! I thought I was going to be sick, I woke up and was still inside the H-Chamber. I just thought it was time to dress for the game."

"That is when the nightmare began; I found the Chamber dark and had to feel my way around for the button to let myself out. When I came out the whole room was dark and empty except for the big screen. Guess what was on the big screen, me making the tackle I had just dreamed about. They were replaying it over and over while they tended to him and took him off the field. Then I saw,… I saw,… I saw myself walking in with the team at half-time! April grabbed his shoulder, "Chris, what are you talking about, I was there when you all walked out of the tunnel onto the field to play!" Chris lifted his hands and cupped her face gently, "April, I never left the H-Chamber!" April just sat there staring at him. "It gets worse," He continued, " I tried the double doors, they were locked so I went to the side door and then I ran into Rachel, Doctor Chase's assistant.

Rachel told me everything was okay. At first I thought I had sustained a head injury and she said as much. I was asked to lie down on the training table and then I saw the text she got on her phone, it said, "Take care of it. Keep him there." As she was about to inject me with something I knew in the pit of my stomach that something was dreadfully wrong and ran right into your arms." They both sat in disbelief, April just kept shaking her head, "This is crazy, I have been here for a year and I have not seen anything out of the ordinary that would describe what you are talking about!" Chris scowled, "April think about it for a minute, why do we need to be escorted by security everywhere, they tell us it is so we do not get lost but, come on, what is really going on here?" April shot to her feet, "Chris we have to get you out of here!" Chris scrambled to his feet and followed her as she sprinted up the stairs.

It was at this point they both heard voices coming from below them on the stairs. Chris pushed April's back, "Go, Go!" They were both in panic mode at this point. Chris could feel his heart racing as if it would pop right out of his chest and his lungs were burning by the time they reached the upper levels. They could still hear voices but they were far below them, "the security teams must be sweeping floor to floor," April added. She then stopped at the next door and turned to Chris, "wait here, I will be back in a minute!" With that she opened the door and was gone. Chris just leaned into the corner trying to catch his breath. He could still hear a voice now and then shout as the security teams opened the next door.

They were still away from him but still Chris could not help feeling like he should keep moving. He turned back toward the door April had exited just a few minutes ago and started to worry again. He started to wonder again if April knew what was happening, how could she work here for a year and not know what the team was doing. It was then that the door cracked open, "Chris," April whispered, "Are you there?" "Right here," he pulled open the door and he grabbed April's outstretched hand as she pulled him into another large room, which Chris recognized. It was the big film room where the team had meetings as a whole team to discuss the game plan.

Doctor Chase felt the vibration of his phone in his hand. He put it to his ear, "Talk to me, what's going on?" He listened for a moment, "Okay, keep making your way upstairs, we need to get him before he runs into someone he knows. Whatever you do, make sure he is not hurt, he is going to be our franchise player for a long time. Of course how the hell are we going to explain this to the board of directors?" The Doctor thought back to when he had done Chris's physical and how his brain scans had raised his eyebrows. He said out loud, "I knew this was going to be an issue for him!" He thought to himself of all the research he could do with just Chris alone. Doctor Chase in what seemed to him to be another life had specialized in genetic research for the military.

The Doctor had made many break throughs in the area of brain function, especially the dream center of the brain. When he was recruited by Professional Football he was still young and thought he would be working with head trauma patients and creating new safer uniforms and helmets. He never in his wildest dreams thought for a moment that he would be working in the most secret, controversial genetic research possible. The phone vibrated again, "yes, please tell me you have found him? Can I just ask why we do not have him on video somewhere? What do you mean most of the video cameras have been diverted to stadium! What to save energy, are you kidding me what happens when we have a serious security breach! Tell them to turn all the cameras back on, now!"

The Doctor stood for a minute and realized that he had to find Chris soon; the game would be over soon. If Chris got out of the stadium with all of those people leaving the game, he would never find him. Sure he knew where Chris lived but he was sure Chris would not go back there. Then he placed a call to Steve, "Steve make your way to the upper levels, Chris will have figured out he has to get up there to find his way out. Unharmed Steve!" "Ten, four," came across the speaker. Doctor Chase walked quickly toward the elevators, he wanted to get to the upper levels and get to a net in place to keep Chris from leaving the stadium. Once in the elevator he began to think about his situation, as a doctor he always hoped to help heal others, however now he felt more like a government agent than a health care provider.

He always kept telling himself that the research he was performing would help untold numbers of people. In the end he knew something like this would happen, the operation had become too large. There were now too many variables to continue to cover their tracks. Their current program had been in place for many years and had worked remarkably well, considering the sheer volume of subjects involved. Then there was Chris, he really liked this kid, he had come from nothing and had built himself into a machine in both mind and body. The Doctor smiled and thought about all the research he could accomplish with Chris finding out how people willed themselves to greatness. The thought of Chris snapped him back to reality, the door to the elevator opened and the doctor sped to his office.

Chapter 7

April and Chris sat across from one another with a, "what do we do now look on their faces." They both looked at the huge TV; it was the fourth quarter with a little over eight minutes to go in the game. The camera man was panning the sidelines and settled on the defense which huddled together on the bench studying computer pads. Chris was beside himself as he again saw himself sitting with his teammates talking strategy. He turned to April pointing to the screen, "See, look right there! I am not crazy! I am right there with the defense! This is nuts, I am good but I cannot be in two places at once."

April could not believe what she was seeing, "Chris, it must be some kind of video imaging, like a super high tech video game. They must be generating your likeness with a computer. With all the injuries to you guys as players sustain maybe this is a way to ensure your health." Chris just looked baffled as he gazed at April, "Could it be that simple, could I be freaking out over nothing!" April started, "I have to believe that whatever is going on here is to prevent major injury to their investment, the team and its players! The board is always all over Doctor Chase about safety, it's kind of creepy actually. The board wants daily updates as to the health of every player. They literally have vital statistics on each of you. You would think the football players were little children being taught safety by a parent."

"Okay April, let us say you are right, why are they sending security teams armed to the teeth after me! Get me out to that field, I have to see for myself." "Chris," April said, "I have to get you out of here, let me find out what is going on and then I will let you know. If what you say is true, I cannot lead you right to them." Chris had a stern look on his face, "I have to know and I am not leaving until I see this video game!" April spun and went in the opposite direction, "hurry the field is this way."

They hustled down the hallway toward the field. After a few minutes April pulled up sharply and held her hand up for Chris to stop. He almost ran into her and skidded to a stop. "Chris, listen to me," she said, "I cannot go with you, I will find out what I can here but they do not know I am with you." Chris looked at her, "What are you talking about there are cameras everywhere, they know." April slyly smiled, "Not on Game day, they focus all their attention on the outside of the stadium and the field itself. To save electricity and money they shut down all video inside during the game." Chris could not believe his luck. "April, just get me close enough to see myself and then we will get out of here."

April pointed to the end of the hallway, "You go to the end of this hallway and take a right, go down the ramp and you will see the press section, just mingle in with them, many are former players anyway. You are dressed like them; you will blend right in with them. When the game is over they all line the tunnel to see the players come in, position yourself and you should have your answer." She started to walk away and Chris was panic stricken, "Where are you going?" "Me," she said, "I am going to run interference for you. I will go up top and make sure they are looking in the wrong areas. This stadium is so enormous that it should be easy to send them on a wild goose chase. Of course the last place they are going to be looking for you is right under everyone's nose. There are so many people

56

down there that no one will even bat an eye with another person that looks like an athlete. Make your way out of the stadium with the press and go right to my house." She turned back toward him and scribbled the address on a piece of paper and handed it to him. She then did something totally unexpected, she full on hugged him!

April pushed away from him and said, "Now hurry, meet me at my house tonight. No one will be looking for you there." Chris just stood there for a moment before he realized she had gone. He did as instructed and went right to the press room. He was very surprised to find no security there, maybe because this was an assigned press spot. Chris did not encounter any resistance and just marveled at the throng of people before him. There were people scrambling here, there and everywhere. Most had headphones and were typing away on their laptops while peeking at the game. Those who were not writing were locked in conversations regarding the play where Chris had tackled the player leading to the dislocated elbow. Looking at the walls he was amazed because he felt as though he was in the midst of the ultimate sports bar as well as being on the floor of the Stock Exchange. There were TV monitors everywhere; many were showing the game from every angle imaginable. The other monitors had stats flowing from every part of the game and every player. This was a Fantasy Football player's dream. They even had the teams who were playing right now.

Chris looked down to see people typing into their phones as though they were being given interviews and others were streaming video of the game and putting commentary into their phones. This sight to Chris was amazing, a few years ago the last major newspaper had gone completely online, no more paper copy. Chris had been a bit saddened by this, he had always enjoyed the hard copy but at the same time he relished the ability to get the news he wanted instantly. Watching the steady stream of swirling bodies around him he started to have a better understanding of what instant news meant. Of course he looked at the game clock, which had come to the two minute warning with the Marauders leading 34-31. The press had to scramble to finish their stories and get them out before the end of the game.

It was then he saw people start to make their way out a side door. Chris followed remembering what April had told him about the press watching the team coming in, trying to get some last minute photos for their stories. As April had described everyone crowded and maneuvered for the best spot to see the players. Chris did not want to be noticed so positioned himself in the second tier of the press and heard the sound of the bell going off signaling the end of the game. Almost immediately following the bell, players starting making their way back into the stadium.

From Chris's vantage point he could clearly see that these players did not look like any video images he had ever seen. There was a major obstacle where the press was stationed making it very difficult to actually reach out and touch the players. The players were entering a tunnel which was huge and the angle of the field seats going up made it difficult for physical contact. At its lowest point the media members closest to the field were still a good eight feet from field level. Then he spotted himself walking in, he looked every bit the gladiator, disheveled, bloodied, and filthy. He knew he shouldn't but he had to do it, he yelled, "Chris!"

The young man who would be Chris looked up. There were so many people the uniformed Chris could not tell where the voice came from. Chris knew as soon as the young man looked up that this was no hologram or video image. Those eyes looking for the person who called his name immediately cancelled any thought of an artificial image being generated. He once again had that dreadful feeling of something being seriously wrong and that he was personal being in danger. That feeling lasted a moment though, anger started to creep in, rage, how could there be someone who looked just like him taking his place on the field. He had spent a lifetime to get on this field. With that thought he jumped over the rail and eight feet down to the field below.

Doctor Chase stood at his desk looking at his computer screen. Upon his command all of the video cameras were scanning the entire stadium. Only one problem, the stadium was the size of a small city, which meant that it could take hours to locate Chris. That thought froze the Doctor in his place, "I don't have hours, Chris where are you, we have to talk!" There was a rushed knock on his office door. "Come in," the doctor looked up to find Rachel standing before him with an extremely worried look on her face. The doctor could tell she had bad news but did not want to be the bearer. "Spit it Out Rachel, where is he?" Rachel responded by handing her tablet nervously over to the doctor's keeping. Doctor Chase looked at the screen in time to see someone jump over the railing near the press room. "Rachel what is that, tell me that is not him!" Rachel looked at him nervously, "I am not sure, the camera angle is difficult and the lighting is not very good in that area."

The Doctor rewound the video slightly, only to look at the player in the tunnel looking up as though someone called him, oh my God, it's Chris!" Doctor Chase watched the video all the way thru again, he thought, "That is Chris but why call out and get the attention of the uniformed Chris? Alright Chris, what are you about!" He turned to Rachel, "if that is Chris then he is trying to get out of the stadium in the Chaos following the game. We have to get down there. If he gets in the crowd we will never find him and who knows what will happen."

Doctor Chase said, "Rachel have Steve and his security team meet down in the press room and double check that all exits are being covered by security and staff, just send them a photo on their phone and text them that Chris has a head injury. Oh, by the way do you still have that sedative ready? I have a feeling Chris is not in the mood to talk right now. I have seen him angry; I don't even think Steve would want to see him angry." Rachel nodded and produced a covered needle. Doctor Chase acknowledged the needle and turned and walked out of his office, "Let's Go!"

When safely inside the elevator Doctor Chase looked squarely at Rachel and stated, "We are definitely going to have to change protocol when it comes to dealing with the players. We have been much too lax." Rachel responded, "We have a long track record, we have never had anyone wake up before." The Doctor considered this for a moment, "I knew when I looked at his brain scan this could be an issue. I should have tested him further; some kind of trauma in the H-Chamber must have woken him. His mind was most likely never truly in dream state or on the other hand maybe his mind in a constant state of dream and therefore makes it difficult to offer such suggestion. He has got to be in a state of shock right now! He just saw himself on the field he worked his whole life to get on! We have to find him, make sure he is okay!"

Rachel was shaking her head, "How do we explain all this to him, to anyone for that matter and make them understand?" Doctor Chase put his hand to his forehead, "I don't know, I just don't know! The only think I do know if we do not find him and he gets hurt or lord forbid starts talking to the press we will be doing a lot of explaining." The door of the elevator opened and the doctor along with Rachel stepped into the large press room. At this point there were the custodial staff cleaning and preparing the room for the next event. They both went to the tunnel only to see a few grounds crew members bringing in a few things into the tunnel. The doctor looked at the jump that Chris had made from eight feet up, "It must be nice to be young, "he blurted out not even realizing Rachel was still with him. He looked down the the tunnel. He finally stood tall and said aloud, "Chris, what are you up to?"

April had made her way to Doctor Chase's office. The offices around the Doctors were still a hub of activity. April asked one the security staff if they had seen the Doctor. The young man, had to be relatively new because April did not recognize him. He was like many in the security force, a no nonsense kind of person. He first asked her for her ID badge and asking many questions of her before answering her question. After being grilled by this little troll, April found that the Doctor and Rachel were headed to the press room to deal with a medical issue. "Medical issue," April panicked, "they found him!" She made her way to the elevator and proceeded to the press room. Entering the elevator she felt as though her body temperature had doubled. The steel box felt as if it were closing in on her and she began to perspire. She had to get to the Doctor, but what kind of story was she going to tell the Doctor. Why had she followed him all over the stadium, couldn't it have waited, he would say.

61

When she arrived in the press room there was no longer anyone there. She took a moment to get her bearings; she could not keep running around. Where would Chris go from here, he would most likely try and find his way out of the stadium. April thought about this for a moment that would be the smart thing to do. Just as April was about to turn for home herself she couldn't help but feel that Chris would be stubborn and want to know what was going on. She had watched this one from afar and noticed his tenacity about everything he did. April had seen her share of driven players on the team before Chris but he was a different story altogether. Anyone who spent any time with Chris at all could tell that he played the game out of desperation. Not the kind of desperation of someone hoping just to play, no, to Chris it was like a veteran's desperation, always looking over your shoulder having to prove yourself day in and day out or like many veterans you would be cut for a younger, faster, cheaper alternative.

Chris, having been a first round pick and as talented as he was had no worries about making the team but whether he was playing or practicing April always noticed that chip on his shoulder. Almost as though he had been overlooked his whole life by those making the decisions. She had become intrigued by this young man and found herself increasingly finding ways to be near him. She remembered when she had come in to take his vitals for his physical. She could tell he was really nervous about the whole process but when he looked into her eyes she felt as though he was drawing her in.

There was something about Chris that made April feel safe and comfortable when he was near. She found herself thinking of his warm smile and his caring eyes. She had told Chris to find his way out of the stadium and to make his way to her home. By all indications Chris had followed her instructions and found his way out with the press. She turned one more time to look down the tunnel and walked back toward the press room. As she left the press room she started to wonder how Chris was going to get to her house. Would he become a stow away with a media member, would he just hitch a ride with someone. There was nothing she could do at this point except find her own way home and to be there to meet him when he arrived.

Standing in the elevator April began to think about what she had gotten herself into, the only saving grace for her at this point is no one knew she had seen Chris or had any idea she was involved. As this thought was passing through her mind the elevator door opened. April, being a petite woman and only 5' 3" looked up to see a large man towering over her. Steve just walked in the elevator looked at April for a moment and pressed a button and the door closed. Steve had turned and put both hands behind his back as if standing at ease during a military drill. Steve's years in the military hand left him with that distinct military bearing in the way he stood, walked, and interacted with others. April just stood staring at Steve's back, did he know something, and was he here for her?

A thousand things whirled around her head, she had worked so hard to get this job and now it was in danger. She began feel anger rising in her, how could Doctor Chase not let her know what was happening. April had worked with the man every day and she never had an inkling that he was doing anything other than working for the betterment of the team's health. April had really felt his caring for his players but was it all a ruse. Her anger still rising she did not even notice the elevator stop and Steve turn to look at her.

When she did realize Steve was looking at her she just returned a nervous smile his way. Steve began, "April, why are you down here, shouldn't you be upstairs with the rest of the medical team?" He left the question hanging in the air. April scrambled for an answer, "I was sent to find Doctor Chase, a player has been injured and needs his attention. I was told to look for him in the press room. I couldn't find him and I called up to them and they handled the situation. So once again I get sent on a wild goose chase, it's a good thing I don't get lost easily!" Steve just nodded with understanding and turned and walked out of the elevator.

When the door finally closed again April felt as though she would burst. She could feel perspiration starting to bead on her forehead with her heart still racing from her encounter with Steve. She always felt nervous around the massive security officer. There was just something about him; he seemed to always be glaring at everyone, trying to intimidate them. April started to gather herself and just about had herself under control when the door to the elevator opened to her floor. The medical suite was still teeming with activity. One of the other nurses noticed her and beckoned her over.

April rushed over and asked what they needed. It turned out that one of the players had broken his nose and had sustained a substantial gouge on the nose that required stitches. She stitched up the young man in no time and performed a few ace bandage wrappings before being allowed to leave. After cleaning herself up, she finally felt it was safe for her to leave. She had known if she left right away that it might seem suspicious with all the had been swirling around her at the moment. She made her way to her car with keys in hand. "Chris, you had better be there," she whispered.

Chapter 8

Chris had landed without incident, but looked up at the eight foot drop with a quick look of, "What was I thinking?" He immediately saw a couple of trainers and moved to a position right behind them. The team had numerous trainers so no one even gave Chris a second look. They were all talking about the other player dislocating his elbow. Chris wanted to smack them right in the head and say to them he was Chris but he had to find out what was going on. His head reeled as he continued to follow the horde of people making their way out of the stadium. He followed the trainers into a corridor with a large elevator at the end; he knew this to be the elevator to bring the players from the locker room to the upper levels of the stadium. He also knew that there was a large supply area just before the locker room, where previously he had grabbed a couple of ace bandages for a teammate. He slipped into the large supply room and contemplated what to do next, as far as he knew he had not yet been noticed.

As he was standing looking around for a place to hide he heard Doctor Chase's voice. "Steve, send your teams to the locker room and search everywhere. Send another team to the media center for the end of game interviews; make sure he is not with any of the media members! Are all the exits covered? I want him found, he could be hurt!" Chris heard that last sentiment from the doctor and was even more confused, "He wants to catch me, doesn't want me hurt or talking to the media?" Chris could not help but feel conflicted by the whole situation; maybe something really did happen in the Chamber to make him see things. He once again thought back to his dream state that he had dealt with his whole life. Many times when he would wake up he would be exhausted as if he actually had performed the acts in his dream. As in most cases he dreamt of playing on the field and it always felt so real that he was always surprised when he woke only to find himself in bed rather than the field. He started to take a step toward the door and saw the knob start to rotate. Out of sheer instinct he spun around and looked for a place to hide. He spotted an area at the back of the room. The area although well-lit looked very dark compared to the rest of the room, he dashed to the spot and hid behind pallets of ace bandages and sports tape.

Not a moment too soon which was evidenced by a small group of three people who entered the room. One was a trainer he recognized, and the other two were security officers. They watched the trainer bring in a few boxes of leftover supplies from the game and leave. The security officers stayed behind and began to look around, "This is ridiculous," one said, "Chris is already out of the stadium by now we are not going to find him here!" "I know," said the other, "just keep looking." They both spent a minute haphazardly looking around the room and glanced quickly at Chris's corner but did not look all that hard. They both looked at each other, "Let's get out of here!" As the door closed behind him Chris breathed a sigh of relief, the only problem now is what to do.

He sat on one of the boxes and thought for a moment, his window of escape had passed him by; there was no way he could get out of the stadium undetected. Of course he just allowed another escape opportunity pass him by, he could have knocked these security stooges out and taken one of their uniforms but he would only get so far that way. He was thinking of various ways to escape and then it hit him, "April!" How was he supposed to get to April's house? The thought of not making it to April's house seemed more horrifying than

66

being caught by Doctor Chase. Sitting in the corner leaning up against the wall he closed his eyes and thought of April.

He pulled up to April's home in his thoughts, April threw open the door and ran to him asking him frantically if he was alright. He assured her he was okay, while April whisked him inside before someone saw him. Once inside, April stood in front of him holding both his hands and looking into his eyes as she pulled him to her and swallowed him in an embrace. Chris felt as though he would be crushed but April was not letting go. When she finally let go he told her once again he was okay. She led him into the living room and asked him to take a seat.

She asked if he was hungry or thirsty, was there anything she could get him. He asked for something to drink and April disappeared into the kitchen. It was at this time that Chris realized he was exhausted. He lay back on the couch with both hands turned back so the back of his hands were covering his eyes. He sat there for what seemed to be several minutes when he got the strange feeling that something was wrong. Where had April gone, was she really getting him a drink, paranoia set in.

That thought brought him to his senses and he sat straight up in a full panic. As he sat up he did so only to see Doctor Chase in front of him. "Hello Chris, you have led us on quite the adventure. I am glad to see you haven't left yet." He looked to Doctor Chase's immediate right where April stood with her mouth covered with a large hand. Steve had a firm grip on her like a snake spiraling around its prey. "Chris," Doctor Chase continued, "We have to talk there are things here that are going on that you do not understand!" Chris was about to charge Steve when he felt the pinch in his neck, he felt a warm sensation run down his back and he tried to move to no avail. April looked at him with tears rolling down her cheeks. The last thing he saw was Steve release April and April streaking toward him and things went black.

Chris nearly jumped out of his skin as he woke up; trying to get his bearings he looked around him only to realize he was still in the training supply room. He was sweating profusely at this point and felt as though he was going to pass out. He could not tell what time it was, for all he knew he could have been asleep for hours. His stomach besides being in knots was growling so loud he thought it might give him away. Once he had calmed down a moment, he began to worry about April. His dreams had an eerie way of coming true and the last thing he ever wanted to have happen was April be involved and harmed in any way. The dream once again felt so real he put his hand on his neck to see if there was a welt where the needle had gone in. Feeling nothing, he thought carefully about what his next move should be, when he heard voices outside the door.

Steve turned to Doctor Chase, "We have all the exits covered and every camera in the entire stadium is on. We should locate him shortly. Doctor Chase responded, "What if he is already out there somewhere," he pointed outward, flourishing his arms in a wide arcing movement. "Honestly, Doctor Chase, he is probably freaked out hiding in the stadium somewhere, waking up from the H-Chamber and finding out the game was going on and someone else playing in his stead is enough to freak anyone out. It still freaks me out and I know what is going on." Doctor Chase looked at Steve with an understanding look, "Steve, I hope he is okay, this is exactly the reason we do not tell the players what is really happening, even those of us who do know still have a difficult time coming to terms with the truth! Find him Steve, he is really important to our research and our team, this dream state of his is absolutely amazing!"

Steve just nodded and walked away but he could not help think about the Doctor, here he was in the middle of a huge crisis and what is he thinking about, research. Steve smiled and pulled the phone to his face; he would find his man and keep all their butts intact as he always did. This is exactly what he was trained for, missions of great importance! It was during times like these that he felt as if he was back with his unit hunting out targets. He could not help feel energized. Steve thought to himself, "alright Chris, if I was freaked out and had to decide whether to leave or find out what was going on, what would I do?"

He had watched Chris with great respect since he had arrived. To Steve, Chris was not one of those athletes who had been coddled and had smoke blown up their backsides their whole lives. Athletes who thought they were the cat's meow really bothered Steve. He had worked extremely hard in life at everything he had ever done and had anything handed to him. Steve would watch their smirks and hear some of the comments about him and his security staff, "Rent a Cop's, etc. the athletes were always looking down on him.

Steve would become furious and then think back to his intense psychological and physical training as an Army Ranger. He was trained to ignore pain both physically and emotionally, his military bearing had always been a brunt of jokes since he had taken the job at the stadium. It was also the reason for his quick assent through the ranks and into the director's position.

His expectations and attention to detail kept the security in the stadium the envy of all the other professional teams around the various leagues. Steve had been asked on numerous occasions to train staff from other teams. He had also turned down many offers to take over other teams because of his fierce sense of loyalty.

Steve was so sought after and trusted that he was asked to be the coordinator of the disaster plan for all the clubs in the league. In this climate of terrorist groups looking to make a public splash, one could never be vigilant enough when it came to stadium security. In the military Steve's training had covered many counter terrorist tactics and large scale security protocol. This intense training provided the leadership needed to protect the thousands of people who came to see the games each week. Protection included not only the fans but the team and staff. He would think of the extreme discipline and strength of will it took to ensure everyone's safety. Steve also would look at many players seeing their toughness on the field but often wondered if they had that same toughness should a real disaster arise. His insights said many would run for the hills. Steve just smiled, if worse came to worse he could just bend them up like a pretzel and kick their ass! This thought brought a wide smile to his face.

Continuing to wonder where Chris might be brought an idea about an area in which Chris might be found. He had last been seen with the media. That particular area was what one would call high traffic and might be easy for someone to blend in with the crowd and walk right out of the stadium. He wondered what might be going on in Chris' mind with all that was swirling around him, this would be quite overwhelming for anyone. What if he has spoken with any media member but this did not seem feasible. Steve shook his head what would Chris say to anyone, he had no idea what was really going on and he would just sound crazy. No, Chris was stubborn, an athlete with a chip on his shoulder. As someone who came up the hard way Chris would want to find out everything he could.

Chris had always been respectful to Steve and the two seemed to have a genuine like and understanding of one another. Steve's eyebrows went down, "I have to find this kid, this really could ruin everything!" Steve gave the matter a little more thought. He was bound and determined to lose this position as it had been extremely hard to attain in the first place. Steve was not about to let anyone jeopardize his standing in the least. With a new look of determination he turned to a computer station in the hallway and pulled up the maps for the tunnel and the media area in which Chris was last seen.

He continued to look at the video of the area when something caught his eye. Steve was looking at the locker room, "No, he wouldn't try to make it in to the locker room, he wouldn't risk being seen right?" There was no way Chris could find the, "Sanctuary." Steve thought for a moment, the Sanctuary had two entrances/exits, one extremely secure. The main door to the Sanctuary came in through the locker room but the other had been designed for more secrecy and stealth. That entrance/exit was through the large supply closet. "That couldn't be it, my guys already searched there, or did they," he said to himself. He immediately ran in the direction of the supply room.

Chapter 9

Chris sat on the cardboard box with his back leaned up against the wall in the back corner of the supply room still trying to come to terms with his current situation. He knew there were video cameras everywhere so how did he get out without being discovered. He then heard the door open and two men dressed in Lab coats came into view. He heard one say, "Do you know what is going on? Security is running around like crazy. Did one of the C-Players get out?" The other answered, "No way! We would have known about it. Let's go! Doctor Chase will have our heads if we are late for the Slumber Party!" In response his friend said, "Yeh, we don't want to be late for bedtime," he started laughing, "Oh crap, I forgot my tablet; I will meet you in there!"

The man turned and ran back toward the door. "Alright hurry up," the other said and turned toward the wall that had all kinds of tools hanging on it. Chris watched in surprise as the young walked right up to the wall and reached up to one of the hammers and pulled it down slightly. As soon as he pulled Chris heard a click and then silently a large door opened inward and the young man disappeared inside. The door closed silently and swiftly behind him. When the door was closed once again Chris walked over from his hiding spot to stand in front of the door, the way everything was organized on the wall he could not even tell where the seams of the door the man had just gone through.

He returned to his box and contemplated what he had just witnessed, "What are C-Players," he heard himself say,

"And what the hell is a Slumber Party." Chris once again heard the door open; he saw it was the other young man went past him. As he passed Chris whacked him on the back of the head with leftover piece of two by four that was leaning on one of the boxes. There was an eerie crack sound as the piece of wood struck the man's head. The man went down in a heap and crashed into several boxes which went tumbling everywhere.

Chris bent down to look to look at the man; he was out cold, but otherwise okay. He then dragged him to his secluded corner and secured him with athletic tape and even taped his mouth shut. He grabbed his lab coat and put it on himself. He also picked up the man's tablet, clipped the ID badge on and put the man's glasses on his face. If anyone looked quickly Chris looked similar to the unconscious man, hopefully that would be enough. Chris stood before the tool wall and as the man had previously done pulled down on the hammer. The same click and the door opened before him, without a moment's hesitation, he walked through the door into another hallway.

The hall itself was only dimly lit and by no other source but that of light at the end of the hall itself. Chris moved forward cautiously as the door silently closed behind him. He could see the light and the end of the hall, at first it just looked to be glowing but as he inched closer he could see a larger well lit room starting to emerge before him. Staying close to the wall keeping to the shadows, Chris could make out a huge medical lab. There were people with lab coats walking from station to station. What struck him was the sheer size of this lab; from his vantage point he could see various stations. There were people moving from station to station with vials and flasks.

One station in particular caught his eye; there was a young lab technician who was carrying a clear cylinder. It was not the cylinder that was odd to Chris but what was inside sent chills down his spine. Inside the cylinder Chris could clearly make out a small form in the liquid. At a closer glance Chris could clearly see that the small form was that of a baby, such that you would find in a mother's womb. He could not believe what he was seeing, the lab tech took the cylinder to another station. She carefully placed the cylinder on top of a large boxlike structure; to Chris it seemed like another H-Chamber. As the lab tech placed the cylinder click into place. The young lady went to the computer and started typing information, when finished Chris heard a whining sound emanating from the top of the chamber. He could not help but stare daring not to take his eyes away from what he was witnessing. When the whining stopped he heard a snap and watched the young child get sucked into the chamber. He felt himself let out an, "oh," sound out of his mouth. He crept a little closer and continued to watch the chamber. At a closer look, Chris could see the chamber had a Plexiglas viewing area on the front. Chris could clearly see the young child now floating in the middle of the chamber and moving its arms and hands slightly.

He also noticed for the first time that the baby had a small belt around it's waist with a small silver adapter attached where the child's belly button would be. Chris watched as a snakelike structure much like a fiber optic camera that law enforcement would use to find out what kind of dangers were inside closed rooms. The snake found its way to the babies' waist and attached itself to the silver adapter like an umbilical cord. Watching the baby Chris was mesmerized, once attached the baby immediately stopped thrashing about. The child's arms and legs seemed to float freely in the liquid and the baby seemed more calm. The child then began to bring its arms and legs closer to its body as though it would be sleeping in the womb.

Chris found himself moving toward the chamber. Before he even knew what was happening he found himself in front of the chamber unable to take his eyes off of the child floating comfortably. Someone tapped him on the shoulder ad he whipped around to find he was looking at the lab tech that had taken care of the child. She turned to Chris, "You're new," she smiled, "its okay this is a lot to take in when you first encounter this entire process. Where have they assigned you?" The question hung in the air for a moment. Chris looked at her and replied, "I don't know they just sent me down here, something must be going on because people are running around like crazy upstairs." She said, "Sure I know, game day can be crazy. That's alright, come with me they probably need you in the Stage Three Lab." She beckoned him and he followed her, keeping his head bowed slightly as to not have eye contact with anyone else. The last thing he needed was someone recognizing him and finding himself in harm's way.

Chris followed the lab tech through a brilliantly lit hallway thinking the whole time how he kept putting himself in difficult situations today. He should have just followed April's instructions and found his way to her home. He was just so intrigued at this point by what he had seen, he felt drawn by his own curiosity to find out what was happening to him and around him. Following the young lady he was able to get a good look around. Moving through the room, Chris noticed that the whole lab was devoted to the small infants floating in the chambers. Continuing on, he really started to realize the gravity of the activities surrounding him. Chris thought, "This has all been happening right under my nose this entire time. I have seen things like this on TV but this is not Science Fiction this is real life."

What really bothered Chris however, was why in the world is this happening in a sports complex. He thought for a moment, being a student of history he started thinking about athletes and their constant to battle to get bigger, better, and faster. Throughout history athletes had always had to battle the ability to play the game and the constant challenge to win. The notion of winning at all costs was given new meaning in this climate of outrageous contracts and billion dollar teams. Of course that thought followed Chris back to where he was now. He had grown up in a climate where PED's surrounded everything athletes were involved in today. So much so teams actually issued their own standardized amino acids and recovery agents.

What Chris saw in front of him however brought him back to WWII during a time when Germany experimented on its athletes to create the ultimate performer. Of course that was before American athlete Jesse Owens went on to disprove the German stance on their athletes by becoming victorious during the Olympic Games. Chris froze, "Am I witnessing history all over again. Is Doctor Chase trying to create the ultimate human?" Then it hit him, "Oh my god, they are creating US!" He could not move, this thought caused him to stop midstride and his head began to spin. The young lab technician noticed Chris's plight and turned to him, "Are you OK?" He looked at her forcefully and grinned, "Just a little nervous I guess." She smiled warmly, "You'll do great, don't sweat it. The folks around here are very cool and they are willing to help you in any way you need." Chris just nodded and continued to follow sheepishly.

She stopped in front a large double door and placed her security card on the reader and the doors silently opened. She looked back at him, "I will bring you through Stage Two and then introduce you in Stage Three. I just have to talk to one of the other technician's here in Stage Two." Entering another large lab he noticed the chambers were much different. The chambers he was looking at here in Stage Two were quite large; they were larger than the size of a man. Similar in construction to the chambers he had just viewed they also had Plexiglas viewing areas on all four sides. Unlike Stage One, these chambers contained human male figures of various sizes but yet not full grown. Chris looked at the figures and saw that they ranged in ages from three to adolescent.

Each seemed to have what amounted to an intricate football helmet with many wires and tubes coming from the helmet and the figures mouths. Chris looked at one particular young man before him who was naked except for what amounted to a speedo. He could not help himself and edged closer to the chamber to get a better look at its inhabitant. A closer look revealed a good look at the young man's eyes. The eyes themselves were covered to what amounted to a pair of night vision goggles. Being a hunter, Chris was familiar with these as he had used them on hunting trips with his friends in the past.

Each young man was floating in the same clear fluid as the small infants, the only difference being this fluid had a greenish tinge to it. Chris stood in awe as he looked around the room, he could see at least a hundred of these chambers, each with a young man inside. The young lab tech went quickly to speak to one of her colleagues. While she spoke to the tech Chris continued to look around the room scanning each chamber to see if there were any differences. What he could see was the normal differences in hair color and facial structure, very subtle but not huge differences.

Chris walked cautiously in front of one of the chambers and caught sight on the young man inside. The young man had a familiar appearance. Chris walked right up to the glass itself and looked closely at the figure before him, although he could not see the face of this individual he knew without a doubt what he was looking at. He slowly backed away from the chamber almost stumbling as he did he noticed the name on the computer screen in the upper right hand corner of the chamber, he almost screamed!

Chapter 10

Steve arrived with three members of his security team and opened the door to the large supply closet. He entered and told his team to leave no stone unturned and let him know if they find even the smallest thing out of the ordinary. They all agreed and fanned out around the room with flashlights in hand. The supply room was extremely large and it took some time for everyone to look in every corner. It was Steve that noticed some movement out of the corner of his eye. Steve made his way slowly and stealthily to the spot in which he had seen movement. At first, Steve just noticed the darkness of the corner and approached with his flashlight raised. He continued toward the movement until he began to make out the outline of a man. The Head Security officer quickened his steps and moved with his hands outstretched to grab the escapee. When he did get to the man he noticed it was one of the lab techs that worked in the Sanctuary.

The man was twisting and turning to try and loosen his bonds. Steve with one massive hand grabbed the tape and tore it from the lab techs hands and mouth, "Oww that hurt!" Steve just glared at him, "What happened!" The lab tech just shrugged and responded, "I was going into the lab and the last thing I remember was the pain of getting smacked in the head with something. The next thing I know I am here in a dark corner all tied up. I have no idea how long I have been here but I woke up about an hour ago." As the wobbly lab tech stood Steve reached out and steadied the man. Steve asked, "Where is your lab coat?" The young man looked down at himself as if he were wearing no clothes, "My security card is gone!"

Steve told one of his officers to take the young man to the nurse's station for treatment. He motioned for the other two officers to join him by the secret door. He proceeded to pull down the hammer and enter the hallway moving toward the Stage One Lab. The trio moved quickly down the hall and nearly slipped and fell on the smooth highly polished floor of the lab. Steve regained his bearings and went over to the Lab Supervisor. The supervisor looked with a questioning glance as the mammoth man loomed over him. Steve led with, "I am looking for someone that may have passed this way recently, someone new, someone who might look a bit out of place." The supervisor answered, "Steve, you know as well as I do that on game day there are people everywhere, in many cases there are people who I may not know simply because they work in other labs or areas of the complex. You know we are always drawing resources from every inch of this place. To answer your question though, we had a computer glitch and almost lost a whole crop of newborns. That has taken up most of my time today. I have not really been in a position to notice anyone, sorry!"

Steve just turned in an attempt to keep himself together; he wanted to scream but knew how important the work was here in the lab. To lose a whole crop of newborns would be devastating and Steve knew it. He simply waved as he walked away and said, "Thank You!" As he was walking away another young tech came up to Steve and said he had seen a female tech taking a new male tech to Stage Three. Steve yelled thanks as he hurried across the room and went into Stage Two. He came to an abrupt halt, "Chris has got to be beside himself about what he is seeing right now." He scanned the room; it was an unbelievable sight, even for himself that has been here at the facility for some time now. There was still a sense of awe when Steve looked at the young man in one of the chambers and he still found himself wanting to touch the creature in the chamber to prove reality. Of course if anyone outside this complex found out what was really taking place here, the implications would be extremely far reaching. He imagined the public with this knowledge that they were funding human experiments, it would be a nightmare. Steve walked toward Stage Three, he could not allow Chris to slip through his hands and ruin everything.

Chris found Stage Three to be very similar in design to the other labs. The chambers here were much the same as the ones he had previously witnessed in Stage Two, the only noticeable difference being the size of the chambers. These chambers to him seemed to be at least eight feet tall with a larger surface area of clear Plexiglas. Chris noticed a large screen that resembled a flat screen TV. On the screen, Chris could see what looked to him like a diagnostic of the human brain. Although Chris did not truly understand what he was seeing, he was in awe of the electrical pathways being shown on the screen. It could have easily been mistaken by some to be a video game with the electrical currents flowing in all different directions and with such fabulous colors. As in the previous labs human beings took up residence in the chambers. The young man that Chris saw in the closest chamber looked to be in his late teens. He continued to look around the lab to see again a variety in the age of the subjects in the chambers ranging from late teens to early twenties. All the young men had similar equipment such as the helmet, the mouthpiece, and the goggles.

The young lady brought Chris to a station where there were a few other lab techs working at a computer station. One looked up pleadingly, "Awesome, some much needed help! Alright come with me!" He motioned for Chris to follow; Chris did not even notice that the young lady that had helped him was already gone. The new lab technician brought him to another door and entered into once again a cavernous room. Chris looked at the room; to him it looked like an extremely large warehouse. The walls and ceiling were painted black with striking white fluorescent lights everywhere. What was most noticeable to Chris was the fact that he really could not make it out the end of the room because of its sheer size.

Chris just stood with his jaw dropped and mouth wide open. As he was looking at the sight before him he could not even begin to understand how many H-Chambers he saw before him. The chambers just stood in row after row; column after column, Chris did not even think he could see where the room ended. The lab tech continued on until he came to another computer station. He beckoned Chris to sit; Chris looked at the computer screen and saw it was some kind of monitoring program. He was informed that since he was new he could monitor the chambers for a while and then someone would relieve him shortly. He further explained to Chris that if an issue arose and the red light goes off and flashes that he had to press the large red button. Also he was to contact anyone he could raise on the intercom next to the computer.

Chris sat at the station as instructed and watched the young man start to walk away. The tech walked about ten steps forward and then sharply turned around and ran back up to Chris. He stood before Chris with a stunned look on his face, this look suddenly turned to panic. "You, you are Chris (Strong) from the Maruaders!" Chris stood to his full height towering over the little man. Chris started, "Listen, I really am Chris and I have no idea what is going on here, this is just crazy! This is something out of a science fiction movie." The young tech excitedly said, "Chris I love how you play, you are awesome, how the hell did you get down here. You can't be here, I have to tell someone," he turned to leave when Chris grabbed him in a full nelson head lock and would not let him go. The little man began to squirm and tried to shout only to have Chris put his meat hook of a hand over his mouth. It was then that the man bit Chris' hand and started to run toward the door as Chris instinctively released his grip from the bite. Chris had no choice and ran toward the fleeing man and did what he does best running the man down while tackling him as he would on the football field. Both men tumbled to the ground in a twisting mass of humanity ending with them propped up against of the chambers. Chris looked up and saw the young man he had just taken down was leaning with his head up against the chamber in an awkward fashion unmoving. To Chris's relief he leaned down to check the man and found he was still breathing but was unconscious.

He scrambled to his feet and went quickly back to the computer terminal he had been at minutes ago. With trembling hands he typed in his name and waited a moment. He hoped for a milla second that nothing would come up but that idea quickly left his mind as he looked at the computer screen. To his horror he saw his name on the screen along with a sheet of information on him including a chamber number. Turning to look at the nearest chamber he began looking for a chamber number. At first Chris could see nothing but he walked up to the chamber and started on one side and continued to circle around the chamber until he found what he was looking for. On the right hand top corner of the chamber where the control box was had a stamped number in plain sight. He looked at the number when he saw for the first time the young man inside. The figure was floating in the liquid with his array of helmet, mouthpiece, and goggles he had seen in the other labs, gone however was the greenish liquid.

Chris began to walk up the row in order to find how the sequence of numbers on the chambers was organized. Quickly figuring the general area in which his chamber would be situated he began jogging toward the area. When he came to his chosen area he frantically began to look at the numbers until he came to the chamber he was searching for. Staring at the number, at first he was paralyzed and could not bring himself to look inside. The sheer weight of the moment was pressing on his chest. How were these people in these chambers being used by the doctor? Remembering back for what seemed to be a day ago, Chris, thought of seeing himself walking off the field into the tunnel which made him cringe. That thought sobered him up and he began to feel his body temperature rise at the thought of what was going on without his knowledge or permission. He finally brought himself to look inside the chamber.

The sight chilled him to the bone! Even with helmet, mouthpiece, and goggles, Chris could still recognize his own facial and body features. Coming face to face with himself, he studied the figure before him. Chris had of course viewed himself in mirrors as anyone would shaving or grooming. This however, gave new meaning to looking at one's self. He put his hand on the glass as if expecting the young man inside to notice him. There was no movement in the chamber other than the rhythm of the man in the box's heartbeat. Chris could not help but have a pang of sadness for the man in the chamber, what was to become of this man before him. As he stood in front of the chamber he felt a hand on his shoulder. He spun to find another lab technician looking at him.

The lab tech asked Chris if he could help with an equipment issue as Chris realized he was still wearing a lab coat. Chris just motioned that he would follow and turned toward the door. Following the young man into the next room, Chris became totally overwhelmed. He was back in the locker room! He could see a few last straggler players taking themselves to therapy. Looking around the locker room he looked directly at his own locker and there sitting on a chair taking tape off his ankles was a player that looked exactly like Chris. Chris could not help himself he made his way over to his locker with his head slightly down so as to not draw attention to himself. Standing in front the young man who was still working on his tape and did not look up but did respond, "I will be done in just a minute you can help me in a second." Chris just grabbed him under the arm and hauled him up. The man shot a glance at Chris. As the two men came face to face the shock and tension between them was enough to make anyone in the room lose their breath. They both stared at one another and each seemed not to want to say the first word. As they continued to take each other in, the back door slammed open and in burst Steve with his security team.

Chapter 11

April drove as fast as she could home without drawing attention to herself driving just slightly over the speed limit. Her travel home was pretty uneventful and she opened her door and rushed into the entry way. She walked back and forth in the hallway looking for Chris, "Chris are you here," she called. She walked into the living room, a very warm room with curtains going straight to the floor. April threw herself on the plush leather couch sinking down with a whoosh of air releasing from the pillows. She sat up slightly and kicked off her slip on shoes and felt the softness of the rug on her feet. Unsure as to whether Chris had heard her call the first time she hollered his name one more time to no avail. April thought he should have been there by now, what could have kept him. Her directions had been very easy to follow and it would have been easy to find his way out of the stadium with the crowd.

Sitting in the elegance of her beautifully decorated home she suddenly had a profound sense of loneliness. She thought about each of the times she had spent time around Chris, he most definitely affected her in ways that still had her quite confused. Each time she had seen Chris his eyes just looked into her soul and she could see genuine affection stream from them. To April this was quite unnerving. April was used to other men looking her up and down as if they wanted to devour her. Of course this made April feel very uncomfortable because she wanted people to see her as an intelligent hardworking woman, not an object of desire. April felt as though Chris was looking at her with x-ray vision and was hoping to learn anything he could about her. He was always interested in her as a person and rarely talked about himself, quite the departure from the selfish athlete stereotype. Having been around sports

86

figures talking of nothing but their imagined greatness this to her was a breath of fresh air.

April thought back to an interview she had seen Chris give, she could not recall a single time he spoke about himself. The entire interview he spoke about nothing but his teammates, his team, and how they all needed to push each other to get better. The only time she could recall him talking about himself was a play he messed up causing a touchdown against his team. He was furious with himself for hurting his team and letting his warriors down as he referred to his teammates. April also always felt comfortable and safe anytime Chris was near. It was almost as if she could do anything or say anything when Chris was with her. That comfort level surprised her because as she had sunken into her couch, she realized she really knew next to nothing at all about Chris the man.

Steve sprinted across the locker room toward the two Chris's as both young men just looked at each other and charged the massive security officer. The two men hit Steve square in the mid-section spearing him with a huge thud. Steve could feel the air expel from his lungs as they all hit the floor in a heap. To Chris's shock Steve was back on his feet almost instantly. He turned to Chris with a sneer and pulled out an extending baton and clicked it open to its full three foot extension. By this time the other two members of Steve's security team were closing in on Chris's twin circling him. Chris could not worry too much about him with Steve looming before him with an angry look of revenge on his face.

With a quick flick of the wrist Steve's baton found its way toward Chris's head with shocking speed. Chris dipped his head just in time to avoid the ball of the baton hitting him square in the ear. Instinctively he brought up his forearm and deflected the rest of the blow, bringing his other arm around in the same motion and catching Steve on the chin with his elbow. Steve's head absorbed the blow and snapped back violently. Steve countered with a leg sweep and he felt Chris' leg give way underneath him and fall to the ground. He brought his baton around and downward with terrific force in order to subdue Chris and render him harmless. The blow never made it to its target with Chris rolling out of the way and hopping to his feet as though he were doing an up down at practice.

Chris brought his own hulking frame to its full height and turned once again to face his attacker. Chris's twin had his hands full spinning around from one attacker to the next warding blows. His twin was remarkably quick and spun out of the way of one combatant while both attackers ran into one another. He grabbed one of the security officers by the collar and the back of the belt swinging him head first into the wall. The man's head struck the wall with shocking force. The man did not rise and lay in a heap on the floor. While getting his bearings Chris' twin felt the other officer jump on his back and then felt the metal of the baton across his throat. Immediately he leaned forward and flipped the unsuspecting man through the air and onto his back on the cold hard floor. He spun around to find Chris had come to his aid.

The two large men looked like lions circling one another, each other battling for supremacy. Steve feinted forward and then spun with a forehand punch aimed at Chris's face. Chris dipped and crouched into a tackle position and took Steve down to the ground. This seemed to surprise Steve; he was not used to sparring and fighting with someone with this combination of size and strength. Once again Steve found himself on his backside and getting more frustrated by the second. Up on his feet again facing Chris they both looked like linebackers ready to make a tackle. As Chris went to attack again he saw movement quickly approaching Steve from behind and saw a chair strike Steve square in the back of the head and shoulders. Chris watched the big man go down limp and he stood once again with, HIMSELF! They both were red in the face and looked at each other with the look that said they needed to get out of there now.

Both men ran toward the door and raced into the next hallway. They saw another lab tech at the end of the hallway and ran up beside him, one on either side. Chris asked hurriedly, "Dr. Chase needs us upstairs right now, what is the fastest way?" The man unquestioningly told them to follow him and they all entered the elevator. As the door was closing Chris could make out one of the security officers had made it to his feet and was racing toward the elevator door just in time to have the door close in his face. The lab tech was about to open the door when the powerful hand of Chris's twin grabbed his arm and pulled it away from the buttons.

The lab tech looked up in confusion at the two men first at one and then the other with a look of recognition, "Chris, what are you doing?" Chris scowled at the tech, "We are getting out of here now, you can help us or I can just knock you out! I am in no mood for any crap; just get us out of here!" He looked at Chris, "I can get you out no problem; your friend here is another matter. Even if I get him out with you they will know where he is as they can track him." "Track him?" asked Chris. At first the man looked as though he would say no more until he saw both behemoths glaring at him like a juicy steak. "Chris, he has a chip in the back of his head connected to his brain stem, I am not sure if there is even a way to deactivate it without harming him. I just help maintain the chambers. I am an engineer." Chris looked at him, "Are you sure there not anything we can do?" The man thought for a moment and then his face brightened, "Give me your cell phone!" Chris looked at him cautiously but the man just nodded with his hand outstretched.

Chris took out his phone and handed it over to the young man. The lab tech grabbed it and began to move his thumbs in a frantic typing motion. A few moments later he handed the phone back to Chris. Chris looked at him with a questioning look. The man responded, "I cloned the GPS signal of the chip in his head. I cannot turn it off without doing damage to his brain but what I did is transferred the active GPS signal to the phone. What that means is wherever the phone is, that is where they will think he is, cool huh!" Chris looked at the man with a look of genuine gratitude, "Why are you helping us?"

The man looked at Chris with tears brewing in his eyes, "I lost my brother recently to illness and I could only watch him slip away while I could say or do nothing about what I know about what happens here. Now that my brother is gone none of that seems to matter much anymore. If I had been stronger I could have done something to help my brother." He starred at the twins, "People need to know!"

The door to the elevator opened and Chris could see that they were at entrance level. They stepped out, the lab tech looked at both and said, "Chris, look after him, all he knows is football, he does not even know where he is right now" Chris let that statement sink in for a moment. The other Chris had not even said anything to him during this whole ordeal. He suddenly looked at his twin and placed his hand on the man's shoulder to reassure him. The lab tech had told Chris he had to go before someone saw him with them. Chris told the young man that it was okay he knew how to get out from here. The tech just bolted in another direction and was gone. Chris turned to his counterpart and said, "This way, we have to get out of here right now!"

Surprisingly there was still quite the crowd left in the stadium making their way to the exits. Both men just began to walk toward the exit as would any fan leaving. Chris spotted a large mass of fans leaving and veered toward the group. Once near the group both men were absorbed by the swarm of people and anyone looking would just see normal fans leaving. Chris just followed the mob straight to the exit. As he approached the exit however he noticed that at each exit stood a security officer. At this point Chris was not about to allow one security officer to stop him, so with unmatched determination he continued to approach the exit. With his head slightly turned down he walked right out of the exit just looking slightly over his shoulder to see his twin walking out as well. Having a great feeling of relief, Chris continued to follow the crowd.

The mass of excited fans returning to their vehicles brought back a lot of memories of Chris attending games with his father as a youngster. The sights and sounds, along with the smells brought Chris back to a great place of innocence and joy. He remembered coming to the stadium to see the games and the energy filled walk back to the car to tailgate after a big win. Of course there was always the stinging feeling a defeat brought, especially at home where your team was supposed to defend its honor. Somehow the extra tailgating after the game made always made things right. Just spending time with family and friends for the game, always had a special place in Chris' heart. For a few moments he felt almost normal. He had not spent much time thinking of the state of his life lately. He was so busy worrying about making it to the professional level that everything else was left behind. It was at that moment that he realized that his twin must be completely overwhelmed by this situation and he was surprised the young man had not completely freaked out.

He turned to his twin, "Are you OK?" The man turned to him with a look of someone overly stimulated and responded, "I have no idea what is going on, who are you!" Chris looked at him with a look of unending sympathy, "I am you! You were made, from what I can piece together, to replace me on the football field." Chris shook his head as if he could still not believe what he was saying and continued, "This is really screwed up, I have no idea what to say here! I am just as confused and angry as you. I just cannot wrap my head around what is going on right now. I do want you to know that I will do all I can to help you. We have to get to my friend April's house but I have no idea how we are going to get there. My car is in the player's parking lot and there is no way I am going there right now."

Chris looked at the man next to him, "Although, we are going to have to call you something other than Chris because this whole thing is totally freaking me out. How about Christopher so it does not seem too weird for you?" His twin smiled, "Christopher, yeh that will work. What do you mean I was made?" Chris turned to his mirror image, "From what I just saw the Team is creating clones of its players and using them in place of the real players on the field. When we get to April's we will talk to her and I will explain more about what I know and what I have seen to you and April. All I know right now is we are in danger and lots of people are going to be after us. They do not want us loose telling anyone what is going on here at the stadium." "No Chris," Christopher said, "I understand, it is just too much like a Sci-Fi movie!"

Chris saw a large group milling around a huge tent with a roaring fire in front. He waved for Christopher to follow and started toward the tent. The thought in his head was to just casually hang out with these people and then hitch a ride. What he had failed to realize is the commotion he could cause after a big win and being recognized by fan. Which is exactly what happened to him as he approached the tent. Almost immediately a person with Chris's jersey came flying up to him going crazy with recognition. As soon as the man approached Chris the whole tent just engulfed Chris and Christopher in a human shield.

The excitement enveloped them. Any other time Chris would have just eaten up the attention. Chris took a look around the tent and could tell right away these were veteran tailgaters with quite the set up going here. He wanted nothing more than to be just another guy hanging out with his buddies enjoying a game. Today was different. He held up his hand and asked for quiet so he could speak. It took a few minutes but everyone eventually relented and quieted down giving Chris their attention. "Listen," Chris started, "My brother and I wanted to sneak out and tailgate with some fans but if we make a huge deal of this then we will not be able to do it again." As he said this he could see the small crowd get protective glances and they all started nodding.

After a few minutes of small talk Chris found out that the owner of the tent was named Pete. Pete and his friends had been coming to the games for years. Chris looked around at Pete's site; he was extremely impressed at his in-depth setup. Pete had a very large pop up tent that went right over the top of his tailgate of the truck. In the back of the truck he had a huge flat screen TV and everyone was standing or sitting watching the next football game. There were several tables set up around the site filled with foods of all sorts. It was then both twins realized it had been a long time since they had eaten. Pete told them to dig in.

He said he was just about to fire up the grill and cook soup, chicken, and wieners. Chris looked over at the grill; it looked like a professional grade catering grill. The grill itself was attached to a box that had a working refrigerator and a storage area to it and a large umbrella completed the ensemble. Chris asked Pete where he had gotten a hold of something so intricate. Pete had smiled a prideful smile and informed Chris that he had built and fabricated the whole unit. Chris continued to compliment Pete on his accomplishment informing him he should market the contraption.

Chris and Christopher ate very well that day and felt much better after having some food in their stomach. After eating Chris took Pete to the side and asked if it were possible for him to give the two a ride to April's house. Pete was okay with it and said April's place happened to be near his place. As the afternoon wound down Chris helped the guys break down the site and began the drive to April's. During the ride Pete had asked about why a player needed a ride home. Chris explained he had too much to drink and that he would never drive home in that condition. Pete accepted this and the rest of the drive was uneventful. Approaching April's home it was late in the evening and everything was quite dark.

Chapter 12

Doctor Chase arrived in the locker room to find utter chaos. People were frantically running around the room. There were security officers everywhere with all the players having been evacuated. Steve walked up to Doctor Chase with an apologetic look but the doctor could tell that his anger was brimming just below the surface. Steve was holding ice on his head and went on to explain the situation. The doctor took it all in and just responded, "Well this is just a Cluster Bleep, he is GONE!" Steve looked at him and shook his head, "It gets worse, a lab tech was forced by Chris to show him the way out. Which is bad but there is more, Chris was not alone!" Doctor Chase's eyes perked up, "What do you mean he was not alone? Who was he with?" Steve grimaced, "He had his twin in tow, in other words he had himself with him. That is how he got away from me. I underestimated Chris, which will not happen again!"

The doctor instantly turned a ghostly white looking as if he had been shot. He grabbed Steve's shoulder, "Are you telling me not only is Chris out there but one of our C-Players is also not contained? This could destroy everything! We can control quite a bit here in the stadium but once they leave the premises we are screwed!" Steve responded, "I have as many people as I can pouring over the video feeds of the exits." As he said that another security officer came over to Steve and addressed him, "Sir, you need to come and see this!" He followed the officer to a nearby computer screen. The officer said, "I think we got them."

Steve viewed the images and after a few times looking at it he asked the officer to enlarge a particular clip. He turned to Doctor Chase, "They are heading toward section H of the main parking lot. Doctor Chase yelled, "Let's get out there, bring your Tasers! I want them subdued and brought back unharmed!" They began to run to the door behind Doctor Chase when he suddenly stopped. The doctor twirled around and faced Steve and grabbed him by the arm. "Enough," he said, "enough running around, think for a minute, where is he going to go? He is not going to go home; he will probably try to go to a player's house. Wait, does he have a girlfriend?"

Steve looked at him, "I have not noticed him with anyone specific, but now that I think of it he seems kind of sweet on April, the nurse. Every time I see him look at her his eyes light up like a Christmas Tree!" The doctor took that information in for a moment, "You are right. I have been seeing the two of them together quite a bit lately. Have all the nurses gone home?" He looked at his watch, "Yes, she would be home by now. Alright let's start there first, take a few security officers with you, I do not want to create a huge scene. I want to keep this under wraps as much as possible."

Steve waved them on; he grabbed two officers and led them to the security garage. He then climbed into a huge Hummer. The doctor started to laugh aggravating Steve and prompting to ask what was so funny. The doctor smiled, "this is quite subtle Steve," as he pointed to the large vehicle. Steve patiently replied, "I know but this is the only vehicle that does not have a light bar on top." Doctor Chase nodded, "Alright, let's go!"

They arrived at April's home and Steve parked about a block away as to not be discovered. He told his two officers to cover the back of the house and make sure no one gets away. He turned and handed a Taser to the doctor flippantly adding, "Do you know how to use this?" The doctor smirked, "Don't make me tase you back to the Stone Age, Steve!" They stealthily walked to the house and noticed a light on in the living room. As they approached and took a closer look Steve could clearly see April quietly resting on the couch. "I do not see anyone but April," Steve whispered. The doctor responded, "Let's ask her and Steve I do not want her harmed all!" The doctor had made that last comment with so much steel in his voice that it even gave Steve pause and he nodded with understanding.

They approached the door and Steve nonchalantly knocked on the door. Steve could hear felt feet padding toward the door when he heard April say, "Chris is that you?" Without even thinking April opened the door. Steve looked right at her and said, "Hello April, may we come in?" April stood frozen looking at the hulking security officer and Doctor Chase. She stumbled, "Doctor Chase, what are you doing here?" Doctor Chase stepped into the doorway as Steve grabbed April's arm with a vise like grip which drew an ow from April. "April," he began, "We must find Chris and from every indication he would come here. By your own response you have confirmed our suspicions. When might we be expecting young Chris?"

Steve roughly brought her into living room forcibly sitting her down on the couch. She just continued to look at Doctor Chase with an angry scowl. "April, come now, Chris has no idea the scope of what he has gotten himself into. We have to bring him in and talk to him about this situation. Many lives are at stake here, not just his!" April looked at Doctor Chase with venom in her eyes, "You are supposed to be a doctor, you are charged with the care and wellbeing of the players not using them for profit!" The doctor looked at April with sympathy, "April, I understand how you feel, I really do, I have much the same feelings. I genuinely like Chris and do not want to see any harm done to him or anyone else for that matter." April did not look up, "How can anyone believe you. Just look at what you have done." Doctor Chase continued, "Obviously Chris was coming here, we did see him leaving the stadium. He will make his way here and we will be waiting!" April tried to scramble to her feet but was abruptly put back in place by two powerful hands on her shoulders holding her down.

Pete pulled onto April's street and the first thing he noticed was the huge Hummer parked on the side of the road, "That thing is huge, you don't usually see that kind of vehicle around here!" Chris asked why he said that. "Well most people around here are what you might call earthy crunchy, they are very environmentally friendly. No one in this neighborhood would be driving a gas guzzler like that around here."

Chris thought for a moment, "Pull over right here, Steve, it must be Steve! He is a big military man it has to be his vehicle! Listen Pete, Christopher and I are going to go get April, wait here for us." Pete just looked at him, "Dude I have to get home." Chris pleaded with him, "Look Pete I do not really want to get you involved in anything but we are in a bit of trouble here. It is very hard to explain and right now I do not have time to even try. Please, just do me a favor and wait for us here for ten minutes. If we do not come back in ten minutes please call the police and let them know we are in trouble." Pete looked at him with a million questions on the tip of his tongue but just said, "OK."

Chris and Christopher walked stealthily from house to house being careful not to be noticed by anyone. The cover of darkness greatly helped them arrive at April's fence undetected. Both men crouched down and peered over the fence to assess the situation. They could see light in the house and assumed April was definitely there. Chris made a move in the direction of the house but was quickly grabbed by Christopher, "Wait! Let's see if Steve is here first, just watch for a minute."

Chris found his place next to Christopher again and they both began to observe the house. What was surprising to both was the lack of movement in the house. They could not see anyone, April, Steve or anyone else. Chris began to have a sinking feeling that April was in serious trouble. He turned to Christopher with a pained look, "OK, you go around the back and I will go in the front. Be careful and watch out for April, don't let her get hurt." Christopher gave him a quick pat on the back and moved quickly toward the backyard. Chris remained semi-crouched as he walked around the fence line and worked his way to another car parked in front of April's house.

He looked from his position behind the car and determined it was safe to continue. Creeping toward the front door he suddenly veered to the right when he noticed an open window. If he could go through the window he might have the element of surprise on his side. He snuck up to the window unnoticed and quietly pushed up the screen which surprisingly offered little resistance. He proceeded to climb in and tried to feel around the pitch black room.

A moment later he saw a small sliver of light coming from underneath the room's door on the opposite side of the room he was now in. Slowly and carefully as to not make a sound he made his way to the other door successfully. He ran into what turned out to be a bed and felt his way to the door. Grasping the door knob he slowly and silently opened the door just a crack and surveyed the hallway. Chris could not see or hear anything, the house remained eerily silent. He proceeded into the well-lit hallway squinting to let his eyes adjust to the bright light moving toward what he thought was the living room.

Chris came around the corner coming face to face with April. The sight before him made his heart sink. April was standing in front of him being restrained by Steve with his hand over her mouth. Chris's eyes went directly to the sight of Doctor Chase standing next to Steve and April. "Hello Chris, We need to talk!" The Doctor informed him. Chris felt a surge of rage building within him. He began to lunge forward and as he did so he felt a painful jolt of electricity go through his body. To Chris if felt as though a million tiny fires were running through his body as he tried to move toward Steve. With a Herculean effort he took two steps toward Steve until another shot of electricity poured into his nervous system rendering him immobile.

Chris could hear Doctor Chase screaming, "No More! Do not hurt him!" Chris looked up as he felt himself crumble to the ground to see April running towards him. He could her arms wrap around his head cradling it close to her chest. Chris could not help but be taken in by her scent, her smile felt like apple blossoms in the springtime. April positioned herself protectively around Chris' body. He heard April shout, "NO!" Then he felt a warm sensation going to his head. The last thing he saw was April's beautiful face covered in tears with one falling on his face and then everything turned black.

Chapter 13

Opening his eyes at first all he could see were fuzzy shapes and he could feel his head pounding and throbbing in pain. He closed and opened his eyes blinking several times until shapes began to clear and become more identifiable. As the room came into view, Chris realized he was strapped to a chair. He tried to turn his head but quickly realized that his head was also strapped in and movement was extremely limited. He peered down as much as he could to see his hands strapped down to the chair as well. Trying to move his legs was futile and a feeling of helplessness and panic began to settle in his mind.

He started to try and shake free and struggled to wiggle and get any movement at all. After a few moments he was sweating profusely and breathing very heavily. Then a thought of horror crossed his mind, "April! What had they done to her? If they had hurt her in any way I will personally snap them in half!" He began furiously to wiggle again in the chair to the point of drawing blood from his wrists. When he could feel the warm sticky blood start to drip down his fingers he started to see the gravity of his situation, he was powerless to help her right now. It was at this point Chris began to realize his head was killing him and all of the sudden he felt dizzy and nauseous. He could feel his face heat up and he could feel his stomach rolling as a moment later he turned his head slightly spewing vomit from his mouth all over the lab floor. The feeling of desperation, pain, and exhaustion overwhelmed him and he began to feel his eye lids become as heavy as ld weights. He blinked a few more times until his body relented too much needed sleep.

Coming to, Chris immediately felt as though some pain and tiredness had left his body. He began to scan around the room. To him, the room looked like any other doctor's office. The room itself was very plain with white walls and a few charts on the walls showing various bodily systems. Chris could also see a blood pressure gauge and an eye/ear light. In the corner stood a small counter equipped with a small desk and sink. On top of the desk was a small laptop computer, which Chris could see had his medical records uploaded on the screen. He looked down to realize he was strapped to some kind of examination chair.

For the first time he began to smell things around the room. Doctor's offices to Chris had always had that sanitary smell but today was mixed today with the smell of blood, sweat, and vomit. That putrid mixture almost made Chris sick again but he quickly gathered himself and began to wonder about April and Christopher. He also had to face the harsh reality about what might happen to him next. He just kept thinking back to the ultimate joyful promise of this day when it had begun.

This was supposed to be one of the greatest days of his life. This was to be a culmination of a lifetime of work, to be able to walk out onto the field and make his professional debut. He had imagined that walk to the field a thousand times over and over again in his head as many young people do growing up. He wanted to feel the roar of the crowd as he was introduced, to run down the gauntlet of his teammate's high fiving him on the way. To feel the sweat build up as he went through warm ups and have the coach come up to him and pat him on the back to help get him fired up was something that would not happen now. What about that first tackle he thought. What about, "laying the wood," on someone and the perfect hit. He began to think about his team mates and all they had sacrificed to get here and how they had the same hopes and dreams as he had.

He stopped for a moment and saw the face of Christopher in his mind, this thought brought tears to his eyes. Chris felt even more helpless at that moment. Although he was in an extremely dangerous situation of his own, he knew that he would try to make an opportunity for himself to get away. Christopher did not have hopes and dreams; he was a pawn in a huge web of lies. What would happen to Christopher, would he be decommissioned, destroyed, put down like a dog! The thought of that fate crushed Chris; this twin had done nothing to warrant any of this kind of treatment and seemingly had no rights of any kind.

The problem for Chris is how to get out of this chair and make Dr. Chase accountable paying for his treachery. He again looked down at his wrists only to see dried, caked up blood along the edges of the metal clasps holding him into the chair. Knowing that force was not going to release him he started to think of other ways to escape. He would definitely have to come up with a well thought out exit strategy. Going over different scenarios in his head he determined he was going to need some kind of divine intervention at this point.

He began to look around the room once more and realized that the door had a regular handle on it not a card reader key lock. This gave him a sense of hope, however being strapped to a chair like a mummy was not a comforting thought. As he continued to evaluate his situation, he heard voices in the hallway. The handle to the door began to move and caused he to tense up like a lion ready to pounce on its prey. His eyes shot directly to the edge of the door. The door slowly opened and in walked Doctor Chase.

He looked at Chris with a genuine look of sympathy. Moving over to a swivel chair near the desk the doctor placed his tablet on the desk and sat down. The doctor sat with both legs apart with his elbows on his legs and head bowed down for a few moments. Chris could tell just by looking at him that the doctor was struggling mightily with whatever decision he had made. Of course right now all Chris wanted to do was get out of this chair and pound the doctor into dust.

Finally, the doctor raised his head. And for the first time Chris got a good look at the state of the doctor. His hair was a mess and greasy, his eyes were blood shot and red. He looked as if he had not slept in days. Doctor Chase spoke, "Chris," he paused, "I do not even know where to begin." He shook his head for a moment and continued, "As a man of science I find myself in the most wonderful age of scientific discovery. We have made such amazing advances in technology to the point where we can literally copy another human! As a doctor charged with helping others to remain healthy and happy I am fighting a losing battle, in the process of looking to help others I have ultimately hurt a lot of people as well.

He put his head in his hands and then proceeded, "Do you know why I became a doctor? I became a doctor to save my brother's life. My older brother was a football player like you and like you played his whole life. He was ready to turn pro when he was diagnosed with a form of ALS brought on from repeated blows to the head. Like you, he was a man of great strength and character. He would have been someone you would have loved to be a team mate of. When he got sick, he never even told anyone. The only reason my family found out about his illness, is that his doctor had to call my parents to check family history related to head trauma. I was a freshman in High School when I found out and knew I had to find a way to help him. I dedicated my life from that moment on to helping my brother and others like him. My brother tried every treatment available and even seemed to be responding and doing well with one in particular.

My brother Joseph never let anyone see he was in pain and was always the life of whatever room he was in. As I entered college things looked stable and Joseph even took a job coaching as an assistant on a high school team. He moved very slow and was a little shaky but one look in his eyes and you knew he would fight this disease with every fiber in his being. When I became a resident, I was doing an overnight shift in the ER when my brother and parents came in. I had not seen him in some time because of my studies and the residency. He looked like death warmed over, I was in shock because the last time I had seen him several weeks ago he looked healthy and full of life.

His face and body were drawn with his skin pulled taunt; he had lost a great deal of weight. I could tell just by looking at him that body functions were beginning to shut down. We stabilized him and brought him to ICU. In consultation with his Medical team, it was discovered that my brother had not been taking his medication. It turned out that he was not taking it, not because he did not want to but rather because in his mind he kept remembering that he had already taken it. He was in a state of full-fledged Dementia and no one had noticed.

My parents were distraught. They had been taking care of Joseph since the beginning. My parents said he had looked so good and it seemed to them overnight he came to this state. Lately Joseph argued with his parents so profusely over medication my parents just relinquished assuming if he was that upset he must have really taken his medication. Of course taking a moment to examine him, it was obvious that he had not been up to date with his medicine. Once back on his regiment of medicines we thought he would return to form. While in the hospital we brought him back to enough health that he was able to go home with visiting nurses.

That is when he became physically and verbally abusive, no nurse would work with him. We had to put him in a nursing facility and from that point that was the beginning of the end for him. Not seeing his family all the time and no recognizable surroundings made his mind continue to falter to the point of not being able to recognize his mother. Even with frequent family visits he seemed to fall further and further into the recesses of his own mind. I went to visit him as often as possible but seeing me set him into severe mood swings. During Joseph's struggles I finished Medical school and since I had a genuine interest in genetic research I took a job with a large pharmaceutical company that specialized in ALS and Alzheimer's research. "Chris, the research I saw gave me hope I could save Joseph and all others like him!"

"In most cases if detected early enough we were able to slow the progression of both diseases so much so that each person lived a much longer and much richer life." Doctor Chase put his hand on his head, "the main issue here is the brain itself, what does the disease do to the brain? We still do not have a way to regenerate brain cells. This means that slowing the disease does not replace the cells lost and at some point the brain rebels and does not work properly or not at all. Research on the process of growing brain cells became paramount. Just growing the tissue would not be enough. Having the tissue function correctly and having the subject learn and remember things that once were a part of them would only hamper the research. With all our genetic research and stem cell research we knew it was possible to clone a human, what we lacked was funding and a venue.

My colleagues and I begged and pleaded with every major money outlet available to fund us so we could save lives. I even went so far as to get my parents' permission to clone my brother in order to save him. Everywhere we turned the answer was the same, the science is incredible but the ethics is something we cannot support! Of course I was livid, obviously being so close to the situation my ethics were much different than theirs. I had even taken all of my brother's genetic samples and asked the next possible benefactor, the government to meet me at my lab. I thought if they saw everything and allowed me to demonstrate they would fund us.

I could not have been more wrong. When the representative arrived and listened to my presentation he stopped me half way through and told me as impressive as all this was the American people would never OK cloning of humans. Three weeks later my brother passed away." Doctor Chase's eyes started to well up; he stood up and walked back toward the door stopping with both hands leaning against the door. Chris just stared at him and the room remained dead quiet for what seemed to be forever. Doctor Chase slowly turned and sat down and looked pleadingly at Chris, "After I lost my brother I vowed to never let that happen to anyone ever again.

I was going to do whatever it took to see that families had the opportunity to save the lives of their loved ones. I continued to work for years to recruit funding to no avail. I even had to start taking on some teaching positions in order to make money to live. Doctor Chase's face became even more lined with worry and his brow furrowed which made him look much older than he was. "I was at wits end when one day I came home to a suit literally sitting on my door step. Of course I automatically assumed the government had come looking for me to do some more research for them. To my surprise the man introduced himself as a representative of the Professional Football League.

He asked if he could have a few minutes of my time. At this point, what did I have to lose? I was almost broke having tried to save my brother and spent most of my money trying to fund my research. We both sat across from one another when the man got a serious look on his face and said this conversation was off the record and if asked about it he would deny everything. I asked him if he had worked for the government or the football league and he just smirked at me with a sparkle in his eye. At that moment I knew I had a former government man in front of me. I assured him I was used to the whole idea of plausible deniability. He just continued to lay out the plan. His football league had a very real use for my research.

He went on to describe the issue the league was having with regard to injury issues, especially head related trauma. The depth to which the football league had planned out their strategy was surprising but yet not totally unexpected. A league that profitable was used to covering all the bases. The plan began with of all things, supplements. For years the league had struggled with PED's and had really gotten to the breaking point. As an entertainment industry the league needed to continue to produce a top level product.

The issue of what supplements were acceptable in order to enhance performance legally has always been an extremely difficult problem when policing the players. Most of the controversy centered around the use of HGH and testosterone. The major difficulty with policing these substances was the fact that the body naturally produces each substance. Since these substances are natural in the body it became extremely difficult to prove what was enhanced and what was natural in one's body. Chemists however, constantly contend they can test for these substances. These same chemists continue to argue that their tests were fool proof, yet most legal substances also increase testosterone in the body. With this in mind, the banned substances were also put on the banned list because they increase testosterone in the body. It has become a very fine line between what is legal and what is not.

In the end, the league along with the players union had agreed on a regiment of proteins and natural supplements that would continue to increase testosterone naturally. They had also agreed on a baseline of acceptable testosterone increase based on these legal substances. The league had also agreed they would provide the supplements to the players providing they included language in their contract that outlined if their levels spiked while taking issued supplements players would be punished with fines or suspensions based on baseline levels of individual players. This was easy language to include because the levels based on these new legal substances were much easier to track.

HGH was and continues to be another matter altogether because there are many ways to mask the hormone. The leagues view on this was if more players started using the league regiment other players would continue to buy in so as to have a more level playing field." The man looked at Dr. Chase through steel eyes and continued his entrancing proposal. Dr. Chase told Chris how the man began to recount the leagues plan for his research. The doctor had been quite distressed with the knowledge of how his research had already been used by the league. He was just as alarmed at the casualness by which the league, in essence had stolen his ideas and had already begun to make their own.

The more the doctor listened the more intrigued he became by the possibility of seeing his research brought literally to life. Doctor Chase had always envisioned his research helping the medical community prevent unwanted loss of life or at the very least extending one's life. The ultimate carrot for the doctor was the funding he needed to make his dream of saving people's lives a reality. To Dr. Chase if he could keep one family from having to face the devastation of losing a loved one, then his life's purpose would be fulfilled.

When the man went into more detail about the use of cloned players Dr. Chase winced but continued to listen. The implications of using a clone on the field almost ended the meeting. Doctor Chase was just about to get up from the table when the man looked at him and said, "Imagine a world without football!" Dr. Chase blinked several times and looked confused by the man's comment. The man then continued, "We are at a huge precipice of losing this game forever! Yes, a lot of very rich and powerful people stand to lose not just money but an entire American culture! Most importantly football is the highest rated sporting event going. If we lose football, many people will no longer have any heroes to route for in their lives'. Football is entertainment yes, but to many in this country and around the world it is a way to take themselves from their normal everyday lives and allow themselves to dream about being a gladiator on that field!"

The thought of life without football was too much for Dr. Chase to bear and was hooked. As a physician, he was well aware of what was at the forefront of research that threatened the game. Although the injuries continued to be horrific, it was the head trauma that threatened the games very existence. Despite every effort to create safer equipment and create rule changes, severe head injuries still were a constant reminder of the barbaric nature of the sport. The doctor knew the man was right if they did not try something outside the box the game was in grave danger of being lost for good. When Doctor Chase was finished sharing the plan to Chris, all Chris could do was shake his head in anger and frustration. His stare could have cut Dr. Chase into two pieces. Chris's face must have been several shades of red because Dr. Chase held up his hand as if to say he understood.

Chapter 14

Chris could only blurt out, "How could you!" He gained his composure and continued, "You are playing God with people's lives, all for the sake of a Game!" As soon as this statement came from his mouth realization set in that he had spent his life in pursuit of playing a game to entertain the masses. A game that had been the cause of so much joy to countless people over the years. The game he loved that had also caused so many of his predecesors to have devastating lives after football. He could not help but feel sorry for those who had come before him and had to leave the game before their time. His sadness deepened thinking of what the doctor had agreed to do with all of their lives. Dr. Chase could see it on Chris's face. He said, "Chris, yes it is a game but a game by which has been built a large empire that goes well beyond that of wealth and power. This Empire offers hope, hope to millions that watch those Gladiators on the field pummel one another week in and week out until only one is left standing.

Chris just kept shaking his head, "What happens to the clones if they are hurt and can no longer perform are they put down like dogs? Their lives are not their own, they are just fodder for entertainment. Do you realize how sick and twisted this whole situation is?" Dr. Chase pulled himself together for a brief moment and stared at Chris, "They were going to do this without my help or not! I chose to help so I could control the situation, so it would not get out of control!" Chris shouted, "Look around you Doc does this look like things are under control?" Chris could feel the fasteners around his wrists continue to bite into his arms causing a burning sensation and more blood to seep down his hands.

At this point, Dr. Chase saw this and had a greatly panicked look on his face, "Chris," he said, "You are right, this has gotten way too big and out of control! You have no idea the lengths to which these men in charge have gone. Military use is just the beginning; they intend to keep making versions of themselves so they may live forever!" Chris just let his body slump back into the chair and looked at the doctor, "What have you done with April and Christopher?" The doctor's face returned to the sad look he had when he had entered the room. "Steve was taking you out of the vehicle to transfer you here and April bolted. She took off into the night. In all the confusion we had all we could do to get you squared away and we could not find any sign of her or your counterpart, Christopher!"

Chris snarled at him, "I don't believe you, what have you done to them?" "Chris," he said, "I assure you that they last thing I would ever want to do is harm April in any way! She is very special to me and I could never do anything but help her!" "Are you out of your mind?" Chris snorted, "It looked like Steve wanted to crush her windpipe when I came through that door!" Doctor Chase looked at Chris, "Yes, there is something seriously wrong with that man. When he is on duty there seems to be nothing he would not do if asked! I cannot repeat enough how I would never let anything happen to April!"

Chris looked at the doctor and could see in his face a genuine smile someone makes when they are proud of an accomplishment. Chris just continued to get more upset, "what now, what are your plans for me?" The doctor stood and said,

"My plans for you, are for you to have a long and fruitful football career and fall in love marrying the woman of your dreams!" Chris was stunned by this response, "What are you talking about!" The doctor smiled, "Oh, not what you were expecting, the only reason you are still restrained is because I am afraid you will hurt me. I assure you Chris the last thing I want to do is hurt you or anyone else!"

Chris, for the first time since talking with Doctor Chase realized just how exhausted he was and he just let his head lean back on the head rest. He said, "Where does this leave me?" "Well," the doctor said, "the owner would like to speak to you and then you need to decide whether your football career is over or is it just beginning! In the end Chris these men will get what they want one way or another, they always do!" As he said these words the door opened and in stepped Steve with the owner of the Marauders Mr. Peters. Steve walked over to Chris and looked down at him and said, "I am going to release your restrains, Mr. P wants to talk to you." Steve reached down and began to release Chris. Chris felt the pressure of the restraints loosen; he took one hand out then the other. He looked at his wrists; they were enflamed, red, and raw. He wanted to rub them but just looking at them he knew it would be useless. Dr. Chase already had gauze and cleaning solution in hand and started to work on Chris's ravaged wrists.

Chris began to stand when the doctor was finished and was shaking as he steadied himself to his full height. Standing eye to eye with Steve they looked at one another with an uneasy feeling. The two could have been ready to square off against each other at any moment. Not one intimidated by the other but yet quite leary of the other. Steve waved his hand suggesting that Chris follow him. Mr. P led the way, followed by

Doctor Chase, Chris and Steve covering the rear. Chris thought it odd after everything that had happened that a whole squad of men were not swarming all over him. As Mr. P opened the next door and stepped into the hallway Chris saw his answer, they were back in the stadium!

Chris was mystified, "Why would they risk bringing me back to the stadium?" At that moment Chris felt nothing but panic, where were Christopher and April? Mr. P led them through a series of halls and finally to a set of elevators that had Mr. P's name on the plate. Mr. P took a special circular key out of his shirt that hung on a chain. He then fit the key into a circular hole accessed by swiveling the plate up to reveal the lock. Chris heard a series of clicks as Mr. P turned the key until the elevator doors opened to reveal what looked like a Hotel Suite rather than an elevator.

The sheer size of the elevator struck Chris as he entered the mammoth elevator and the stimuli of the amazing photographs covering the walls. Chris's eyes adjusted and stared at the photographs in awe, they were all his heroes. Growing up watching the Marauders he had such fond memories of each photograph. The ornate walls were equally supported by the plush surroundings inside the elevator. He was reminded of the elevators in some of the five star hotels he had stayed during various trips. None, were as elaborate or large as the one he now stood. As Chris brought himself back to his current situation, he could not help but be extremely sad to think of where his beloved game had gone.

He understood the league to be a business but he was totally unprepared for the depths to which that business was willing to keep the money flowing. Chris sat down on one of the four leather couches in the elevator and leaned his head on the back panel and closed his eyes. He let himself back to the first time he had seen April, "those eyes," he thought. Almost immediately he opened his eyes and shot straight up with his fist raised to strike whoever got in his way. He saw Steve and launched himself pinning Steve against the wall with Chris's forearm across Steve's neck. Steve was caught off guard and was helpless against Chris's brute strength and adrenaline. Having Steve pinned Chris growled, "April had better be alright or I swear I don't care how many guys you send after me they will all end up in the hospital!" Steve looked into Chris's crazed eyes and began to understand what was happening for the first time.

Chris felt a hand on his shoulder and flinched, he just barely heard Dr. Chase. He blinked and looked at Steve realizing what he had done. He released Steve apologetically and looked at Dr. Chase. Doctor Chase put his hand back on Chris's shoulder, "It is okay Chris, I feel the same way! I am very worried about April! I have not seen her since we went to her house." Chris shook his head, "There it is again, that genuine concern for April," he said to himself. Chris could not help but wonder what Dr. Chase's relationship with April really was. Chris knew that April felt the same way about the Doctor. He thought for a moment and did not remember April mentioning her family even once. He had spent some time with April but probably not enough to warrant the family talk, so he dismissed it out of hand. For the life him he could not place this concern by the Doctor for April, it certainly was not that of an employee.

He had expected Steve to retaliate and put him back in cuffs but one look from Mr. P and Steve backed off. Chris looked at Steve and apologetically said, "I don't know what

118

came over me, this is just too much all at once." Surprisingly Steve looked at him in an understanding way, "Chris," he said, "I have been working here for a long time and I still feel that way sometimes!" That completely caught Chris off guard. Here was this military man struggling with the very same ethical issues. Chris had played against and with military family members. All the military members he had dealings with had the same integrity and approach to honor he now saw in Steve. Duty was what drove these people but here was one highly duty driven individual that had a difficult time dealing with such an ethical dilemma. Steve had much more time to digest what was happening and still was at odds with it.

The door opened and Mr. P walked into a palatial room even more decadent than the elevator. Chris thought to himself, "It must be nice to own a team!" Mr. P motioned Chris to have a seat in a leather recliner. Chris sat and almost immediately a stunning woman dressed in a pant suit came and placed a bottled water on the table next to his chair. At that moment Chris felt his parched lips screaming for the water. Chris looked at the water suspiciously. Mr. P saw the look and responded, "Chris it is ok, if I wanted to harm or drug you, you certainly would not be here right now!" Mr. P sat down in a chair that reminded Chris more of a throne rather than a place to sit. Chris looked at the chair and just started smiling. This did not go unnoticed by Mr. P, he started, "Yes, I understand this is all a bit much but I learned early on when I first purchased the team, that in some ways we were expected to be over the top." Chris leaned over in his chair and reached for the water. He quickly undid the cap and gulped down the entire bottle within seconds. As he put the bottle down he realized everyone was watching him. He looked at them smiling sheepishly, "I am so thirsty I could probably drink another gallon right now!"

Mr. P nodded and continued, "Chris we have an unbelievably difficult situation to deal with here! I truly care a great deal about each one of my players. So much so, that I agreed to be involved with this type of research to save the team. I was so frustrated with seeing players that I had invested so much into getting permanently disabled. I know what you are thinking, when I say invest your first thought is of money. I will not lie to you money is awesome, I love having money! I made my own money having begun with nothing. I certainly understand what it is to earn your own money. No, I am talking about the emotional attachment I have to this team and my players. Honestly the last thing I want to see is one of you hurt or get hurt. Believe me Chris if we could have come up with another way to do this short of having robots out there we would have already instituted it."

Chris looked at the owner of the Marauders and began to say something and then stopped. He thought and then said, "Mr. P, we are players; we have been players our whole lives. We have lived out our fantasy by making it to the Show. Every one of us to a man understands the risks involved in playing this game that we love!" He began to get very frustrated, to the point that he could feel his voice start to get louder, "You took my dream away from me! You have destroyed everything that has taken me a lifetime to build! I will never be able to play the game or view the game the same way ever again!"

Mr. P looked at Chris compassionately, "Chris, I understand, I really do! That is exactly why you are not supposed to wake up during the game. No one but us was ever supposed to know what was really happening!" "Which means what exactly?" Chris cried, "You have to kill me because I know too much?" Mr. P starred at Chris in horror, "You can't be

120

serious right now! Of course not! But what the hell are we supposed to do with you! We certainly cannot have you running around alerting everyone to what is happening here!"

Chris just put his hands on his head as if to hold it up from sheer exhaustion. The weight of the world seemed to be crashing down on him and his head felt as heavy as medicine ball. "Mr. P what happens to the players once they have been hurt to a point where you cannot use them anymore?" A shadow passed over the owners face and he turned ashen. "Chris," he stammered, "They are handed over to the government." He paused, "What happens after that I am unsure." Chris could tell by his guarded answer that he was not telling the whole truth. Mr. P continued, "The government actually owns the rights to the clones. They really just allow us to use them for a time and then they take them."

"Chris we really have to discuss our options here. Doctor chase has developed a way to erase certain memories based on his research of the brain. I have to remind you in the contract you signed with us you are pretty much under a gag order when it comes to certain aspects of the team. So this incident comes under these provisions in your contract and I am spending this time with to see if you are willing to abide by your contract or should we discuss Dr. Chase's solution?" Chris was beside himself by the request that was just made of him. "Mr. P I really have no answer to that right now. I cannot even fathom this whole situation. You are asking me to keep my mouth shut about one of the most horrifying situations I could have ever imagined in my life! Oh and by the way if you don't like that we are going to erase your memory!" Mr. P held up his hand to stop Chris, "Chris I could have already wiped your memory and saved myself a lot of trouble in the process. I have already told

121

you that you are much more valuable to me intact and playing for my franchise." Chris took that last comment in for a moment and just stared in disbelief. What had he gotten himself into; it seemed he had definitely been dropped mid-scene in a Science Fiction Movie.

Chapter 15

April pounded her hands on the steering wheel with tears streaming down her cheeks. She tried to steer the car blinking to keep the tears from blurring her vision. Her anger and frustration had reached its apex. "Christopher, I can't see their car anymore, I lost it! I can't let them take Chris; I will never see him again! She pulled off to the side of the highway and broke down. Her tears became free flowing rivers of agony. She put her head on the steering wheel and started crying hysterically. Christopher stared at her with a pained sympathetic look. He really could do nothing to comfort her having no reference point from which to guide him in this situation. He did what came natural and placed a reassuring hand on her shoulder.

She flinched at his touch and then realizing where she was and she relaxed and slumped in her seat. April wrapped her fingers around the steering wheel like a vise and turned to Christopher and said, "Christopher, I can't lose him! I just found him!" Christopher just gently clasped her hand and smiled. April looked out the windshield and with an angry look on her face and said, "I think I know where they are but I am going to need some help! I am going to strangle Dr. Chase! He is going to help me or I am going to hang him up by his toes and pull out every one of his fingernails."

She put the car back in gear and slammed the pedal straight to the floor. The car responded immediately with a jolt and wheels spinning. The car swerved out sideways into the road almost hard enough to turn the car sideways. Quickly picking up speed, April turned the car toward the highway. As they closed in on the stadium April had a look of panic on her face. As if wrestling with herself she whispered, "they could not have done anything to him, they need him? Right?" Suddenly she turned to Christopher and grabbed his arm with visible authority, "they are not going to do anything to him, Right!" Christopher looked quickly at April, "April I am the last person to be asking anything of right now. I just found out my whole life is a lie!"

April could see his eyes moisten and she put a soft hand on top of his, "Christopher we are going to figure this out but first we have to get Chris out of there!" Christopher looked at her with a confused look on his face, "how are we supposed to do that? They are never going to let us back into the stadium. I know I do not even want to go back there! Even if we managed to make it back in, the stadium is so immense, and where would we begin to search?" April with steel in her voice responded, "Oh, I know where they are bringing him, the owner is going to take care of this himself. He has a secret Penthouse that not many people are aware of in the stadium. Dr. Chase and I have been called there a few times. It is more like a small palace rather than a Penthouse. The explanation Mr. P gave was that when he constructed the stadium and found that there were so many unused nooks and crannies he could not waste the space! Of course in some twisted way that does make sense! He will have brought Chris there to try and impress him and make a pitch for Chris to see things from his point of view. As delusional as Mr. P is, he genuinely cares about his players. Sometimes he seems as though he lives through the ball players almost as if he wishes he were one! You could almost say he is infatuated with Chris more than any other player.

"Ok," Christopher said, "How do you propose we get in? That place is going to be in complete lockdown! I have every faith in you; however might I remind you that we just escaped from there barely with our lives! Is there anyone that can help us? April shrugged, "I know a way in only very few people know about. Doctor Chase showed it to me when we had to bring Mr. P medicine for his heart during a game. Mr. P did not want anyone seeing his doctor bring him medication. He is very secretive when it comes to his health." "That is great," said Christopher, "but what about the cameras everywhere?"

April gave Christopher a sly look, "Christopher you my dear are going to be a janitor tonight! Third shift is about to start, security may be extra tight in and around the stadium itself but I have had to come in the service entrance during that shift. Most of the employees that enter that way have low level security clearance and the security officers are new and just happy to have jobs. Many times when I have to come back to work at night those guys just wave me in. The service entrance is also set off to the side of the stadium and is usually not very well lit. Even if the cameras see us we will look just like the custodial staff walking in nothing will look out of the ordinary!"

"Believe it or not Mr. P goes in that way sometimes so he is not recognized and bothered. He has a special elevator where the entrance looks like a service elevator. The code, believe it or not, is the year he bought the team!" Christopher looked at her in disbelief. "What," said April, "he boasted about it one time when Dr. Chase and I were in the elevator with him. To this day I am not even certain he remembers saying that to us. We have no choice, we have to get in there and get Chris out! Remember this is a game night so there will be extra staff on tonight. We will get in safely. The question is whether or not we can make it out again!" Christopher winced as she said that, up to this point everything told him they had a chance. Then his face hardened and she said in a hushed tone, "Chris needs us, let's roll!"

April parked in one of the last rows of the staff parking lot. Christopher immediately noticed what April had mentioned about the area being dimly lit. He could just barely see where he was going. There were very few light poles until you arrived at the security station. Even the security station was rather dim with just the lights coming from inside the small metal and glass box that was made for no more than four personnel. April and Christopher were in luck as there were only two guards on tonight and they were only glancing at security badges here and there. As April had already told him the next shift was arriving and it was quite large group having to clean up after the game day crowd.

As they approached the gate they just fell right in behind a large group of staff members. April and Christopher kept their heads slightly down and walked in with purpose. They did not even slow just a little as they walked through the gate. The two continued to follow the crowd to the service elevators. As they approached the elevators April grabbed Christopher's arm and led him down a short hallway to some rest rooms. "Christopher," she started, "we cannot go right in, it will look suspicious if we go in the other elevator right now, let's wait about ten minutes. That will give everyone enough time to take their elevator to their departments!"

Christopher did as asked and walked into the men's room and made for a stall. He opened the nearest door and locked it behind him and sat down. He couldn't help but shake his head; he still could not even begin to grasp what was really happening to him. He leaned back with his head against the wall and closed his eyes. He thought he heard a woman's voice but it sounded so far away. He heard his name and felt hands grab his shoulders. Immediately he shot straight up and wide awake! Feeling very disoriented he stared down into the eyes of a woman. It took him a moment to realize he was looking at April. April with her hands up in the air in front of her thinking to fend off a blow started, "Christopher! It's me, it's me, calm down, everything is alright!"

As Christopher realized who was before him his shoulders visibly slumped and his eyes became less crazed. "April, I am so sorry! I must have fallen asleep, you startled me!" April was already moving toward the door and waved him to follow, "Come on we have to get to Mr. P's elevator." April opened the door and walked out into the hallway. As she began up the hallway her head was down and she failed to notice the man standing right in front of her. April's head literally banged into the man's chest and she looked up directly into Dr. Chase's eyes. A look of unrelenting horror took April's face and twisted it. Dr. Chase wrapped his arms around April. Immediately Christopher grabbed one of Dr. Chase's hands and twisted the hand and arm until the doctor was forced to release April. April fled down the hallway. Christopher, seeing April flee safely continued to twist his captives arm until he went to one knee in pain.

The Doctor wincing in pain yelled, "April stop! I want to help! Stop Please!" Christopher could see in the Doctors eyes he was telling the truth and released the Doctor's arm. Dr. Chase stayed down grabbing his shoulder and looking down the hallway. April stopped mid-stride determined not to leave

Christopher behind. Turning back toward Christopher she hastened her step and found her way back. Doctor Chase was just returning to his feet when April came into view. Still holding his shoulder he looked straight at April, "April listen to me, we have to get Chris out of here!"

By the look on the Doctor's face April could tell that he was serious. April started to panic! If the doctor had come to warn them, was something already happening to Chris upstairs? The doctor could see the fright in April's eyes, "April, Mr. P brought Chris upstairs to convince him to follow protocol and keep his mouth shut. At first I do actually believe he had Chris on the ropes and just for a moment I breathed a sigh of relief. Just for a moment though because as soon as he realized what was going on you could see his blood start to boil. Everyone was so fixated on Chris no one even noticed me leave. Now I am smart, but it will not take those guys long to figure out what I figured out the moment we brought Chris back here. I knew you would come after him and I was sure you would figure out Mr. P would bring him here. I just hope Chris has not done anything stupid in my absence!

Christopher put a powerful hand on the doctor's shoulder and clamped down. He put so much pressure on his shoulder the doctor started to go down again. "Why should we believe anything you say?" The doctor looked up into Christopher's eyes with tears streaming down his cheeks. "Chris is in there right now because of me, I need to get him out! Enough is enough! I cannot allow Chris to be punished for my mistakes!" Christopher saw the confused, pained look in the doctor's face and knew at once the Doctor meant every word. Christopher released the pressure on the doctor's shoulder and lifted his hand leaving an imprint of his hand on the doctor's shirt.

The doctor still wincing in pain rubbed his shoulder and began to rise. When the doctor returned upright to his full height he immediately looked at April with concern in his eyes, "April we have to get Chris out there but I do not want you two involved! It is already going to be hard enough to get Chris out safely. I want you two to head to my office. Everyone has been sent home and I will remotely turn the cameras off. They will think it is some kind of computer glitch and will work for some time to figure it out. In the meantime just lay low there until I come for you." He gently held April's hand and smiled at her, "I will not let them do anything to Chris, just meet me at my office. Go now, hurry, I don't want any unwanted questions, this is complicated enough as it is!"

April and Christopher turned, April waved Christopher down the hall to follow her. They quickly moved out of sight while the doctor sat watching them and said quietly, "Take care my heart." The doctor then entered the secret elevator and ascended to the penthouse. As the doctor rejoined Mr. P and his guests he noticed Chris was now standing and pacing with his hands on his hips. He had an exacerbated look on his face and red splotches were starting to appear on his face. The look on Chris' face told the good doctor he needed to act quickly before Chris took matters into his own hands. Dr. Chase worked his way to Chris and stood right in front of him.

Doctor Chase looked carefully into Chris's eyes trying to disarm him without words. Dr. Chase was about to say something, however, before he could Mr. P spoke instead. "Dr. Chase, Chris seems to be struggling with this whole situation a lot more than I expected!" Dr. Chase turned to look at the Marauders owner. "Mr. P, I think we have no choice than to continue with our plan. We have to wipe his memory so we can get back to business as usual. We have a game to prepare for next week and to be quite frank, I am sick of this whole situation. I have important research that needs to be attended to. The last thing I needed was some rogue football player who has a conscience!" Dr. Chase made that last statement with such conviction Chris actually shuttered from the shiver that went up his spine.

Chris turned to look for an escape route but all he saw was the elevator he had originally come upstairs with everyone. He felt panic well up inside him and as he looked at Dr. Chase. He felt powerful hands grab his left arm and twist it until it was pinned to his back. He could feel the pressure on his arm increase and a sharp pain shoot up his arm. Chris tried to spin and face his captor but he felt his other arm being grabbed and felt the pain of metal digging into his skin. His other arm was immediately forced behind his back and he heard an ominous click as the other handcuff locked around his wrist. Chris felt his body forcibly turned as his eyes focused to see Steve with a sly smile on his face. All Chris could bring himself to say through his teeth was, "You are a real piece of work!"

Steve just continued to smile and responded, "Chris it does not matter what you think in a few minutes you will not remember anything. I will see you every day and just smile and know what you will not. So you and your righteous attitude can go to hell. I do not need you or anyone else judging me! Everyone has to do what they have to in order to survive and quite frankly you are lucky they are letting you live. You will not even know any of this ever happened. You cannot even

understand how lucky you are, your life does not even change."
Steve had a perplexed look on his face as he made this
statement. As much as Chris wanted to physically harm Steve,
he was beginning to see his captor as being in a no win scenario.
He continued to stare at Chris. "My life remains the same and I
have to go on and know every day that this is all going on right
under my nose!"

Chris took that last comment and digested it for a
moment. He really had not even considered how difficult it was
for staff members that knew what was going on to deal with the
whole situation. Steve just pushed him ahead and into the
elevator. Steve forced Chris against the wall opposite the door
and gave him an extra shove in the back. They were joined by
Doctor Chase and Mr. P. Dr. Chase pushed the button and the
door closed with the elevator beginning to move. The elevator
stopped and Mr. P walked through the door, he stopped and
turned toward Chris with a sympathetic look. "Chris I am truly
sorry that it had to happen this way. I will make sure you are
well taken care of during your career and beyond. You will not
have to worry about a thing!" That took Chris by total surprise,
he really felt so disturbed by the whole situation he did not
know what to think.

Mr. P looked one more time at Chris and then shuffled
off down the hallway. Steve led Chris down the hall following
Doctor Chase. After a few minutes, Dr. Chase stopped in front
of his office. He looked up at Steve, "You can leave him with
me, in a few minutes he will forget everything and I will no
longer need you guarding him." Dr. Chase could see the
apprehension in Steve's face and responded in kind, "Steve just
leave me the keys to the cuffs, I am going to cuff him to the
chair anyway. If you have an extra pair of cuffs I will use those,

he is not going anywhere!" He looked at Chris and started, "Alright Chris let's get this over with I have better things to do than babysit you!" Chris turned with hatred in his eyes, "Doctor I don't care what it takes, you will never take my memories. They will be burned into my mind, I will find them and then I am going to find you!" Chris said it with such venom that Dr. Chase stepped back for a moment and looked at Chris in disbelief. Steve just looked at him, "You sure you do not need any help? I could quiet him down a little first. He wouldn't remember it anyway! He has been such a joy to be around I would take great pleasure in teaching him some manners!" Chris growled, "Take these cuffs off and we will see who teaches who a lesson!" Steve just smiled, "I am sure you would but in a minute it won't matter. Be sure to say hi to April for me!" Steve started walking down the hall and stopped, peered over his shoulder, "Never mind I will tell her myself!" With a sinister grin he then turned away and continued down the darkened hallway.

Chris followed Steve with his eyes burning holes in his back as he walked away. As Steve rounded the corner and was out of sight, escape came back to Chris' mind. He quickly turned to Doctor Chase, knowing he was going to have to tackle him to the ground and take the keys; he thought right now would be a good time. He prepared to launch himself at the doctor when he heard the doctor say, "Thank God that idiot is gone, honestly I still wonder where the heck Mr. P found that guy. Someone needs to beat him senseless, although I don't even know if that would help him get perspective." Chris thought this a very odd comment coming from a Doctor who was about to wipe his memory. The doctor seemed genuinely relieved that Steve was gone and did not seem worried about what Chris might be planning.

132

Chris towered over the doctor and outweighed him by at least eighty pounds. Chris knew he could easily subdue Doctor Chase but something held him back from pouncing. Something in the back of his mind kept telling him that there was something not quite right about the way the doctor was so casually handling this situation. Dr. Chase opened the door leading to his office and waved Chris in which again confused Chris. Chris thought, "Why isn't he dragging me in there?" Almost as if the doctor read his mind, he looked at Chris, "Chris come on, we really need to get this done!" Everything about this was wrong to Chris, "Why had the doctor not let Steve guard him and make sure he was secured? Why was the Doctor acting so non-chalant about Chris when Chris could easily escape?" Chris could not get a handle on this whole situation and what was more, is the fact that the doctor did not seemed concerned in the least.

Doctor Chase unlocked the door to his office and gestured to Chris to enter. Chris went through the doorway and watched the doctor lock the door behind him. After looking around the outside of the office to make sure they were not followed. With the door locked, Chris could almost feel the tension in the room immediately lessen. Dr. Chase started to walk toward the back of the room and did not even look at Chris. He called over his shoulder, "Well you coming?" Curiosity won out and Chris followed closely watching every move the doctor made. Dr. Chase bent to open the door he was standing in front of. Chris went into a panic as he came to the realization that this was the room he had listen to the Doctor spill his guts. This was also the room he had been held captive.

Chapter 16

Doctor Chase walked into the room as he had done a thousand times knowing the lights were attached to a motion sensor and would automatically turn on. As he entered the room the lights did not turn on and the doctor walked into a heavy object on the floor falling forward into the blackness. Chris watched in horror as the doctor disappeared into the abyss. It seemed to Chris as though the darkness swallowed the doctor whole. Chris sat motionless for a few moments, not sure of his next course of action. Should he run or should he help the doctor. Chris struggled with his conscience. This is the man that held him captive, the man who was going to wipe his memory, and the man that kept him from April. In the end, Chris used the old adage that you do not leave a fallen man behind. He cautiously worked his way to the doorway. As he wrapped his hand around the door jamb he heard a groan. Out of the darkness he heard a hoarse voice call his name.

Chris responded, "Doctor Chase are you alright?" There was no answer. Chris inched his way into the dark room with his hands outstretched in front of him to feel for anything that might be ahead of him. A few feet into the room he peered over his shoulder to make sure the doorway was still there. Chris half expected to see only unending darkness but to his surprise he could still clearly see the outline of the doorway. There seemed to be an ominous light flooding into the dark room as if dark and light were struggling for domination. The weight of the darkness seemed heavy on his shoulders. Chris continued to cautiously move forward. With his arms still in front of him hoping to touch something, he realized he must be a least halfway across the room by now. He still had not run into or touched anything and started to get a panicked feeling in the pit of his stomach.

As he was about to turn around and walk out the still open doorway, a hand reached from nowhere and wrapped around the front of his face. Chris felt a powerful arm grab his left arm and pull him toward the unknown assailant. With darkness all around him Chris had been caught off guard and felt hot breath in his ear. He heard a familiar voice, in the dark it could have been his ghost but Chris knew at once who is was. Chris immediately went limp and relaxed all his muscles including his frantic brain. He felt the giant hand unwrap from around his mouth and face. As he was about to speak the lights sprung on blinding him instantly. After blinking furiously for a few moments images began to come into view. Through the bright haze of new light an angelic face came forth.

At first Chris just stared at the shining beauty before him. April stood before him and cupped his face with both hands cradling him softly. The warmth of her hands seemed to wake him from his dream state. Chris could feel his face start to heat up at the thought of April being so close to him. "April?" he felt himself say. "Yes, Chris I am here!" She released his face and enveloped him in a huge hug. He felt her arms wrap around him and felt his arms find their way around her torso. Chris just stood for what seemed to be eternity holding April. He could not even imagine letting go. Without even a second thought he brought his head down close to hers and released the most passionate kiss on her lips. For Chris time stood still, he felt the moist warmth of her full lips pressed to his. He could feel their intertwined bodies held together by the sheer electricity of their attraction to one another. When the two

135

finally, gently pushed any from one another, they just stood staring into each other eyes.

It wasn't until Chris felt the clap of a huge hand on his back that he snapped back to reality. Christopher stood next to him and Doctor Chase, although a little bruised was standing in front of them all. As he took in Christopher he started to move away from April while holding on gently to April's hand. As they moved further apart their fingertips were touching and at the last moment their fingers passed from one another. The spell seemed to be broken and reality set in very quickly. Chris looked at April perplexed and then sheer panic. "April what are you doing here, you have to get Christopher as far away from here as possible. You are both in grave danger while you are here with me!"

"April," his eyes started to well up, "in a few minutes this will be all over. Doctor Chase is going to wipe my memory. I can go back to just being a ball player!" April looked enraged at him, "Are you insane, I am not letting Dr. Chase do anything to you! As a matter of fact, now that I have him here I was thinking about wringing his little neck!" Dr. Chase turned to her with a hurt look on his face, "April wait a minute now, you know I would never do anything to hurt you or Chris!" April looked as though she was going launch herself at the doctor's throat, "Dr. Chase, look around you, this is all you're doing! You're playing God has led us all here and shattered our lives. Even if we survive today, what kind of life can we lead from this point on? A life on the run, one of constantly looking over our shoulder wondering if another one of Mr. P's thugs will be waiting for us around the next corner!"

April paused, "Well say something! Never mind, there is nothing you can say that will lessen the devastation you have caused!" "Christopher," she ordered, "find something to tie him up with, he is coming with us!" Christopher smiled, "It would be my pleasure, can I gag him too?" April though about this for a moment, "No, he has a lot of explaining to do to us when we get out of here." To all of their surprise the doctor did not resist as Christopher tied his hands in front of him. They wanted to blend in as much possible, if his hands were tied behind his back that would be quite noticeable. April turned and grabbed Chris by the hand, "we are getting out of here right now." They started back the way they came. April was in the lead holding close to the wall with Chris and Christopher pushing the doctor in front of them. April announced that they would be using the service tunnel to escape and because of the time, not many would be in the tunnels or even notice them. They had little trouble getting into the large service elevator; the whole complex seemed deserted at this time.

The elevator began to work its way downward as April began glaring at the doctor. The doctor looked extremely ragged, worn out, and defeated. His sunken eyes and faraway look told April that he was resigned to his fate. She felt a pang of sorrow but it quickly dissipated as she came once again to the realization that he was the cause of their current situation. The doctor just silently kept his eyes turned toward the floor. When the elevator stopped they all disembarked and once again April took the lead. She walked at a frantic pace which almost turned into a jog but she still did not want to alert anyone that anything might be amiss. As they worked their way through the maze of tunnels Chris noticed how much each tunnel looked like the last. The walls were smooth concrete painted gray and overhead were a series of tubes all labeled.

The labels read, grey water, drinking water, waste water, electric, and computer.

Chris could not help but to be in awe of the engineering marvel he was now stuck inside of. He had been coming to football games his whole life but had never once given any thought to the inner workings of a huge stadium such as they were now trapped. The sheer magnitude of everything involved just to bring a three hour football game to the world was mind boggling. For a brief moment he began to think of what Mr. P had told him about everything regarding the team. He could even begin to understand how easily Mr. P could have come under the sway of the doctor and the ability to continue to bring everyone the game they loved. This thought was short lived as he looked at Christopher, who until very recently just thought himself a ballplayer. What a shock to the system to find out your whole life was made up and worse, you had no life of your own.

Chris took a moment to contemplate, he found himself very much in the same predicament. His life had been very straight forward to him. He had done everything he could to become a professional football player. All that seemed a distant memory to him right now, he could barely focus with the blond angel in front of him leading him to safety. April brought them to a storage room that all types of custodial supplies. April scanned the room quickly and got a serious look on her face as she tried to decide the best course of action. After a moment of thought she nodded her head yes and beckoned them to follow. She led them to the door straight across the room. April stopped as she was about to grab the handle to the door. "When I open this door follow me quickly to the car. Once we are on the road I will tell you where we are going."

Chris glanced up at her as she was looking back at them, her beautiful hair cascading down her shoulders. She struck a picture of many heroines that Chris had read about, a tall statuesque woman of strength. A great feeling of pride welled up in his heart and at that moment he happened to glance at the doctor. Chris saw an odd look in the doctor's eyes; to him it looked like one of pride the way the doctor smiled to himself. This had happened many times during the ordeal he found himself in the middle. That look and those responses continued to confuse Chris. April considered this man a colleague but yet there seemed to be more under the surface. The doctor was always looking and smiling at April.

Even though Chris himself had felt in grave danger during this whole time, something in the recesses of his mind assured him the doctor would not harm April. April opened the door and they all sprang through and continued their fast paced walk toward the car. As when they had gone in the stadium the lights were dim and spread out. The companions found their way through the parking lot with no resistance. As they neared the car Chris dared hope they had made it out without being noticed. Hope quickly faded as April began to open the car door and they were all promptly blinded the striking high beams of several cars surrounding them.

Chris just caught movement out of the corner of his eye and was ready for the tackle to his mid-section. He felt himself being taken to the ground and began to feel punches rain down on his head. Instinctively covering his head with his own fists to lessen the blows, he lifted his knees and struck his assailant in the mid-section with tremendous force. Chris sprang to his feet to face his attacker only to see his opponent was Steve. The two circled each other like mountain lions ready to square off for supremacy. They launched themselves at one another simultaneously, the impact matching that of two bulls colliding. Both men tumbled to the ground exchanging blow after blow. Grappling at one another neither combatant could gain the clear advantage.

After several attempts to lock up as if in a wrestling ring both men were on their feet once again stalking the other. The two men cut a picture that would bring one back in history to the Coliseum and the period of the Gladiators. Each man with sweat pouring down the sides of their faces had a mixture of dirt and blood covering their faces. Neither man looked winded; these were two superb specimens ready to fight to the death.

April had just reached to open the car door when the lights had come on. Luckily her eyes where down and focused on the lock. She opened the door and quickly got in the driver's seat as Chris and the others were attacked. April could see Chris and Steve going after each other as if they were in the middle of an ancient arena. If not for the situation April would have marveled at these two behemoths pounding the life from one another. She did however notice Chris' power, she knew Steve to be an extremely strong and well trained man. Yet Chris was stride for stride, blow for blow with Steve, not hesitating in the process. After a few minutes of fighting to what seemed to be a draw the two men just circled each other measuring their opponent for their next move.

Christopher had his hands full with two of Steve's security detail. He hurled an elbow to the face of one attacker who had grabbed the doctor and connected with terrific force stunning the man as the doctor ran to the car. The man he had struck was quickly back on the attack joined by another assailant. Both attackers grabbed one of Christopher's arms not expecting the powerful man to use their momentum against them. As both men came at him and grabbed each arm Christopher just pulled them in toward each other. Each man continued toward one another unable to stop. They collided head to head and crumbled to the ground in a heap. Christopher saw the men immobilized on the ground and quickly looked for Chris.

He could see his mirror image engaged in an epic struggle, the two gladiators sizing each other up when he felt something crash into his right shoulder. A sharp pain followed and Christopher turned to see another security officer with a baton coming after him. Christopher recovered and met the next blow with a grunt and one of his own. He hit the man squarely in the jaw with his own huge closed fist. The strength with which the blow found its way to the man's face was frightening. Christopher could feel the crack of bone as his fist struck the man's face. Christopher did not relent and continued with an upper cut the man's chin. The newest blow caught the man just right and he crumpled to the ground motionless.

Christopher turned quickly looking for the next attacker but none came. He saw the doctor make it to the car and he could see that April was in the driver's seat with the car running. Turning his attention to Chris and Steve he could see they were both exchanging blows, going toe to toe. Christopher thought to himself, if this had been a prize fight people would have paid huge money to see this fight. These were two prized heavy weights pummeling each other into submission. Christopher wanted to help but could not help but be enthralled by the violent nature of their brutal encounter. No man had a clear advantage but Christopher wondered how much more punishment each man could endure. He cautiously moved to Chris's side to assist if needed.

Chris not noticing his cohort spun with a back fist and connected with Steve's face. Steve's head snapped back but rather than throw another punch Steve went low. Steve whipped his legs at Chris' and took his legs out from under him. Chris was caught by surprise felt himself fall backwards. He landed with a thud on his back momentarily stunning him. That was all Steve needed, he pounced on top of Chris and rained punches on his exposed face. Christopher was about to jump in when he saw Chris' legs come up and catch Steve's arm in between his legs. The punches ceased and Christopher could see Steve was in trouble.

Christopher knew if Chris could get those legs around Steve's neck it would be all she wrote for Steve. Christopher was surprised to see Chris content with Steve's arm pinned against his body. He could see the pressure continuing to mount on the arm. Chris was in clear control at this point and Christopher could see the determination on Chris' face. Chris continued to ratchet up his grip squeezing and bending Steve's arm. Steve knew he was in a great trouble and tried to squirm away but could do little to escape. Christopher watched in horror as Steve's arm suddenly snapped. Writhing in pain Steve remained on the ground as Chris regained his footing and stood. Christopher reached for and grabbed Chris' arm and led him to his car. Both men threw themselves into the back seat. April stepped on the gas and the car screamed off through the parking lot.

Chapter 17

One of Steve's officers was up at this point and rushed to Steve's side. Steve stood hesitantly with his injured limb hanging by his side and his face full of rage. He looked at his man, "Get in the car we are going to finish this!" Steve got in the passenger side and told the driver to follow April. Steve's car quickly caught up to April's. Steve screamed in the driver's ear to ram April's car. Pulling up alongside April's car that is exactly what they did, smashing into the passenger side of the car. This caused minimal damage and did not slow the car in the least. The security officer swerved to the other side striking the driver's side front fender. Again a huge crash ensued without slowing April's car. This time Steve's vehicle rode directly to the rear of April's car and rammed full speed into the trunk of her car. As the car struck, April's car swerved to the side and spun around. Steve's car sped past and turned to finish the job.

April was frantically trying to start car after it had stalled during that last exchange with Steve's battering ram. Chris screamed, "April we have to get out of this car!" "No, Chris, I can start it, hold on!" As soon as she announced this the engine roared to life. As she did she could see Steve's car turning and coming straight at them. "April!" Chris yelled, "Get out of here!" "Wait Chris, watch!" Chris started, "Whatever you are going to do, you had better do it now!" April smiled, "I got this!"

The lights from Steve's car were almost on top of them. April gunned the gas and the car lurched forward and April spun the wheel to the right. Steve's car just missed hitting them and continued passed them striking into a light pole! Steve's car struck the pole with a deafening crash. The light pole stood for a moment, teetered and fell right onto the car. Sparks flew everywhere and the light pole landed directly onto the middle of the car crushing the roof. April started to speed away but she felt Chris' hand on her shoulder. "Chris, what is it?" Chris said, "We have to make sure they are ok!" "What, are you nuts, they just tried to kill us!" Chris just continued, "He would not have killed us, just captured us, he is an honorable man!" April just shook her head and brought the car alongside Steve's car. Chris jumped out and looked inside Steve's car which by now was on fire. Steve had begun to stir but Chris could see the driver was not so lucky and was already gone.

Chris went around and tried to pry the door open without success. Instead he reached inside unbuckling Steve's seatbelt and dragged Steve out through the window. Steve stood assisted by Chris leaning heavily against his rival. Chris could see that Steve's injuries were not life threatening but he was in rough shape. Chris brought him a short way to another light pole and let Steve sit leaning up against the pole. Steve looked up at him as the damaged car exploded. Steve sat stunned for a moment and then looked at Chris, "Why?" Chris turned to Steve, "You are an honorable man and I couldn't leave a fallen man behind!" Steve just looked shocked to hear a civilian make this statement, "Thank You, you saved my life, but don't expect me to stop trying to catch you! I will capture you again!" Chris smiled, "I would expect no less from you!" Chris turned and called over his shoulder, "Until we meet again!" Chris ran to the car and jumped in. Steve watched as the car sped away too stunned to do anything and whispered, "Until we meet again."

April turned the car onto the highway and they drove for much of the next hour not saying anything. They kept looking in their rear view mirror to see if they were being followed. When they finally were sure they were not being pursued April broke the silence. "Doctor Chase, I am turning you in. I have a friend at the FBI and I know I can trust him. You are going to expose this and return all our lives to us." Chris just looked at April in shock, "April you cannot be serious, you do not know how high up this goes. According to Mr. P he is just a piece in a larger puzzle. When the clones are no longer needed they are transferred to military use. In other words, the government is involved, which means any attempt by us to implicate the government would be futile!" April continued to drive and said, "Chris this is different, this is about justice, this man lives for honor and justice. Trust me Chris; I would not even consider this if I even thought there would be danger, considering all we have been through. Chris you know yourself what the court of public opinion can do in a situation like this! However, the problem we have is who do we trust in the media?

Chris sat thinking for a moment. He could not think of any other way to get out of their current situation. Chris honestly hoped April was right and they could trust this agent. Unfortunately every fiber of his being was screaming that no one could be trusted. Chris thought of the media connection and how that would work. He had dealt with the media ever since he could remember. To sports figures the media was heaven and hell all rolled into one. The media always claimed to be giving people the truth but to many in the sports industry it always seemed the truth came at the price of an agenda. Everyone in the media loved to build people up only to enjoy even more destroying their creations.

Chris thought of all the prospects he had gone through the combine with and the constant media barrage. He remembered clearly how one prospect was projected as a top ten pick and then the media picked up on an assault he had committed as a minor. The media ran with the story and a first round pick became toxic to every team going undrafted. The fact that the media revealed a court sealed incident mattered not. It was later discovered that the young man's father had actually committed the assault and blamed the boy because he was a minor and would get a slap on the wrist. The young player because of his sports status had his file sealed and received community service. The media tried to backtrack and issued all kinds of retractions, however the young man had lost millions of dollars at this point. Eventually he caught on with a team as a free agent and became the first round player he was expected to be in play but was a value pick for the team.

Chris thought about the sheer devastation the media could cause and realized that would be the only way to get themselves out of the situation they were currently a part of. He turned to April, "Listen if you want to get your FBI friend involved let me talk to a friend of mine first. I have a reporter, an old friend of my Dad's; let me tell him our story first. I know he is with the media but he is old school and believes in facts. Besides, he is connected with everyone, if we want our story told he is the one we need to tell it to." April glanced at him and nodded with approval, "Chris, I agree we will need help from the media but we are going to have to rely on someone with government connections to expose how high up this goes!" Chris, with a worried look on his face said, "I understand, the problem is if we make the wrong choice a lot of people will be hurt!" April clasped his hand warmly, "Chris, I will not let that happen! One thing that you can count on is I am never letting

146

you out of my sight again!" Chris turned cupping her face with his hands and kissed her passionately. Releasing his lips from hers he peered into her eyes and saw unbridled determination. He could tell she meant every word. April blurted out, "Let's go see this reporter and see what he says."

April pulled up to a small Cape style home. The lawn and surrounding area were meticulously landscaped. There were flowers all over the front of the house. The explosion of color was very welcoming and inviting. April had a bright smile on her face, the first Chris had seen in quite some time. As Chris reached for the doorbell he hesitated for a moment. As if battling with himself, he finally shook his head yes and rang the bell. After a few moments Chris could hear some stirring from inside the house. He could see a blurry figure start to come into view through the frosted glass of the door. Chris seemed to wait forever and listened to quite a few chain removals, along with what sounded like dead bolts being unfastened, the door finally opened a crack. "What do you want?" Came from the small opening. "Gus, it's me, open up," cried Chris, "I need your help!" The door shut quickly and once again they heard more rattling before the door opened the entire way to reveal a small frail man. He was almost completely bald except for two small patches of hair near his ears. He was slightly bent and leaned heavily on the door jam. He eyed April and Christopher suspiciously and then turned to Chris. Almost as soon as he took Chris in he then turned to Christopher and his eyebrows shot straight up. "Chris, I have known your family for a longtime would you mind telling me how come I did not know you had an identical twin!" Chris could tell by the hawk like gaze that the old news blood hound was already on the case.

Chris and company stepped through the entryway closing the door behind them. The house was neatly arranged, with a clean fresh smell. Chris took in the wall to wall carpeting and the knotty pine walls. The furniture was sturdy, plain, and a little dated. Chris thought he had stepped into the seventies. All that seemed missing was a disco ball and bell bottom jeans. He looked at Gus with an extremely serious look on his face. "What if I was to tell you Gus, that this is not my brother? Seriously, take a good look at him!" Gus with eyes trained from years of investigative reporting looked Christopher up and down as if he were a computer scanning a document. When complete with his scan Gus' face twisted with confusion, "Chris, there is no way he is not a blood relative!" Chris just laughed, "Gus, blood relative is a perfect description, you do not know how close to the mark you actually are!" Gus turned waving them completely in, he moved over to the couch and offered them seats.

Gus chose a leather lazy boy for him and the companions took up residence on his plush couch. From out of nowhere a small notebook and pen appeared in Gus' hand. "Tell me everything; do not leave out a single detail!" Chris could not help but smile; he had seen Gus work numerous times over the years and knew he would not leave any stone unturned. He had always pictured Gus as a throwback to a lost era of journalism and reporting. Chris expected Gus to come out of his house each time in a trench coat and a fancy brimmed hat. As Chris recounted the incredible events of the last twenty four hours, Gus never once looked up or stop to ask Chris to repeat any part of his tale. When Chris finished his tale he sat up straightening his back and looked at Gus for some sign. Christopher and April sat on the edge of the couch and waited for Gus to respond to the epic story.

148

Gus peered up from his notebook with one eyebrow slightly raised, "I have been reporting the truth for a long time. I have heard many fantastic stories and claims through the years where each story teller wanted me to believe their story true. I have been witness to some of the greatest conspiracy theories known to man. Chris, you have truly outdone yourself with this remarkable tale. I honestly have never heard such a well-constructed story in all my years! This Gridiron Conspiracy of yours would make a remarkable fantasy novel." April and Christopher looked as if they had each been hit in the gut. Chris just quietly got up from the couch and started for the door. He never once looked back in Gus' direction. At the front door Chris reached for the handle, stopped for just a moment as if to say something and then continued out the door.

Chris walked briskly to the car, slid into the passenger seat and proceeded to pound on the dash board unmercilously with his fists. He smashed until the plastic cracked and gave way revealing the inside of the glove compartment. His fury was so unchecked he did not realize April stood next to him yelling for him to stop. It was not until he felt a sharp jolting pain run up his arm did he stop. He raised his red raged eyes to see April staring at him in disbelief. Chris glanced down to assess the damage caused by his onslaught to the dashboard and his own body as well. It was then he realized the extent of the damage to both the car and especially his hands. The knuckles on his right hand were a bloody pulp and for the first time he noticed sticking out of the large knuckle of his middle finger was a jagged piece of plastic. He sat in shock taking in the devastation and real pain began to set in.

April knelt down and took his hand in hers. Gently she pulled the piece of plastic from his hand, as he winced April just looked at him as if to say, "Stop it you baby!" April continued to assess the damage to his hand and shook her head. His hands looked like baseball mitts compared to her hands. Chris' hands were scarred, bent, and calloused from years of abuse on the field. April wrapped his hand in gauze after cleaning him up. Chris could not even recall April taking out the First Aid Kit and completely spaced out on how he ended up in the back seat resting. He found himself looking out the window watching the light poles pass by. It wasn't until he heard Doctor Chase's voice that he was brought back to reality.

April looked in the rear view mirror and asked Chris, "What happened back there, I thought you knew this guy? He seemed to completely dismiss you and what you were telling him." Chris just continued to stare out the window, "I have known Gus for a very long time, if I cannot convince him about what is going on, there is no way in hell I am going to convince anyone else of significance that could help us! This guy is used to the most outrageous stories imaginable! Sometimes, I think he would rather write for tabloids instead of his newspaper. Some of the stories he has told me over the years are just as fantastic as our current situation. That is exactly the reason I wanted him to hear from us before we told anyone else." April continued, "Chris, I know you were counting on this to work out but let's go with my plan and see what happens." Chris just sunk lower into the back seat, "It would seem we have no choice, but if a guy from the media does not believe us what makes you think the FBI is going to be any better. April looked back with sorrow, "Chris we will make it work. If we have to travel the country until someone listens, we will have our story told!" Chris could tell by the determination in her voice that she was never going to let this stand. Justice is a swift lady and the lady had just spoken.

The ride to the FBI field office happened without incident. April asked that everyone stay in the car and she would go in and see about contacting her agent. The anxious occupants of the vehicle did not have to wait long before April walked out of the building. She opened the door and sat back in the driver's seat. "Agent Bradley is on the road," she offered, "they did contact him and he said he would be here in fifteen minutes." Chris asked, "April you seem so sure of this FBI agent, how can you be so sure? How do you know him?" April paused and then answered, "Well every now and then Mr. P will ask the FBI to investigate a prospect that the team is interested in drafting or a potential free agent. Agent Bradley always seems to be the one that comes out to the stadium to complete and pass on the results of the investigation." She stopped and looked at Chris with apologetic eyes, "He is constantly asking me out, honestly I think he would do anything for me."

Chris' face twisted and he looked ready to explode, "April are you out of your mind, this agent Bradley is on Mr. P's payroll! April, he is bought and paid for; we will be the ones that will find ourselves behind bars. How could you even consider talking to this guy?" April waited for Chris to finish his mini-rant and then calmly replied, "Chris, first off, he is not bought and paid for, he hates Mr. P! He has mentioned to me more than once how shady he thinks Mr. P is but he has a job to do which he takes very seriously. Trust me when I tell you, Agent Bradley hopes one day to find dirt on Mr.P and bring his downfall. Honestly Chris he played football at some Division II college and just loves coming to the stadium to catch a whiff of what it must be like. Every time he comes to the stadium no matter what time of year, he wants to go down on the field. He treats the field as though it were his altar of worship. No Chris, this is your guy he will probably worship you as if you were a

Bishop, the moment he lays eyes on you! I really think he wanted to be here the day they signed you. He was here for another prospect and when he found out they were considering you, I thought he would never shut up. Chris, I think he knew more about you than did our scouts!"

Chris starred at April, he knew she was a nurse but having spent this time with her and learning all she had been involved in, he could not help have a great feeling of awe. April was turning out to be a much more complex, important woman than he previously thought. Chris just happened to glance at Doctor Chase during his exchange with April only to notice he had a proud glow on his face. Each time he looked at April it seemed as though he wanted to cry out with pride! Chris could not explain this connection April and the Dr. shared. April had worked for Dr. Chase for many years but from what everything April had told him Dr. Chase never really said all that much to her outside of the typical work banter. Chris continued to ponder this relationship and then thought about what April had said with regard to Agent Bradley being a fan boy. "April, you trusted me and my plan was a flop, we will follow your lead." April smiled, "Chris, I am serious about Agent Bradley; he might pass out if he sees you right now! When he arrives please stay in the car with everyone and I will talk to him for a minute first."

Chapter 18

Chris had nodded his head in agreement and fell silent.
Doctor Chase and Christopher had very little to say during this
whole exchange. Dr. Chase just sat contemplating if there was
an exit strategy that he could envision. The Dr. had been
impressed with their resolve. He saw the determination in this
small group and marveled at how tight knit they had become,
especially Chris and April. Not sure how he felt about that
situation, the Dr. continued to evaluate their current status.
Everything in his body told him that they had to leave. He
could not stay with this group. They really had no idea the
danger they were in and he did not want to be anywhere near
them when the hammer came down upon them. Of course to
make matters worse they were sitting in the FBI's parking lot,
the very last place they should be. He had thought about April's
conversation with Chris regarding Agent Bradley.

He did believe April may be right about the agent, the
problem was all the other agents that were on Mr. P's payroll.
For years Doctor Chase had played along and continued his
research hoping to get to the point of independence. The issue
that always arose was funding. Dr. Chase patented many
aspects of his research, even incorporating himself and had
various working deals with Pharmaceutical Companies
regarding the use of portions of his research for medicinal
purposes. He had incorporated his own company and was now
on great financial footing. It seemed as though he finally had
things the way he had always envisioned they should be. The
only real issue at this point was the research itself. The problem
that kept popping up was the continued advancements in the

field. There seemed almost unlimited applications for medicine and more research based on his current work. With continuous advancement came an increase in staff and lab facilities which all led to a constant requirement to find funds, in turn meaning more government assistance.

The doctor thought about privatizing his research but found he was in too deep with his current benefactor, the government. Each time a breakthrough was imminent, almost immediately someone from the government would show up on his door step with another contribution to ensure his participation. Having this seemingly endless wallet to fund his research he found himself constantly sucked into whatever his research would bring next. When he began his research, he looked only to enhance human life. What he found was, when he solved one human ailment another screamed for his attention. With the governments' financial backing, he felt his possibilities were endless. He had definitely sold his soul for what he hoped in the end would be an ultimate win for the human race. In his mind he never wanted anyone else to ever have to deal with losing a loved one to disease or age.

He continued to look out the window and saw the dark sedan pull up next to their vehicle. The unmarked government vehicle had pulled alongside and stopped so both drivers' side windows were parallel to each other. April started talking to the agent across from her. In the dim light the Doctor could see his handsome features. His strong chin and chiseled face were no match for his sparkling intelligent eyes. He politely listened to April as she announced she needed to speak with him urgently in a secure location. His attention was so riveted to April, he failed to notice her counterparts. The agent just kept smiling and bobbing his head up and down. He proceeded to tell her to follow him as talking here was not a safe situation.

April looked at Chris in the rear view mirror while turning on the ignition at the same time. "Chris, trust me, he will help us!" Pulling out of the parking lot Chris could not help but look back at the federal building and wondered if they really should be leaving. Chris had that sinking feeling in the pit of his stomach which made him think they were even more in danger than they initially realized. It was at that moment that he noticed Doctor Chase missing. "April stop!" he cried in panic. April pulled over to the side of the road quickly turning to Chris, "Are you all right? The way you cried out I thought someone was hurt." As she took in the empty seat beside Chris she whispered, "Oh, No!" Chris looked apologetically at April, "I am sorry I was so focused on making sure you were ok I didn't even think to keep an eye on the doctor." April quickly looked up the road to see if she could still see Agent Bradley's car. She could see his car pulled over; he must have realized April was no longer following. Chris could clearly see in her face that she was wrestling with her decision. She shook her head and turned and drove the car toward Agent Bradley. "We will deal with the doctor later!" By the tone in her voice, Chris could tell he would not want to be in the doctor's shoes when April caught up with him.

Christopher had not said much this whole time but finally chimed in, "Do you think Doctor Chase is going to turn us in to Mr. P's goon squad again? After all he pretty much knows our entire plan!" April thought for a moment, "I don't think that is it, I honestly think this was all about him staying out of this and not involving himself. It would be easy to deny everything and play both sides. Which might be what he was doing all along." She scowled, "No, this was definitely about him saving his own skin," she smirked, "just in time for me to skin him!" She continued, "The doctor is not going to be very happy to see me the next time."

Having caught up to Agent Bradley, April opened her window and signaled to keep going. Agent Bradley pulled out and April followed right behind staying close as to not lose him. Chris knew his way around the city but the neighborhood Agent Bradley had brought them to was one Chris had never seen before. The apartments they pulled up in front of were old but not in terrible disrepair. This was not the hood but it wasn't exactly the high rent district either. Except for the fact that they were clearly apartments one would think these were college dorms. There were small balconies with grills and chairs. It actually looked fairly appealing and inviting. To Chris this seemed a little odd, why would an FBI agent bring them to a neighborhood where people might ask questions or worse be extremely nosey. In most low income areas that Chris had been in people minded their own business and went about daily life without even flinching when an unmarked car showed up in their neighborhood. Going unnoticed would not happen in the neighborhood to which Agent Bradley had led them.

Agent Bradley pulled into a parking spot in front of one of the apartment buildings and got out. He quickly motioned for April to pull in next to him which she did smoothly. April practically jumped out of the car and Chris scrambled out quickly to joint her side. As Chris pulled alongside April he noticed Christopher had not joined them. He grabbed April's wrist, "wait, why don't you talk to Christopher he probably still does not really comprehend what is going on right now." April turned back toward the car and went around to Christopher's door. She didn't say a word but opened his door and held out her hand to him. Christopher did not move at first but then looked into April's determined eyes and grasped her hand. He stepped out of the car, "April I have a really bad feeling about this!" April put her hand on his shoulder, "This whole thing stinks but we don't have much of a choice!" Christopher responded, "I know, couldn't we just go to a TV station and be interviewed so everyone could see?" April smiled, "I actually thought about that but you don't just go on TV and tell people about this. Many of the TV people are directly connected with Mr. P in one way or another because of all the TV money the league gives to all the stations. Christopher that is the problem, there are so many people tied to this situation. Everywhere you turn someone is going to be adversely affected when this all comes out."

April walked up to greet Agent Bradley with what would look to most people like two huge body guards. This was not lost on Agent Bradley who viewed the two large men with a raised eyebrow. Chris and Christopher stood just behind April right over her shoulders. Agent Bradley greeted them very cordially but advised them they should get inside before someone saw them. All three looked at one another as if to see if one of them would just say, "No," and leave. Whether no one could say it or they did not have a better idea they just followed Agent Bradley as he walked toward the apartment complex.

The trio followed through a series of doors and a maze of corridors until they arrived at a large brown door. Agent Bradley opened the door flipped on the light and motioned them in. Chris cut in front of April protectively with Christopher right behind. Chris scanned the apartment quickly; to him nothing seemed out of place. The apartment was neat and well furnished with the smell of being freshly cleaned. Agent Bradley led them to a living room with a very warm, soft looking couch. The agent was first to sit in a matching love seat. He seemed very comfortable and waited patiently for his guests to join him. As they all sat he could see the trio looking around taking in the apartment. "This apartment is a kind of buffer zone for the Bureau, we use if from time to time as a half way or safe house." Agent Bradley continued, "Sometimes the last place people would expect to find someone hiding would be an everyday quiet neighborhood." Almost as soon as he said these words the tension in the room lessened greatly. Everyone seemed to breathe again. Agent Bradley smiled and said, "Ok April why don't you tell me what I am doing here with you, one of Mr. P's prized players and his twin brother." He stopped for a minute and then raised a questioning hand looking at them both again with confusion in his face, "Chris, you don't have a twin brother! I am not sure if April has informed you but I am a bit of a fan of yours. I have been following your career closely for a long time and I know you do not have a twin brother. So, would someone mind telling me who this young man next to you is and why he is your mirror image?"

April stood up and faced the agent, "I am not really sure where to begin. You are well aware of the nature of Doctor Chase's genetic research. What you don't know is the extent to which the doctor has succeeded!" Agent Bradley chewed on that statement for a moment and then turned with an astonished look toward Christopher. "You are not his brother or a family member at all are you?" Christopher sprang to his feet and looked as though he would launch himself at the agent. April stepped in front of Christopher with an outstretched arm as if to prevent any unwanted incidents. Chris reached for Christopher and put his hands on the big man's shoulder,

"Christopher, it is okay, we are here to make sure this does not happen to anyone else ever again." Chris could feel the tension in Christopher's shoulders lessen and in turn felt himself relax. It felt to Chris that he had been on the edge of exploding all day. He did not know how much more in the way of surprises he could take today. Chris could not even imagine what was going through Christopher's mind right now. Christopher sat back down without taking his eyes off Agent Bradley once.

The agent put his hands up in front of him, "alright everyone just take it easy, I can see we are going to have to spend some time coming to terms with all this and figure what to do next. Who wants to begin?" April leaned forward and proceeded to illustrate for Agent Bradley the events that had taken place over the last twenty four hours. As was such when they told their story to Gus, there was no detail no matter how small left out. The surprising part to Chris was the inclusion of Chris' own admission that trusting the FBI Agent was a bad idea. Chris noticed that Agent Bradley's eyebrow raised but his expression remained stoic and he said nothing. When April finished Agent Bradley stood and looked at all three smiling the whole time. April and her Cohorts had been through this already and it seemed to them they were in a dream repeating over and over with the same outcome. Agent Bradley put his hand out questioningly, "just one question, you said Dr. Chase was with you however I do not see him now." April went on to explain that she believed the doctor had gotten spooked by the possibility of dealing with the FBI and found an exit strategy.

Chapter 19

Chris answered his phone and was shocked to hear Gus' voice on the other end of the line. "Listen Chris, I have known you your whole life and you have never once given me reason to doubt you as you have always been a straight shooter with me. If you say all this happened no matter how crazy it sounds, then I believe you to be on the level. If what you say is true and after thinking about it I realized how closely Christopher resembles you, I am inclined to believe you. You know me though, if I am going to run with a story I need proof to back up everything. I am going to need to do some digging before we go any further. Let me check with some of my government contacts." As if he could sense the apprehension through the phone, he said, "don't worry, once I know something I will give you a call. Be sure to keep your phone on you, I am sure I will be calling soon!"

Chris hung up the phone and April looked at him longingly. He turned to her, "That was Gus; it seems he had a change of heart once he realized Christopher is flesh and blood and not my twin brother. He is going to do some digging and get back to us with what he finds." He flopped down on the couch and looked extremely relieved. He eyed Agent Bradley, "April is trusting you with our lives, can we count on you?" Agent Bradley got an extremely serious look on his face, "listen Chris, I would do anything for April. I always thought she would see me as a man she could trust. I have spent a long time hoping that she would see me as more than just a friend. April has always been very gracious and never dismissed me as some jerk. I knew my feelings for her were more intense than were hers toward me. I am not sure when I realized she would never see me romantically but from that moment on I thought of myself as more of a protector or even big brother to her! Seriously Chris when I tell you I would do anything for April you can count on that!"

He shook his head before continuing, "The problem is not me Chris, I will do everything in my power to help you. The issue here is not my willingness to assist you, it is what form can that help take. Make no mistake I know the system and the right channels to help you. I am just not so sure once we go down this road that I can be of much help to you in the end." April looked at Agent Bradley with raised eyebrows, "What do you mean you might not be able to help!" The agent did not look up from his hands, "April, I will go to hell and back for you but I am just one man! If everything you say is true we are going to find our road blocked and we will very much be on our own. The other part of this which you may or may not have given thought t is the fact that who really knows how far up this goes. You are going to need an army of people not just one FBI agent!" He paused for a moment, "I am however, really good at research and I can find out almost anything you need. I am going to have to be very careful; I do not want anyone knowing I am snooping around. One thing I have learned in all my years with the Bureau is you always follow the money. Every time I have visited the stadium and talked to Dr. Chase he always seems concerned with funding for his research. After speaking with you I am quite confident I know why he was always so concerned about how he would finance his work. Let me see what I can find out. For right now I want you all to stay here and keep a low profile. The only thing I ask is that you stay out of sight tomorrow and I will see you after my shift."

161

April looked at Chris for some guidance and felt reassured when Chris nodded his head in agreement. "Agent Bradley, I cannot tell you how grateful I am to you! We have had every door slammed in our face and really had no idea what to do if this failed!" He just held his hand up as if to stop her, "Don't thank me yet, if we make it out of this alive then you can thank me, until then let's hold that thought!" Chris chimed in, "Agent Bradley, I think what April is saying is until now we had no hope. You have given us a glimmer of hope and that can be a powerful spark! I have seen small sparks in football ignite remarkable things. This might just be what we need to bring it all together!" April looked at Chris with such a prideful stare you could have easily mistaken her for his spouse at that moment.

Chris and Christopher watched intently as April closed the door and locked it behind Agent Bradley. He had warned them not to go out of the apartment until he summoned them. April returned to the couch and looked at Chris with a slight smile on her face. "I don't know about you boys but I am taking a shower and going to bed, would you mind keeping watch for me?" Chris looked at Christopher and at once they both said, "Yes ma'am!"

Watching April saunter off toward the bath room, the two mirror images just sat looking at one another. They had been dodging and ducking danger all day. Finally with a few quiet moments to themselves, the two still did not know what to make of each other. The awkward silence continued until Chris could no longer stand the tension. Instead of launching into a tirade he chose to stretch out on the couch and get comfortable. With his feet on the arm of the couch, he put his arms behind his head comfortably and drifted off to sleep.

Morning broke with the first light of day seeping through the edges of the shades. Chris had been up for a few minutes and stretched out on the couch. He sat up with the blanket resting on his knees. Sleep had little problem finding them all last night. They all had not realized the extent of their body's exhaustion. Chris' body still felt very heavy but his head felt much clearer and focused. He scanned the room and noticed the beautiful morning silence. After the previous days chaos this serene setting was a much welcome departure. Chris pondered for a moment; his life had been on warp drive for as long as he could remember. He could not even think of the last time his day was not planned out to the minute. He had spent so much time in pursuit of his goal of becoming a professional football player that there was little time left for any outside distractions.

Rising slowly from the couch he reached out and opened one of the blinds to reveal the most spell binding sunrise he had ever seen. As he stood there mesmerized by the natural beauty before him he felt the warmth of another's hand join his. April had silently joined the others and instead of ruining the moment, she stood transfixed by the suns warming rays. Neither spoke, the moment too perfect to interrupt it with mindless chatter. Christopher had risen and walked around the corner and saw the sight before him. It took his breath away, the radiant colors of the sky calling to him. He could not move or speak; he was awestruck and could not take his eyes off this most precious sight. He did peer down for a single moment to see two silhouettes holding hands before this glorious sight.

Each stood, none of them really knew how long they were there watching the sun come up only to have the silence shattered by the ring of the phone. As if shaken from a dream everyone seemed to scramble for the phone. April was first to arrive at the phone hastily picking it up to answer. April's face at first was bright but quickly changed to a serious expression. The conversation continued with mostly April listening and then quietly hanging up. April looked at Chris, "Good news, Agent Bradley found out some things we told him were true, but he said it is going to take some time to gather intelligence. Bad news, he says Mr. P has a small army out looking for you. Also, the propaganda machine has already begun rolling. You were hurt in the last game and have been placed on IR." April started to laugh, "You are listed as day to day. I could never understand that expression, aren't we all day to day? Billions of dollars made in this business and the best they can come up with is day to day, that's just great!" Chris smiled, "What else did he say?" April shrugged, "He says to hang tight, that he would have more for us tonight. He also said if we have to contact Gus, use the house phone, it is clean and bug free. Other than Gus, no contact with anyone else for now. As a matter of fact he wants us all to take the batteries out of our phones so they cannot be tracked, right now!"

They all did as instructed, disabling their phones and placing them on the kitchen table. Chris discussed with April when they should contact Gus again. It was decided that Gus, like Agent Bradley needed a little time to work his magic. April nor Chris were very comfortable with the idea that their lives no longer seemed in their own hands. For them the small amount of control they always thought they had seemed to vanish overnight. Sitting and waiting was something Chris had much trouble dealing with. He was always the person who sought out and found solutions for himself and others. Chris was beginning to grasp the sheer magnitude of their plight and knew help was going to be needed in order to survive even the day.

Much of the day was spent speculating what Gus and Agent Bradley would find. Since they were in the middle of the situation they had a unique perspective that required a lot of, "What if's" in their discussion. To the companions, the uncertainty of what to do next weighed heavily on them. They wanted to be able to offer Gus and Agent Bradley more than what amounted to just a magnificent story. It was decided that they would take as active a role as they could to decide their own fate. This decision seemed to calm their restlessness a little.

April and Chris began to focus on Christopher, who to this point was at a loss with everything swirling around him. Christopher's big question, "What is going to happen to him?" is one they all wrestled with for much of the day. Christopher could feel his friends would not let anything willingly happen to him but it was the odds they were facing that frightened him most. He definitely felt the kinship to Chris growing inside him as he spoke more frequently with his double. What was shocking to Christopher was the more the two spoke the more memories seemed to come back to him. However as he started to realize these were not his own memories, he could not help but be overwhelmed again.

April put her hand on Christopher's arm to reassure him everything would be alright. Christopher looked at April with a warm smile and put his other hand on top of April's. Chris also put his hand on Christopher's shoulder and stated, "Christopher we all ask ourselves that same question of what will happen to them. The question too many is just phrased differently, "Why are we here?" It is the question of questions. Many of us live out our lives never really having answered that question. Honestly Christopher, too many people spend too much time worrying about the answer to that question. What they should really concern themselves is what type of life they have lived." Chris himself thought about that response, "Christopher, the awesome part about all this is you will be able to lead your own life, when all is said and done! Spend your time thinking of what you can do to live a good fruitful life!" (Life, live it, face it, don't fake it!)

Christopher reached around and bear hugged his double embracing the other as if never to let go. For the first time, he felt a surge of hope spring through him as though it was an electric charge lighting a dark room for the first time. Chris returned the warm embrace and April could not help her watery eyes watching these two towering men before her. The whirlwind that had been the last few days had left little room for what one might call tender moments. This magic moment in time was exactly what Chris was describing to Christopher when he had told him to live his life, not a life someone else had programmed for him to lead.

Chapter 20

In an instant that feeling of hope was shattered. April heard the noise in the hallway first. She was up and rushed to the door to make sure it was secure. As she checked the door she peered through the peep hole and saw Steve and a security detail behind him. Her heart stopped, "how could they have found us," she whispered. Whirling around she could see her two companion's right beside her. The trio moved to the back of the apartment and went immediately to the bathroom in the master suite. Chris threw open the window and dislodged the screen. April, being a thin and athletic woman had little problem fitting through the window. The men on the other hand had quite the time twisting and turning their bodies to get through.

They found themselves in between two apartment buildings. Just as Chris made it out the window he heard the door burst open and he could hear shouting coming from the vacated apartment. The three ran toward the back of the complex hoping Steve had not brought a large contingent of security personnel. A few of the smaller security officers were already through the window in pursuit. Knowing Steve was seriously hurt in the last exchange; Chris felt a little relief knowing he would only have to face a less worthy opponent. With that knowledge they stopped at the edge of one of the buildings until they heard footsteps. As two men ran by they were struck from behind by Christopher and Chris at once. The unsuspecting security officers were no match for these two and were quickly dispatched.

Chris looked up to see three more men running toward them full speed. Instead of running, Chris turned and ran straight toward the men. He launched himself through the air at the first man and speared him right in the midsection. Being a football player had its advantages, Chris thought as he felt the man's ribs crack. They landed with terrific impact but Chris was up instantly looking for someone to hit. The Linebacker mentality fully on display, these amateurs did not stand a chance. Chris was facing the two remaining security officers now. He felt Christopher join his side and they charged. They could clearly see Tasers in the security officer's hands. Without slowing the two behemoths bowled into the officers with devastating effect. Chris and Christopher were pummeling both officers when two more security arrived with night sticks.

Chris felt the crack of the night stick on his back and rolled off his victim falling with a thud to the ground. On his back he saw his attacker bearing down on him. He quickly raised his legs and kicked out as the officer was about to hit him. He struck the man right in the chin and the man went down in a heap. Rising to his feet he saw Christopher had made quick work of his target. The scene was one of writhing bodies all over the ground around them. They scanned the area for April and their hearts skipped a beat. April stood with Steve whose arm was in a sling but the other was holding a gun with the barrel pointed at April's head.

The only thing Steve did not count on however was there was no one left to deal with the two massive men. Chris and Christopher approached from opposite sides carefully. Steve had miscalculated; both men with adrenaline still pumping were ready to destroy Steve. Seeing his situation as dire, he shouted, "Stop right there!" For the moment the two stopped mid-stride within an arm's length of Steve. The men could see the nervousness in Steve's face, that unbending confidence seemed to have broken with his arm. Chris stood right in front of Steve, "You are as good as your word, you have caught us once again!" Steve just stared at him. "Now what," continued Chris, "you get your man, what happens now? You know what they will do to Christopher! They will erase April and my memory. Is that how it is really going to end! Not now, too many people now know what is happening. You and Mr. P. can no longer keep this quiet. As a matter of fact if I were you I would seek other employment. I certainly would not want to be anywhere near Mr. P. when the fireworks start!"

Steve opened his mouth to speak but then shut it almost instantly. Chris could see his internal struggle. A man of honor, duty, and integrity such as Steve was really at odds with himself over this whole situation. He was not beyond taking a life in combat but these were innocents. He thought about Chris, he had seen him come up in college, had seen his ascent to the pros. He had never known this man to do anything but the right thing. That meant a lot to Steve, if it weren't for his duty he would have walked away. Keeping the gun still pointed at April he spoke, "Chris, I understand, I really do but when I got out of the military I could not find work. Mr. P. took me in and has treated me like family. Loyalty is something you don't just throw away! He was there when no one else was and he helped me take care of my family." Chris looked at Steve with genuine sympathy, "I know when I was a prospect Mr. P. came to me and asked me if I could see myself playing for him? Steve, I had been dreaming about this my whole life. Playing for Mr. P. and the Marauders was a dream come true which has turned into a complete nightmare!"

Steve looked at Chris, "What now?" That is when Steve felt a crack in the back of his head and then blackness. When he came to, he was in the back of his own car. He could see April driving, Christopher was in the passenger seat and Chris was right beside him. Steve now realized while he was talking to Chris he had not kept an eye on Christopher. "What did you hit me with?" He managed. Christopher turned, "A trash can cover, sorry you had a gun pointed at April, I could not let that stand!"

Steve, almost relieved that the chase was at an end just laughed. Chris looked at him seriously, "What do you find funny about any of this?" Steve just went on, "You don't understand Chris, I have been working for Mr. P. for a long time, nothing exciting really ever happens. Oh now and again a fan gets out of hand or I have to investigate a prospect but that is about it. You my friend have really screwed up Camelot! This is a gravy train for these guys; they practically print their own money at the stadium. Think about it Chris, if you had just woken up when you were supposed to none of this ever happens. We would all be going about our normal everyday lives." Steve chuckled again, "Boy this whole thing really sucks! Honestly, in the last few days I felt like I was back in the military on missions. Chris not only are you a worthy opponent, you gave me my life back. I am a man of action not someone's pet!"

A wave of surprise ran through the entire car. Everyone expected Steve to flip out and try to escape. The shock continued when Steve spoke next, "Alright what do you need me to do? This is twice you have saved my life and I will give you a life for a life. What can I do to help!" There was a stunned silence for several minutes. Finally April spoke, "Is you phone clean? We need to contact a friend." Steve said, "As clean as a phone can really be, I am sure Mr. P. is not tracking me but that does not mean he couldn't." April turned to Chris, "grab his phone and call Bradley."

When Agent Bradley answered he was noticeably nervous about being contacted, he had left them with specific instructions to wait for him. He quickly calmed when he understood the nature of their plight. Agent Bradley realized they had been compromised. "Don't worry," he said, "I have been in contact with Gus and he will be running our story later today. He has been doing some digging along with me and we have found some government contractors that are directly connected with the Marauders." There was a pause, "Chris, you got them!"

There was dead silence. Then Agent Bradley's voice brought him back, "Chris, are you there?" "Yeh, I am here! Listen Agent Bradley, we have Steve with us and I think at some point you are going to want to want to have a discussion with him." Agent Bradley responded, "Chris you be careful with that man. He is an extremely resourceful man. Sure, he is a military man but make no mistake he is a very intelligent man. Make sure you do not say too much in front of him that you don't want repeated. There is a reason he is Mr. P's number one man. Loyalty is a very valuable commodity to Mr. P. and he had become such a powerful, wealthy man due to that loyalty!" Chris could not help but take a pause before continuing, "Agent Bradley, I understand, we will be very careful. Would you prefer we just turn him over into your custody?"

After a moment came his answer, "Not yet, see if you can learn anything from him first. Call me at five o'clock and will give you directions to a secure location. If we do that we will have a better chance of not being found." Chris was a little frustrated; he wanted Steve in custody now, especially after the nightmare he had just put everyone through. He also wanted Agent Bradley to find them a safe place to stay. Of course Chris had to think for a moment, the agent was in a very precarious position as far as they were concerned. He had been sure the last location he had found for them had been secure only to have their worst fears come true. Chris hung with Agent Bradley and briefed his companions apprizing them of the agent's plans. April and Christopher agreed they should lay low for the time being. April drove them to a very run down part of town and found them an overpass to hide under. They sat quietly each engulfed in their own thoughts. It was Steve that surprisingly spoke first, "Mr. P. has people out everywhere looking for you, it is only a matter of time before another team finds you!" All at once they said, "We will be ready for them, let them come!" Steve was taken aback by this brash pronouncement, "Yes, I know you are ready, but are you ready for wave after wave that Mr. P. has at his disposal and ready to deploy? Chris I don't think you really understand, Mr. P. is going to do everything in his power to get you back and minimize the damage you have caused his organization. Although I am sure he does not know about your FBI friend or your journalist but he has an army of people that will do all they can to stop this incident in its tracks."

It was April that chimed in next, "Steve, he might have a lot of people on his side but he does not have everyone. All it takes is one person in the right place with this information to bring Mr. P. and his cronies down! People are not going to stand for this, cloning animals is one thing but people that is entirely a different matter. The outrage this is going to cause will be enough to put a stop to this atrocity." Steve looked at her, "April I hope you are right, I hope you are right!" April just smiled, "Steve, if I have learned nothing else in watching Mr. P's Empire grow larger through the use of media, what do you think is going to happen once the media gets a hold of this!" April held up her hand to silence Steve, "Chris come with me, Christopher will you stay and keep an eye on Steve?" Christopher agreed, while April and Chris stepped outside the car.

April brought Chris within sight of the car but yet far enough away so Steve could not hear their conversation. "Chris, we have to be careful what we say in front of Steve. I guarantee he is gathering Intel to report back to Mr. P." Chris smirked, "I know, I will be very careful but we can have a little fun while we are at it. We can tell him things we want him to bring back." April liked this, "Yes we might as well have a little fun with these losers! Right now, however, we have to figure out what we are going to do when we meet with Agent Bradley." Chris spoke, "April we need to make sure Agent Bradley can keep us safe until Gus came perform his magic. Even if we have to hop from place to place, we must be ready to tell our story." April grabbed his hand and led him to a Mini-Mart across from their car. "We need some food if we are going to wait for Agent Bradley." Chris said, "I am certainly hungry enough to eat a whole cow right now. April when we do talk to Agent Bradley we have to figure out how to get Doctor Chase back. I have an eerie feeling the doctor is in even more danger than we are!" April just looked right into his eyes, "Oh, I already know how to get that bastard back; I will take care of him! Don't you worry about that! Let's eat!"

They all spent the afternoon eating and taking turns keeping an eye on Steve, who did not seem the least bit uncomfortable about his captivity. During this time they rested as much as they could. Each imagined what it would be like to have their life back, not for the last time did this cross their minds. The afternoon wore on as they all kept looking at the car's clock. To them it seemed five o'clock would never arrive. It was at this point they decided that they needed to listen to something other than themselves. Turning on the radio they turned to the local sports station. Listening to the local take on last week's game was quite entertaining for these friends. Of course on any normal day listening to these talking heads would be extremely frustrating. Usually the talk shows spent much of their time making inflammatory remarks about the local sports teams all in the name of ratings. Today turned out to be much different. The topic of discussion shocked the occupants of the car. Today's focus for the program was a story that was put out by a local reporter implicating Mr. P. in a huge scandal.

The scandal being described was not news to those in the car but what surprised them was the passion that the callers and hosts alike were talking about the scandal. People were absolutely livid about Mr. P's role in such a human rights violation. Chris just listened intently as person after person called the show with one thing on their minds, bringing the perpetrators to justice. As April had anticipated, the media storm that can occur during situations such as this had already begun to take hold. April thought to herself, "Let's see him get out of this one!" She smiled a small sad smile. Justice would be served but what form would the justice take and how much would they continue to be affected. April turned the channel to another station and they began to listen carefully. The very same conversation was taking place on this station. They listened for a few minutes and then turned to the local news channel. Even on the news station they were talking about cloning and human rights violations. On every channel they checked hosts were talking about football for all the wrong reasons.

Each member of their little party could not stop listening even though every station was reporting the same exact information. It seemed surreal to them as if something out of a movie. They all sat staring at the console hoping to hear more details. As they continued to listen they were amazed how much accurate information was actually being reported. Usually in a case such as this accusations caused quite a stir. In this case there were actual names attached and divulged, including April and Chris. April thought this was brilliant on Gus' part now no matter what Mr. P. came up with to combat the story he would never make it stick.

April finally turned off the radio and handed the phone to Chris. "Call Agent Bradley and find out what our next move is please." They all looked at the clock, it was exactly five o'clock. The phone rang several times and just as Chris was about to hang up he heard someone answer. "Hello Chris, you have led me on quite the chase," came Mr. P's voice. "Now I have to admit this is one hell of a mess you have gotten us all into. This is going to take some time to clean up this mess. You may think you have brought me down but this is all public relations, this is what I do. I put out fires all day every day. When a player is involved in drugs or something illegal I have to fix it. If a member of my staff gets a DUI or if a member of my medical team is caught giving the wrong meds, I fix it! This is going to cost me a small fortune but I will prevail. Chris when I am done with you none of you will be able to show your faces anywhere. You will wish you had let me erase your memory and lived a normal life!"

Chris heard the click on the other end and was in shock. April grabbed his arm, "Chris what is it, what did Agent Bradley say?" Chris leaned his head back, "We are on our own, Bradley is compromised, that was Mr. P., he is coming after us full bore." April screamed, "What are you talking about, how?" Chris shrugged, "I don't know but we've got to move. Let's get out of here!"

April started the car and they drove off back toward the highway. Once underway Chris asked where they were headed. April told him, "I am not going to say just yet." As they continued down the highway the phone rang. At first no one wanted to answer but since the last encounter with Mr. P. they did not seem to have much to lose. Chris picked up, "Chris is that you?" It was Agent Bradley's voice. "Listen we don't have much time, Mr. P's goons are after me too! Meet me at the Club Seat Restaurant at nine o'clock tonight. I have to go, meet me there and make sure you are not followed." The phone went dead. Chris relayed the message to everyone. Steve who had remained quiet this whole time broke his silence. "You know this is a trap right?" April just shouted, "That is not true, a member of your security team has already reported to Mr. P. your whereabouts. He has no idea where Agent Bradley is right now. He is however tracking your phone." She reached over and took the phone from Chris' hand and threw it out the window. The phone shattered on impact. "Let him track that!" she said.

April looked at the clock, "it is five thirty now, we have plenty of time to do what I need to do and meet Agent Bradley." She stepped on the gas and continued to speed down the highway. After ten minutes she pulled the car quickly into a rest area. She got out and Chris followed. April told Chris to put

Steve in the trunk. She did not want him to see where they were going. Chris looked at her skeptically but did not argue and followed her lead. He walked Steve to the rear of the car still questioning himself if this was the right move. They placed Steve in the trunk with surprisingly little resistance and continued on their journey.

Chapter 21

Doctor Chase had seen his opportunity and taken it to slip out of sight during a moment of confusion among his companions. He understood their plight and genuinely wished to help them. His view on the matter was quite a bit different than his friends. Though each had a great deal invested in this situation, Dr. Chase had a much more personal interest in making sure this incident was contained as much as possible. The doctor could not help but wonder if he helped April and Chris maybe they could help him out of his own plight and escape. The doctor envisioned his life much differently and had hoped to be at the forefront of life saving research. He had struggled often with the lure of money to continue his research. A day did not pass by that he did not wish he had taken a different path. Everything he had accomplished in medicine seemed on the verge of complete collapse and being taken away from him. He could not allow that to happen, his legacy was at stake.

Moving quickly down a side street he saw the bright street lights of a major roadway and made straight for it. Once on the main road he gathered himself to gain his bearings. Looking quickly up the road, he recognized a local Italian restaurant that he had frequented some years earlier. The more important knowledge to the doctor was that there was a bus stop not fifty feet from the front of the restaurant. As luck would have it the doctor saw a young couple and an older gentleman waiting for the bus to come. A wave of relief came over him as he walked briskly toward the bus stop. He knew he would be able to make it home on the bus, as he had during times his car had been repaired. The doctor actually enjoyed riding the bus to work on occasion. Sitting back and letting someone else take care of him appealed to him somehow.

The doctor made his way onto the bus and found a seat at the back, so as to observe anything taking place in front of him. He thought for a moment about getting stuck without an exit strategy should the occasion arise. He had been on edge with all that had taken place in the last few days and laughed at himself for being a bit paranoid. Pushing himself farther into the stiff seat, he leaned his head back and looked at the small luggage rack with a smile. He thought back to his own days as a young baseball prospect. The buses the team traveled with back then were much plainer and if possible even more uncomfortable. The luggage rack reminded him of a time when a duffel bag was pretty much all he had owned. There were days when he and his brother grabbed each other's bag by mistake only to find out later on of the mishap. This provided for some fun being that Dr. Chase was taller and thinner than his brother. Having put a shirt on that was much too short for him had made him the object of jabs by some of his teammates.

The doctor had definitely enjoyed that simple part of his life. He and his brother had a typical childhood with plenty of sibling rivalry. They would constantly be on each other's case, but yet were always there for each other when the situation arose that required a brother's touch. It wasn't until they started to get older and found baseball to be their common ground did they grow extremely close. It was as if bonding with his teammates had given the two brother's the okay to show their love for one another. Having that carefree time with his brother was still among the fondest moments of his life. That is until the day he thought he had found a way to save his brother.

The sense that he could save someone's life had always been foremost in his thoughts and losing his brother now prompted him ever forward to save as many lives as he could.

Pondering this thought he noticed that the bus had stopped and looked up from his seat. Two tall athletic gentlemen in running attire boarded the bus. This in itself was nothing noteworthy except that Dr. Chase had become accustomed to security personnel in his line of work. The ear piece is what gave these gave these gentlemen away. It was small but did have a small antenna sticking out and if not for that the doctor would have thought it a hearing aide. Not even stopping, looking around both men sat right up front and went into a heavy conversation. For some reason the doctor felt he must stay out of sight and scrunched himself down in the seat. After a few more stops the doctor noticed the men showed no signs of leaving the bus which made him more anxious. They would be at the doctor's stop in a few minutes and he felt he had to act soon. The next stop was a mile or so away from Dr. Chase's house. If he waited two stops he would literally be on top of his street. As the bus neared the first stop he made the decision to get off at the first stop. When the bus pulled over to stop he made his way up front carefully as not to cause any attention to himself. The two men did not even skip a beat in their conversation which made the doctor relieved. He exited the bus without fanfare and started for home. Closing in on his home something in the back of his mind told him to get off the road, so following his instincts he walked more on people's lawns.

That is what allowed him to see the black Yukon parked a few houses down from his house. He recognized the vehicle as one of Mr. P.'s security team's. Dr. Chase slunk to a large

Maple tree within eyesight and earshot of the SUV. Laughter could be heard emanating from the Yukon and the doctor strained to hear what was being said. A low fast voice could be heard, "We need to get out of here, no one has seen the doctor in a whole day. The last time he was seen was with Mr. P. himself, so why would he hide?" Another more grainy voice chimed in, "All I know is we were told to bring him to Mr. P. personally! I think this is a huge waste of time myself but I am sure Mr. P. will pay handsomely for the return of the illustrious doctor." The other retorted, "That is all well and good but we have been sitting here for twelve hours and have seen nothing but the mailman! I am calling it in." Dr. Chase heard a heated phone conversation that resulted in both men deciding to call it a night. The Yukon started and drove off leaving Dr. Chase still hiding behind the tree. He peered around the tree toward his house only to have the bus stop just to the side of his house. Low and behold who did he see step out of the bus onto the sidewalk, none other than the two men in the running suits. He whispered to himself, "This day just keeps getting better and better."

The Club Seat was a very well known, popular sports bar. When April and the others arrived the restaurant was packed with patrons. Entering the restaurant they could see right away why there were so many people. The décor was amazing. Signed jersey's from the local team's sports stars lined the walls. Autographed photographs of sports legends were everywhere. Each table was glass covered with either sports cards or game ticket stubs under the glass. Every table had its own small flat screen TV with your choice of sports channel. Large flat screens hung in what seemed to be each corner and wall with every sport imaginable. Chris was brought back to the many times he had spent with his friends and family in places such as this very establishment. He wondered how many people had watched him play in this past weekend's game here. The joyful, raucous crowd was dulled only by the robust smell of cooking meats and fried foods. How anyone could not enjoy themselves here would be a mystery to Chris.

He found himself being led through the rows of tables and servers by April. She definitely seemed to know where she was going. To anyone watching these three it would seem to most that these behemoths were her big brothers protecting her interests. To the rear of the restaurant a hallway split off to the side revealing a much smaller room. The room, although similarly decorated, had more of a businesslike feel to it. There was one large table which one might use for a conference. Sitting at the head of the table was Agent Bradley in civilian clothes. April almost laughed; she didn't think she had ever seen Bradley in anything other than a suit and tie. What was surprising to everyone was the person sitting to Bradley's right, none other than Gus. Gus had the biggest smile on his face Chris had ever seen. Standing quickly Bradley and Gus greeted everyone before sitting down almost as fast. April and her friends took seats at the table.

Gus seemed to be chomping at the bit to talk so Bradley waved his hand as if to say go ahead. He started by asking if they had listened to any of the news lately. He smiled a sinister smile and waited for anyone to respond. Chris was first to speak up, "Gus, we have heard on almost every channel what you and I spoke about earlier. I know you have us as sources but I know you would never run with a story unless you had any other confirmed sources." "Chris," he said, "After doing a little digging you would be surprised at how easy it was to confirm your story. The more I look into this it is amazing no one has found out about this before now. Honestly Chris if you had not woken up when you did who knows how long this would have continued. I do know however with a league as large this they have suppressed this information extremely well. I also really believe that many people involved in the league really had no idea this was going on outside of the coaching staff and the medical team.

To most of the other staff and to fans it has seemed like business as usual. They really have not had any reason to suspect anything out of the ordinary. Even the TV people and crews just viewed and showed you as modern day gladiators through the digital lenses. Even you, Chris, who played the game, had watched the game had no idea this was going on right under your nose. I really think one of the reasons they have been able to keep a secret like this for so long is the true fantastic nature of the story itself. Hell, I am a reporter and I am still not sure I believe what is going on here. One thing is for certain, is we have stepped in it now! I hope you are ready for an all-out war because that is what the, "Good old boy network," is prepared to do to protect their product. Also right now the public is very much with us but what if this backfires and their favorite sport is irrevocably damaged? We have to do whatever we can to keep the unruly mob focusing on the owners and their teams.

Agent Bradley looked quite content as Gus was speaking. It was apparent that Gus had spoken to Bradley prior to meeting with Chris and his cohorts. Bradley motioned them to sit and come closer. Each member of the group sat and turned in to listen to the agent. "I have contacted a person high in the ranks of the FBI, way above my pay grade that assures me we will be safe. This contact is also well aware of Mr. P.'s efforts to shut us down. Mr. P. finds himself in damage control mode right now because too many people know what is happening. Soon, damage control will turn to an all-out assault on us and anything attached to us. We are going to offer irrefutable scientific evidence of Christopher's existence." He looked straight at Christopher, "Yes, I and everyone else can see the uncanny resemblance but arguments can be made against those claims. The simplest being a look alike."

Chapter 22

The two men from the bus approached the house and did not go in but rather snuck around as if casing the house. Doctor Chase watched with great curiosity as the two men vanished into the shadows. He thought to himself how odd it was that Mr. P.'s boys just rode off and these two conveniently show up. If Mr. P. did not send them then where did they come from? Dr. Chase felt curiosity rising up from within him but every instinct in his body told him to stay put. It only took him a moment to take note of his situation out in the open.

Moving to his left peering towards his backyard he had decided to find out just exactly what these two men were doing here. The doctor had decided that he knew the terrain much better than these men and that he could stay out of sight. Crouching low, he spotted a large bush at the corner of his next door neighbor's house that would offer sufficient cover. Judging the distance to travel as safe, he moved swiftly toward the bush and the house. From his vantage point he could scan his backyard and out of the corner of his eye he sensed movement. Staying so still he thought he might lose his breath, he watched as a shadowy figure made its way to the set of French doors at the back of the doctor's house. He watched in great surprise as the man took from his pocket what looked to be a small flashlight. The man pointed the tool in between the two French doors and then a concentrated beam of light shot through the air. The doctor stood, transfixed, as the beam seemed to easily cut through the dead bolt that locked the double doors. In a matter of seconds a second equally shadowy figure joined his partner and entered the home with no sound.

Panic set in for the doctor with the realization what these two men might find in his home. He heard the crash of something falling to the floor emanating from his home. This affected him more than he thought, and he started to walk toward his home. He made his way stealthily to the edge of the house without being detected. Entering his house through the same doors as the intruders he began to feel more angry than frightened. The invasion of his private space was something the doctor was not about to let stand. The sheer audacity of these intruders was offensive to his sensibilities. Just through the door on the left hand side stood his golf bag that he had forgotten to put in the garage. As it turned out that was a blessing because he grabbed an iron and continued into the house with the club raised to strike.

The doctor expected the men to search for his computer so he worked his way silently to his office. When he turned the corner, he saw small beams of light coming from the office. He worked his way along the wall until he was at the doors edge. Flattening himself to the wall he stretched his neck to look carefully into his office. Two figures were barely visible in the minimal light given off by their small flashlights. Surprisingly Doctor Chase did not wait to think things through and just bolted into the room with club ready. Caught unaware, the first man took the iron club right square on the side of the head. The man crumbled to the floor unmoving as his partner was fleeing toward the door. With a flick of his wrist he threw the club at the intruder striking him in the back of his right knee. The man stumbled and crashed right into the wall but did not go down. With no other weapons Dr. Chase was at a distinct disadvantage and found himself standing face to face with the stranger. Even in the dark the man cut an imposing figure with significant mass in his arms and chest.

186

The first blow struck Doctor Chase in the sternum and knocked the wind out of him. When he was hit for the second time he had still not recovered and took a shot to his right temple. Still stunned and now seeing stars the doctor did not see his attacker come up from behind him. He felt himself being brought to the ground and landed with a thud on the side of his face. The man swiftly grabbed the doctor's wrists and brought them behind his back with a sharp pain in his shoulders. He felt plastic tear into the flesh of his wrists and was unable to move his arms without terrible pain. With great force his attacker lifted the doctor up and forced him to sit in a chair. The only light at this point came from the small flashlight on the ground after having fallen during the struggle. As the man bent down to retrieve the light the doctor's head had begun to clear and his foot came up striking the man's chin with terrific force. The cracking sound was sickening and the man was rocked but still did not go down. Wheeling around he elbowed the doctor in the face and watched as the doctor fell backwards over the chair and onto the floor with terrific force.

The doctor was beginning to rise when he was blinded by the sudden infusion of light from what seemed to be everywhere. He thought he heard the word, "Freeze," but was so startled by the course of events it was hard to fathom what was happening. Suddenly he was surrounded by police officers telling him it would be alright. One of his neighbors had heard suspicious things happening on the property and alerted the police. With eyes still adjusting to the light he was able to take note of the four uniformed officers looking at him sympathetically. He blinked several times while trying to re-focus his eyes. The one assailant left standing then took out a badge of his own and announced himself as NSA. He then proceeded to inform them that Dr. Chase would be going with him in his custody. The ranking uniformed officer stood before the NSA agent stating that may be the case but not until it was okayed by his captain. The agent started to get agitated which did not go unnoticed by the officer. He alerted the NSA agent that his captain and FBI were at the station and expected Dr. Chase. The officer suggested things could be sorted out at the station. Looking none too pleased the agent began to complain but caught sight of the additional officers behind him and thought better of it.

He agreed that it would be best if they straightened everything out with the FBI first. As he turned to tend to his partner, the lead officer struck him in the back of the head with an expandable night stick. The sound of the blow was sickening and the strike did its job as the NSA agent landed on the floor unconscious with a thud. Dr. Chase watched this whole exchange with great anxiety. He was extremely confused by the actions of the officers. By all rights, they should have handed him off to the Federal agent, no questions asked. When someone from the NSA is requesting your prisoner, they are usually granted that request. Dr. Chase knew from his dealings with various government agencies over the years that each is highly territorial and did not care to share with anyone. The doctor turned to the officers wincing expecting much the same treatment as the NSA agent. To his great surprise the officer asked him to put his hands in front toward the officer. Dr. Chase felt the clasp of hard steel wrap around his wrists. When the handcuffs had clicked for the last time, the finality of being taken into custody began to set in.

As the officer held his head helping him into the squad car, he could not help but wonder about his own fate. He knew Chris and April were about to release what amounted to a nuclear blast on the sports world and who but the Doctor would be at ground zero. Being at the epicenter of perhaps the largest sports scandal since the, "Black Sox," had thrown the World Series made Dr. Chase's face red with embarrassment. He continued to reason it out in his head as to the benefits to humanity outweighing the horror the cloning process being used in this manner had cost everyone he cared about. The Doctor also knew how Mr. P. would approach the situation deny, deflect, and blame others in order to stay clear of the worst of things yet to come. He couldn't help but laugh for he knew Mr. P. to be a ruthless business man and he would throw anyone under the bus in order to gain his own pursuits.

A stark realization occurred to him, he would be the one on whom the most blame would fall. Having his research at the forefront of everything Chris and April had unearthed would be extremely damaging to any defense he might be able to muster. This brought about the feeling of frustration, what good would all his research if he could not continue to see it through to its ultimate end. It was then that the officer who had struck the NSA agent started speaking to him and brought him back to the present. The officer began, "Dr. Chase you are being transferred into the FBI's custody. They will be handling your situation from this point on and from what I know, be glad it is the FBI that has you and not the NSA." The car turned into a parking lot and the doctor was instructed to get out of the vehicle. Doing so, the doctor immediately felt highly suspicious. Why was the transfer taking place in a parking lot and not the office of the FBI. He was shuffled off toward another vehicle and noticed there were quite a few occupants in the car itself. The driver's door of the vehicle he approached opened and out stepped a large man. In the dim light he felt his heart race as he got a glimpse of the man's face.

The man said a few words of thanks to the officers and proceeded to lead Dr. Chase away towards the new vehicle. Stooping down to get into the car he peered at the other occupants only to laugh out loud and sit while putting on his seatbelt. No one spoke for what seemed to be an eternity, the awkward silence only broken by the hum of another car's engine as they passed. Finally the silence was broken, "Dr. Chase I have to tell you this has been quite the day but I am glad you are with us, where you belong." The doctor responded, "Agent Bradley, something tells me I had little choice in the matter!" Agent Bradley smirked, "well I guess I could just turn you over to the NSA, I am sure they are an understanding bunch."

Doctor Chase nodded in agreement and turned to face the heat and rage emanating from the back seat. He began, "Honestly, what would you have done? Every single one you would have run as well!" April's eyes looked as if they could burn holes through the doctor. "I think the difference doctor, is not one of us would have taken off on you! We would have found a way to stick together! We would not have left you behind," she trailed off. Dr. Chase's face twisted uncomfortably with regret, "April," he stuttered, "I really need you as far away from me as possible. You definitely have a much better chance without me. I only put you in more danger, don't you understand that!" April reached over the seat and grabbed him by the collar, "Danger!" she screamed, "Danger! You are the one that put us all in danger! There is no danger with you! You are our insurance policy, our way out!" Stunned and not knowing what to say the doctor just stared at April. April returned his stare with a frustrated gasp and sat back down in her seat deflated.

Agent Bradley piped in, "Listen guys we are not out of the woods by a long shot! We still need to get you all to the safe house. I have arranged this carefully, no one knows where we are going." Chris cut in, "Yes that worked last time!" Bradley countered, "Yes but last time we were stuck in a FBI sanctioned house. No one knows of this place, no one! Dr. Chase what the hell were you doing going back to your house. That is the first place everyone would be looking for you!" The doctor sheepishly said, "There are things I need there that I do not want anyone to get a hold of. Some of those things in the wrong hands could become costly and dangerous for some, while making a lot of money for others."

As he was finishing his statement the window by Agent Bradley's head exploded. The car swerved and struck the guard rail and bounced off. Gathering his wits, Agent Bradley realized his ear was missing several small pieces and blood was streaming down the side of his face and neck. He straightened the car and held it steady while pulling out his side arm. Meanwhile, the car was struck again in the side by gunfire piercing holes in the door panels. Agent Bradley gunned the gas and sped up the street leaving the mystery car behind. The lights quickly caught up and the passengers felt a crushing blow to the back of their car. The blow was enough to lift the back end of the car and make it skip as it landed on the road once again. Agent Bradley yelled for them all to get down. They all leaned forward and kept out of sight as this happened the back window shattered glass everywhere from a bullet. The agent jammed on the brakes, letting the other car ram into the back of the car. The jolt from the collision made everyone strike their heads and glass sprayed everywhere.

The bloodied agent proceeded to jump out of the car and open fire on his pursuer. He put three rounds directly through the driver's windshield. Surprised by the lack of return fire, he kept his gun pointed ahead and went for the driver's door. Opening the door and shoving his gun into the car what seemed to be simultaneously, he saw slumped over the steering wheel, the driver. He lifted the driver's head back to see a bloodied, matted mess of what had once been a face. Not only did the crash cause multiple facial fractures, but what the car did not do the gun shots had finished. The agent swiftly scanned the car surprised to find the man had been alone. He did recognize him as one of the men who had identified themselves as NSA agents. Bradley searched the body to find the dead agent's credentials and a few fire arms. Taking all he could, he returned to his vehicle and slipped into the driver's seat once more. The car was still running and he put it into gear moving forward practically tearing what was left of the back end of the car off. In spite of this the car remained relatively intact and lurched forward. He turned quickly to see if everyone was okay. Despite the shock of the event they were all sound and mainly unharmed.

The agent on the other hand had major lacerations to his ear and upper neck causing him a great loss of blood. The bleeding had stopped but to his passengers he was a ghostly sight straight out of a horror film. April pleaded with him to pull over and let her take over but he insisted he was fine. He continued for quite a few more miles before starting to fade and feeling his eyes begin to close. The agent struggled to keep the car on the road. Reluctantly he pulled over quickly, he unsteadily switched places with April, practically willing himself into the back seat. He told April in general where they were going, but he had to stay awake to finish the directions.

Dr. Chase took bottled water from the floor and went to work cleaning the agent's wounds and helping him where he could. Agent Bradley graciously took the water and sipped it and allowed the doctor's care. With the loss of so much blood the agent was extremely weak. Having gone on mostly adrenaline to this point he slipped into unconsciousness. The doctor took smelling salts out of a small pouch he had and held them under Bradley's nose causing the agent to stir. He stayed awake long enough to give final directions, which they luckily were not far from their destination. Drifting off again the doctor told April to hurry; he really had to examine the agent in better light. April had the car screaming toward the place Agent Bradley had described for them. They pulled up to what looked like had been a restaurant at one time.

Chapter 23

The building was in good shape but they could tell no one had been there in quite some time. The parking lot was cracked and had grass growing through the pavement in many spots. A quick glance of the surrounding area saw various vacant business buildings. It seemed the economic downturn had affected this entire area hard. The road leading up to the building seemed as vacant as the buildings, with an occasional broken down car on the side of the road. The companions pulled into the parking lot looking to see if they were not the only living things within sight. They quickly grabbed the agent who was now in a semi-conscious state. He pulled a key out and handed it to Chris before slumping over again. Moving quickly to the door, they found the key easily fit and the door opened with little difficulty. They entered a front room which still had all the tables and chairs set up. Except for the thick layer of dust and lack of light, it looked as though the establishment was expecting patrons.

April and her small company trudged through the dense layer of dust and collapsed into the nearest booth. Dr. Chase laid agent Bradley carefully onto one of the tables. The agent was unconscious but his breathing was raspy and shallow. A closer inspection by the doctor revealed a large shard of glass still sticking out of the agents head near the rear of his ear. In the dark and in the confusion of the chase the doctor had not noticed the piece of glass until now. The doctor called April over and requested water and any clean linens they could find. Producing a small bag the doctor started to take various small instruments out and layed them on a sterile napkin. Meanwhile

April and Chris washed the areas instructed by Dr. Chase behind the ear to reveal the full extent of the damage. When clean the doctor could clearly see the shard. It did not appear that the piece of glass was imbedded very deep into the tissue around the ear. What worried the doctor was if any fragments may have made their way into the agent's ear canal.

Carefully using what looked like a pair of long needle nosed pliers he wiggled the shard free from behind the ear. The piece came out with relative ease, which made the doctor feel confident everything would be okay. Further examination of the wound did not reveal any further fragments and the doctor closed the wound with ten stitches. The doctor continued his search for other injured locations. When he was satisfied that the agent had no life threatening injuries he rested his hand on the agents head in reassurance. With the major damage repaired all they had to do was wait and hope the agent had not lost too much blood.

April stood vigil over the fallen agent and kept checking his vital signs. She had covered Bradley with a fire blanket they had found in the kitchen and bandaged the rest of the minor wounds he had sustained. She noticed his temperature rise during treatment and put cool compresses on his head to combat the fever. April and company took turns sitting with the agent to both talk to him and watch over him. After several hours of nervous silence, agent Bradley's breathing became less labored and more regular. His body regained a more glowing and less ashen look. Doctor Chase put a prideful hand on April's shoulder and announced the agent would be fine, that the worst was behind him. April, a little more uncertain did not leave her post and continued to monitor the agent's recovery.

Little else was said during this whole ordeal except to assist the doctor and the nurse with their patient. Now that the crisis seemed to be subsiding everyone collapsed into a seat and seemed to breathe for the first time in hours. Christopher had not said much the entire time and stood by and helped when asked by either Dr. Chase or April. Now he sat in a chair with legs outstretched and head leaned back against the wall. Chris had also said little and kept a nervous watch over April. Now, Chris also had a hawk eye on the doctor fully expecting him to bolt again. He had thought seriously about tying the doctor to one of the chairs. Although looking at the doctor relaxed in his own chair, he hardly looked like a flight risk. Chris decided he was not taking any chances and carefully measured each movement the doctor made. Had the doctor known about Chris's willingness to pounce like a predator, he may just have tied himself up.

Chris kept one eye always on the doctor but would not take the other off April. He noticed her slightly bent shoulders, suggesting her fatigue and her hand holding up her head in an attempt to stay awake. April had not once waivered while attending to the agent. She had not complained once while changing dressings and washing wounds. Chris was amazed at how calm and confident she remained while attending to the agents injuries. Chris wondered to himself, "Has she always had that confidence or had she gained it through experience." April continue to enthrall him each chance she got with her kind nature but quiet confidence and strength. He glanced quickly in Christopher's direction and could see the big man had fallen asleep. Scanning back over to Doctor Chase, he saw the doctor's head lean forward and to the side indicating he was dropping off to sleep.

It was then Chris realized no one had had anything to eat in a long while. Of course this was a bit much to handle for Chris considering they were hold up in an old restaurant. He decided to explore and found himself in a backroom filled to his surprise with all kinds of food and survival supplies. There were shelves lined with canned goods and dried foods. It seemed to Chris like he was looking at the isle of a grocery store. The most surprising to Chris was the quite large supply of liquid refreshment, most of which took the form of water and sports drinks. He could not help but laugh, from the front of the building it would look to anyone as though the building was vacant. With the amount of dust they had walked through coming in it was apparent no one had been here in quite some time.

Further exploration revealed a smaller store room with a myriad of cooking supplies. Pots and pans hung from the ceiling. There were cooking oils, flour, sugar, dried beans, rice, and tons of pasta. If they were not in the spot they were in he would love to make a great meal for everyone. He searched the drawers of the cabinets and found utensils of all kinds, along with plenty of lighters to light stoves. Coming to the end of the room he noticed a stainless steel door with a heavy pad lock securing the door. Out of curiosity he gave the lock a tug with no luck, it was locked tight. He shrugged his shoulders thinking it was the freezer for meats and frozen foods and made his way back to the others.

Everyone sighed with relief when Chris announced the news that they were well stocked with food. He even joked and told them they had enough food for a siege. April turned to him and added she hoped they would not have to be held here as if in a siege. To everyone's surprise it was Dr. Chase that offered to prepare dinner. Of course during preparation, Christopher did not take his eyes off the doctor. Doctor Chase finally turned to him, "Christopher if you are going to treat me like an inmate, the least you could do is help me with dinner. You can keep an eye on me and we can get this done much more quickly!" To Christopher's surprise the doctor seemed quite at home in the kitchen. He did not bark orders at Christopher but rather asked him to grab certain ingredients or mixed different things for him. When finished they all had a fine home cooked meal.

Finishing their meal they all cleaned up while April went to go check on agent Bradley. She found him resting quite comfortably and checking his vitals she smiled warmly at him. He seemed out of danger and April grasped his hand and told him he was going to be fine. She sat with him for a few minutes before returning to the others. Entering the dining area she found Chris sprawled out in one of the booths. Doctor Chase and Christopher were quietly talking at one of the larger corner tables. April moved over to her own booth and plopped into the seat and put her head onto the table.

April shot up when touched and was very disoriented, not knowing where she was, she instinctively put her hands up. As her eyes focused she took in Chris, even in his disheveled state he cut quite the picture. His warm hands enclosed hers, immediately reassuring her everything was okay. He smiled at her and looked at her with loving eyes. She felt a shiver go down her spine as he brought her in close to him and was engulfed in his warm embrace. In his powerful arms was the only place of refuge she wanted to remain. She reached up and caressed his cheek and then without warning she grabbed his face with both hands planting a passionate kiss on Chris's lips. The electricity that passed between them seemed to amplify as though lightning striking a tree sending showers of sparks rising into the air.

As if his lips were singed from their combustive kiss Chris sprang back, holding April at arm's length. He paused for just a moment and then charged back in for more almost knocking April over. The two became intertwined as though their faces were one when they heard someone clear their throat. It took a few more throat clears before they separated. Dr. Chase just stood in front of them smiling from ear to ear and announced, "Our patient is awake and taking nourishment." April rushed past the doctor into the room where Agent Bradley was sitting up eating some soup. Most of his color had returned and he looked rather healthy for someone who had to have chunks of glass removed from his head.

He looked at April, "I understand nurse, you took great care of me! I for one am glad that I had a doctor and a nurse to patch me back up." His eyes began to moisten, "Thank You! By the way how do you like my secret lair, pretty cool huh? We will be safe here for a little while anyway. I am not sure what our next move is going to be. Has anyone found the radio, we need some news." They all stared at him in amazement, just a few short hours ago they were not sure he would survive but here he was babbling away! After further discussion it was decided April would go with Chris to the local convenience store to get some newspapers and a Trac phone. When they returned, reading through the newspapers, it was obvious their story had continued to evolve. It was also quite apparent that the PR machine was in full swing for Mr. P. and the Marauders. Deny, deny, deny was the strategy of the day and various statements put out by the team were assuring fans there would an investigation into these baseless as they termed the allegations.

What was so reassuring to Chris and his companions was the continued onslaught of information the media was continuing to pour out about this story, waging a terrific battle of information against Mr. P. Gus certainly knew what he was doing when he unleashed the beast. Almost all the stories relayed the same message, "the public will not stand for human beings, being treated in such a fashion!" There were a few dissenting reports however, trying to debunk the allegations. As they read they were sure Mr. P. continued to work the phones in an attempt to discredit them in the public's eyes. Right , for Mr. P. damage control was in full force. He had even scheduled press conference for the following day to discuss his plans to foil this smear campaign on national TV. Chris slammed his fist on the table nearly splitting it in half, "That's it! I know how to fry his bacon!"

Chapter 24

Mr. P. sat at his immense mahogany conference table surrounded by an army of lawyers and public relations staff. The scene was one of utter chaos and the volume was so loud he could not hear himself think. He had been through unbelievable ups and downs during his tenure as owner of the Marauders. The Championships were still like a dream to him and he wondered if he would ever see another as an owner. That thought made him furious, he had faced scandals before and come out unscathed. This seemed to him a much different situation; the backlash he was receiving was beyond anything he could possibly imagine. He watched his team of handlers scurry around the room in a panic and he knew he was in for a dog fight!

The owner of the Marauders held the newspaper at arm's length and read the headline aloud, "Trouble in Paradise." The story outlined in great deal the actions of the football team's owner and ended with calling into question the entire leagues integrity. Mr.P. had been on the phone with all of the other owners trying to come up with a strategy to combat these allegations. The other owners, like Mr. P. it seemed were constantly facing one scandal or another. Their league being as large and as successful as theirs brought with it many unsavory occurrences from time to time. Like Mr. P. the other owners were ready to fight and in some cases relished the chance to be in the spotlight. Over the years Mr. P had developed a reputation as a Pit Bull when it came to fighting for his team. He also had turned out to be quite a leader and the other owners showed him great respect and deference. It had been decided among the owners that in times of crisis Mr. P. would be their mouthpiece. Over the years he had served the league well and brought them great wealth and fame in the process. They all once again looked to him to save their skins. The only problem remaining, was could he save them all once again.

Mr. P. flicked the newspaper down toward the middle of the table and stood with a determined look on his face and crossed the room toward the hoard of lawyers. The leeches surrounded him as if out for blood and were bombarding him with suggestions. He raised his hand for silence and waited for them to calm down. When they were silent Mr. P. began, "Gentlemen, we stand on the edge of disaster! You are charged with the task of rescuing not only a franchise but possibly an entire league. Our very way of life is being threatened! Can you imagine what weekends would look like without football? That gentleman is Traitorous!"

The lawyers exploded into discussion that rivaled a mosh pit, once more as Mr. P. walked away. He smirked, he knew from experience a lawyer with a cause was a very dangerous thing. He walked to his private elevator to begin his preparation for tomorrow's news conference. On councils advice he would deflect, deflect, deflect and offer plausible deniability when pressed by the media. Riding in the elevator by himself he was stunned by the silence. He had spent so much time lately surrounded by screaming meanies, the silence was deafening. When the door opened Mr. P. stepped out into his Penthouse office. Usually he would be glad to be surrounded by such comfort. He had become quite fond of excess and enjoyed the finer things in life. Now, however, the huge office seemed to echo with silence. Mr. P. sat down in the very chair Chris had sat in when he had tried to convince Chris to help him. He genuinely was very fond of Chris and did not want anything bad to happen to him. The issue remained, could he and the team survive this onslaught of negative publicity. Mr. P. put his hand on his temples and decided Chris and his little group had to be stopped at all costs, no matter how he felt about Chris. He could capture them and erase their memories allowing him to reboot the whole system. If that worked he would easily disprove their story and turn the tables on Chris and company. The only problem with that, was capturing them all. Capture was the first option but Mr. P. was faced with the harsh reality that someone might need to be permanently removed.

Steve had said very little during the time they had brought Agent Bradley in the restaurant. He sat off to the side and into the corner. No one seemed to notice him and in fact they did not even look his way. He listened intently to all their conversations. He was very used to picking apart conversations and determining relevant information. Most of what he had heard was mundane chatter about what they should do to combat Mr. P.'s public relations machine. Steve had seen and been involved with multiple situations in which Mr. P.'s PR watch dogs trampled anyone in their way. He smiled inside, knowing chances were slim that Chris and company would find a way out of their current situation. One thing they had in their favor, which Steve found very surprising was the media had quickly pounced on Chris' story.

The backlash that Mr. P. was facing right now was intense and usually it was the other way around. Mr. P. was usually in the cat bird seat and Steve did enjoy knowing Mr. P. was squirming. Mr. P. had been a good employer as far as work and stability were concerned. It was obvious however, that Mr.

P. cared little for his staff, other than to give orders or to occasionally say hello. No, Steve knew where he stood on the food chain, the players on the other hand, that was Mr. P.'s life. Sometimes Steve was quite envious of the treatment the players received. Oh, Mr. P. loved his team no doubt but his players could do no wrong. Steve had seen many players who should have been suspended or fined have issues swept under the rug time and time again.

He sat holding his chin and contemplated all the various transgressions over the years he had seen Mr. P. take care of and wipe clean. Loyalty and honor were Steve's code and he was loyal to a fault. This was different, he knew Mr. P. would fight with everything he had but would it be enough? An uncertain feeling began to sink into Steve's brain, "Will they come after me too!" Steve had witnessed the forging of this tight knit group first hand. He now began to wonder why they do not just throw him in a dumpster somewhere. The more he thought about it, the angrier he became, his structured discipline life had turned into chaos. For the first time he looked up at his captors and felt ashamed at his part in this real life drama. He watched the group go back and forth bouncing ideas off of one another and his mind went back to his military team members. The comradery he had in the military was nowhere to be found in the civilian world. Yet, he thought he had found it once again working for Mr. P. only to find that he was just another employee. Steve stood up stretching out to his full great height and announced, "Let's take the SOB down!"

Everyone immediately shot a glance at Steve. Chris jumped out of the booth ready to engage his captive. Steve made no aggressive moves but rather stood smiling. April raced in front of Chris and put a hand on his chest to stop him. She could feel his heart racing and put her other hand on his shoulders to calm him. When she felt Chris' tension release she turned to Steve, "What do you have in mind?"

Mr. P. was still in his plush chair thinking strategy when the elevator doors opened and out walked a host of FBI agents. Standing he turned to the agents, "Good Day gentlemen, are you here to apprehend Chris and his cronies?" To his shock the lead agent grabbed him roughly spinning him toward the wall and cuffing him quickly. Mr. P. could not hear the Miranda rights being read to him, all he heard was himself say, "I want to speak to my lawyer!"

He found himself almost lifted off the ground and pushed through halls and elevators. On the bottom floors he was whisked through the front doors just in time to see his lead attorney George Henman rush to his side. George stood shoulder to shoulder with Mr. P., "make sure you do not say anything, I will take care of this, I will meet you at the field office!" Mr. P was forcibly thrown into the back of a black SUV and driven straight to the field office building. He was quickly rushed into the building, finger printed, and processed. Before he had time to blink he found himself in a small dark square interrogation room. With the way he had been rushed in he half expected to see FBI agents in the room already asking for a signed confession.

What he found however was quite different; the room remained very dim and extremely stifling. He waited for the throng of agents he expected to be surrounding him by now and bombarding him with questions. His lawyer George should have been here by now, he had followed him here. As he sat in solitude he could almost see the walls start to encroach upon him. The lights in the room seemed to continue to dim even more creating almost a haze in the room. Nothing adorned the room and searching around the room he could find nothing to lock his eyes upon. He folded his hands and placed his head upon his hands staring at the table. After a while he stretched his hands out above his head leaning back until he could view the ceiling. The ceiling tiles were normal everyday tiles you would find in a drop ceiling, except for one smooth black tile. Mr. P. stared at this tile and realized for the first time there were no two way mirrors in the room, this tile must be a camera, he thought. Mr. P. just leaned back starring at the tile smiling. The smile faded, however when no one entered the room leaving him completely isolated. The heat in the room was stifling by now and Mr. P. was sweating profusely. He unbuttoned his shirt and put his head on the table. The table felt cool to the touch and allowed him some temporary relief.

Mr. P. shot up disoriented when the door opened. He had no idea where he was or how long he had been there. His eyes started to adjust to the dim light to take in Agent Bradley. The agent sat down across the table from him without turning on the light. In the dim light the agent cut an ominous figure. He sat and took in Mr. P. for a few moments before speaking. "I am Special Agent Bradley, and I will be handling your case. You are being charged with Human trafficking, fraud, racketeering, and obstruction of justice, just to name a few charges." The agent said nothing else, stood and walked from the room.

Mr. P. just watched stunned as the agent left the room. The door shut tight and he was once again left alone with his thoughts. The hours passed until he began to wonder just how long he had been there and why had his lawyer had not been present. The answer came hours later, when finally the door opened and the lights came on suddenly, blinding Mr. P. Blinking to adjust to the light he began to make out the hazy outline of his lawyer George. George ran over to him as if a mother cat checking on her litter. He fawned all over Mr. P. yelling at the young agent that had escorted him in to get Mr. P. something to drink and eat. The young man said nothing and stood his ground not moving from his post.

George faced Mr. P., "I am sorry, they would not let me in, they claimed you were being processed. They also claimed to be having electrical issues. Although, that may have been half true because there were several rooms out there with no lights." The lawyer paused, "Listen Mr. P., do not say one word to them without me being present. They are fishing; they have nothing but unsubstantiated accusations." Mr. P. glared at his attorney, "Accusations, you moron, they have three of my employees and if you count the other one, four! What else do they need to sink me? It's not as if it is one rogue employee, these are pillars of the community, a doctor, a nurse, and a football hero! I think there is plenty of credibility there don't you think?" He glanced at the lawyer whose mouth was gapping open, "Well, how do you propose we get out of this one genius?"

George stuttered, "Mr. P...," he composed himself, "listen every case can be won, we just have to find the right angle. A prosecutor's job is to prove the case in court; it is simply a matter of what they can prove. What is the teams, the League's contingency plan?" George looked up and saw sheer panic in Mr. P.'s eyes, "You do have a contingency plan correct? A back up plan in case things go wrong." Mr. P.'s face told the story, he turned ghostly white and his eyes blinked as though he would faint. "George, we have always had everything self-contained, up until now the situation was easily controlled. Our players never knew what was going on and they were all well taken care of, they are heroes to many. Our partners have always done a great job of keeping this all under wraps." George got a stern look on his face, "Mr. P. you can count on your partners to distance themselves from you as much as possible. You are on your own!" Mr. P. nodded his head, "I have forged my own way in this league, I shall have to do it once again." He sounded certain but in his mind his confidence was much shaken. George folded his hands on the table, "Mr. P. it may very well be that we have to come up with a plea bargain, you might have to cut a deal. Otherwise, you may lose the team and do some serious jail time. As your council I highly suggest we work out a deal." Mr. P. shook his head, "George, I cannot lose this team; it is my legacy, my family's legacy!" George frowned, "If we don't do something there will no longer be any legacy. Let's see what the FBI's plan is and then we will mount a great strategy."

The door opened and in walked Agent Bradley with a large file. He stood next to George's seat and tossed the file on the table in front of George. Instinctively George grabbed the file and rifled through it. He looked at Agent Bradley, "You have all of this and yet you have not even once questioned him?" Agent Bradley smiled, "Call it Homework. Think about it George, all that pales in comparison to what is happening right now. Your client has a long list of transgressions when it comes to sweeping things under the rug. You know as well as I that each case is built brick by brick and in this case," he held up the file, "we have enough bricks to build a house already." George put his best poker face on, "What are you offering?" Agent Bradley chuckled, "Offering, well I am offering your client three square meals a day and maybe time off for good behavior!"

"Agent Bradley," George spoke, "You know as well as I that Mr. P. is an upstanding member of this community and any help he can offer would assist everyone involved in this matter." Agent Bradley stopped smiling, "George normally I would agree with you and we would come to some arrangement but right now we are in a whole new legal territory, created by your client might I add. George, your boss thought it was okay to clone human beings for his own personal and monetary gains. This is a landmark case; there is no way this is not going to court. Mr. P. is about to make the judge and the prosecutor rock stars!" Agent Bradley grabbed the file and walked toward the door and turned as he opened the door, "The only question is, are you going to make this easy or hard on your client?" A moment later two other agents came in handcuffing Mr. P. once again and began to escort him to the door. George stood in front of the door barring the way, "Mr. P. don't worry I will have you out of here ASAP, sit tight and don't say a word." Mr. P. just had a stricken look on his face as he was led from the room.

Chapter 25

April and company had awoken to a beaming Agent Bradley. "We have him in custody. I need you to stay put for a while until other arrangements can be made but this is going to be a trial for the ages." He turned to Christopher, "I am going to make sure nothing like this ever happens again!" Christopher crossed the room and clasped the man's hand warmly in gratitude. Agent Bradley held his hand firmly and patted him on the shoulder, "Right now however I would like you to meet the prosecutor in the case, Jessica Reali!" He went to the door opening it reveal a stunning statuesque blond woman wearing a power suit. She came in and playfully slapped Agent Bradley in the face, which raised a few eyebrows. She then got right to business introducing herself, while April eyed her with suspicion, which did not go unnoticed. "April," Jessica said, "Usually it is the boys that are distracted by the fact that I am a woman. I am surprised at your reaction; I assure you I am the attorney for this case. I have tremendous experience with high profile cases. I just concluded a huge Ponzi scheme case, which believe it or not had many of the same elements as this case. Trust me when I tell you that you do not want any crusty old men leading this case. You need brains, energy, beauty, and bravery. I have all of those in abundance as well as a great deal of confidence in my own abilities. I am your man, your woman!"

April just smiled, "So not just a pretty face. You and I will get along just fine. Where do we start?" Chris came up behind April and held her waist, "Two beautiful, strong women in the court room, this could be interesting. Let's get started!"

Christopher and Doctor Chase nodded in agreement. Jessica proceeded to lay out the plan to expose Mr. P.'s ill-gotten empire. She outlined how in many cases the prosecutor has a great deal of difficulty lining up key witnesses. In this case the star witnesses were hand delivered to her and she would have little difficulty having a jury see the mountain of evidence that she already had on hand. She informed them there would be no way the jury would render a verdict of anything other than guilty in this case for Mr. P.

As the small group listened to Jessica's strategy they felt more confident in their situation. From time to time Agent Bradley chimed in and let them know that Jessica's approach was indeed sound, if not brilliant. He even went so far as to say with Gus' media barrage, both the court of public opinion as well as the court of justice had little chance of being defeated. Jessica seconded Bradley's affirmation with a proclamation of her own, "I will not rest until Mr. P. and his cohorts are brought to justice!" Chris was so impressed with her confidence all he could do was smirk. Jessica noticed this and remarked, "alright Chris, what is going on in the head of yours? I saw that mischievous look!" "Jessica," he said, "The world is intrigued with cloning at this moment; I have an idea that will turn this case on its head!" Jessica turned to Chris, "Let's hear it." Chris laid out his plan while everyone listened intently. Even Steve's eyebrows raised with interest as Chris continued to illustrate his plan. When finished Chris waited for a response and everyone just leaned back in their seats with their heads shaking yes. Jessica said, "Chris, I am not sure of the legality of what you propose but then again this whole case is new territory for the legal system. It will certainly give the jury something to think about." Chris knew his proposal was risky but they needed every edge they could muster. Mr. P. was already in the deny,

deny, deny mode and his team of lawyers would not be easy to crack no matter how good Jessica was.

The days that followed were chaotic with media requests and lawyer after lawyer throwing themselves at Jessica to join their team. Jessica stood steadfast, maintaining in this case the more would not be merrier and therefore she would work with her small group of colleagues. At first this worried April and company but Jessica reminded them that the more people that were involved the more chance there was things could get overlooked and mistakes could be made. Mistakes, Jessica contended were the easiest way to derail a case and she assured them that her firm was quite capable of handling anything they might need in terms of resources. Jessica also advised them to continue to talk to only Gus. The group required little convincing here because they knew the media were vipers and anything said to anyone they did not trust could lead to disastrous consequences. Gus was their guy and they all agreed to say nothing to anyone else but Gus.

Jessica did sit them all down and warned them that everything looked in their favor right now but a large celebrity trial such as this was a huge roller coaster ride. The group listened carefully as she advised them to stay the course, "not to get too high or too low," she said. She continued, "The fact is, right now momentum is on our side and I am going to use that but you can be guaranteed Mr. P. will throw everything in his arsenal at us. That means there will be some very low points as well and like I said before we are in new legal territory here. Mr. P. will definitely try to use that to his advantage to show uncertainty in our case. I intend to use the media to help us solidify the legal side of this case because that is how new laws are put to the forefront right now in terms of the people's needs. Just don't get too crazy yet, we have a long way to go and I need you all focused!" By a look at the stone faces before her Jessica knew she had little to worry about.

Jessica spent a whole afternoon meeting with each member of the group to see how each would fit into her strategy. When finished with her interviews she could not help but feel the utmost confidence that they would prevail in this case handily. April, having assisted Doctor Chase as much as she had, made her alone an outstanding witness. Even though she was not privy to the inner workings of Dr. Chase's menagerie, she still had a great deal of knowledge to lend to the case. She also had a great deal to offer on many transgressions hidden by Mr. P. and his cronies. Chris himself having witnessed everything first hand was as strong a witness as one could hope to procure. Christopher was the smoking gun and literally would leave no doubt in the jury's mind. Just in case there were any doubts in the least, the doctor would clear everything up. As with any whistle blower you need to be an insider. Dr. Chase was the ultimate insider; it was his research that was at the very heart of the case. Also just for good measure, Steve had agreed to cooperate with them which added an unbelievable layer on insider knowledge of Mr. P.' empire. These building blocks as she liked to call them were fitting together quite nicely but she knew there were always a few cracks that had to be filled in on occasion.

That evening Jessica was sitting with April going over some of her notes when she received a phone call. When she hung up she asked everyone to join her in one of the large booths. This large table was what they were using as their command center. They all eagerly gathered around in anticipation of news which would come from Jessica or news

213

passed from Gus to them by design. All of them knew how the media could twist any little thing, so she had advised them to keep their intake of information down to just a few trustworthy outlets, Gus being one. Looking at the eager faces starring back at her, she smiled, "We have been assigned Judge Hirochi Azawa. Now this is good news, bad news. The good news is that Judge Azawa has sat on high profile cases before and he does not take any crap. He is a straight shooter and is on no one's payroll, except the taxpayers. The bad news is that being such a straight shooter, he allows for very little wiggle room where the law is concerned. This worries me some because we are embarking into much that will be new in terms of cloning humans and how that fits into the current legal system. The cool part about that is we will all be writing the next chapters in the law books!" Jessica appeared giddy at this last remark, "Yes, I know that is strange to hear but as a lawyer I have spent much of my career dissecting the law, now I actually have a chance to shape the law. That my friends is an awesome feeling and not many ever get to boast that!"

Chris just looked at Jessica in awe. Every dealing Chris had ever had with lawyers, including his own agent, revolved around nothing but money. Here, on the other hand was a lawyer looking to live the law and see it grow. Everything Chris had heard come out of Jessica's mouth was what she thought she could do for them as well as those to come after. She viewed this case as people's lives and not dollar signs. Chris could not help but feel proud and lucky to have such a person representing their interests in this case. As Chris looked around the table he saw much the same look of pride and gratitude when they looked at Jessica. There was one thing for sure; they all felt confident and comfortable with her at the helm.

Chris found himself looking at April protectively. His glance went immediately to Christopher. He had to set this right, Christopher's very life was at stake! With the thought of Christopher being able to assimilate into a regular life on the fore front of his thoughts, he was quickly brought back down to earth. Chris found himself sick to his stomach as he continued to think of how many lives had been ruined up to this point by Mr. P's continued use of human beings as fodder for entertainment. What shocked Chris most is the thought of how long this had been taking place and how many actual human lives had been involved. He once again brought his eyes into to focus. This small group before him was about to embark on an amazing journey to bring justice to the world. Chris could only look at Jessica in admiration.

She told them the trial would start in two weeks which was quite sudden but she thought this was great news for them. Strike while the iron was hot she described to them. The feeling she had was that this gave Mr. P. much less time to mount a media rebuttal campaign and this would allow them to ride the positive media swell that was a huge advantage for them at this time. So with less time for people to change their minds and striking while the iron was hot would work into Jessica's swift strategy. She did inform them that this was quite irregular for such a high profile case but the public was in such an uproar that the pressure was unbearable that there had to be a resolution to this case as quickly as possible. Once again, she felt this was to their benefit considering she had all her important witnesses in hand. The hardest egg to crack would be Mr. P. himself. Jessica knew that Mr. P. was a court room veteran and would not be intimidated by cross examination. She told the group her approach to Mr. P. was going to be his love of his team and players. She thought she could push the right buttons and get him to think about what he was doing to his beloved players.

Over the next few days Jessica began to prepare everyone for the devastation that was cross examination. Granted there was little dirt on Chris or April but Doctor Chase and Steve were another matter. Dr. Chase and Steve were at the epicenter of both sides of this case and if Jessica was not careful they could be used too skillfully by the defense. Jessica was extremely forceful with them to the point of making them feel as though they themselves were on trial. She informed them that this was a tactic used by many defense lawyers in order to break down the case by making the witnesses seem less credible. Jessica kept on them to the point of exhaustion but in the end, she was content with her witnesses' preparation. All, except for Christopher. She had done what she could to prepare him but he had no frame of reference with which to discuss his responses with Jessica. Christopher remained a mystery, being a cloned human being left him with practically no legal backing what so ever.

As the start of the trial approached Jessica came to them and said everything was set. She however, they could tell was a little upset. When pressed she alerted them to the fact that Mr. P. had filed a motion for dismissal based on the very thing she was worried about, cloned human beings. The defense's contention was that the case had no grounds due to any legal parameters to deal with the situation. This had been Jessica's fear all along and she had told the group that in her opinion this was Mr. P.'s only shot at winning. She had also suggested to her group that this might also work in their favor. That public support was so pressing right now that she felt, the case would have to be heard. Jessica told them that the judge received the motion and would render a decision tomorrow.

April woke to the sound of quick chattering voices. She quickly pulled on some sweat pants and stumbled toward the dining room. Rubbing the sleep from her eyes she entered the dining room and saw the reason for the commotion. Jessica was in the middle of everyone speaking quite quickly and animated as illustrated by over exaggerated hand gestures. April took Jessica in; the stunning woman was dressed in professional attire and beautiful Prada heels. Her hair was pulled back in an exquisite bun with not one hair out of place. April wondered how early this woman must rise to put herself together so flawlessly. Starring, April could not help but chuckle, most times at work all she was required to wear was scrubs and a lab coat. This was quite a different picture compared to Jessica all together. April wondered if Jessica ever even wore sweats or let her hair down for that matter.

Almost as if on cue, Jessica spotted April and almost ran over to her, stopping just a few inches from her nose. With kid like enthusiasm Jessica filled April in on the mornings court proceedings. "April, I have the greatest news!" Jessica's beautiful eyes sparkled with electricity. "The trial will go on as planned. Judge Azawa has concluded that there is plenty of grounds for a trial and that there need be no more delay. The Judge explained to council this morning that since Mr. P. had done these acts to his human players without their knowledge this constituted enough grounds to proceed with the trial. In essence the Judge seemed fit to focus on what Mr. P. and the other owners were doing to Chris and his fellow teammates."

April blurted out, "what about Christopher, Mr. P. has to pay for what he is doing to those people!" Jessica did not hesitate, "This is part of the game April, the judge right now is telling Mr. P. there is going to be no mistrial. No, Mr. P. is going to have to face Chris and his teammates. The door however is open for plenty of discovery! Remember those building blocks I was telling you about, this case has many different facets to it. We will have to work Christopher in to solidify our case but not to make it. Mr. P. is really up against it here, now that his motion has been denied. He is going to go into full press mode and use any dirt he can against us." Jessica smiled again, "We are ready, I have prepared you, so let's rock and roll!"

April watched Jessica walk out of the room, her shapely body swaying in a purposeful manner. Chris came up to her and put his hand on her waste. As if waking up again she looked at Chris carefully, his bright smile was infectious and she returned his with a warm smile of her own. "April, this is what we were hoping for, a chance to get our lives back, a chance for justice. I would not want to be Mr. P. right now. Honestly April, I do believe Mr. P. did not really want to hurt anyone. I can see where the lure would snare him into this whole mess. Football is, I believe the greatest sport going but it is ultimately one of the most dangerous. I always knew what I was getting myself into but I never imagined I would be fighting for my playing career quite so early before it really began." April responded, "Chris I am with you. I think Mr. P. really is a good man caught up in something bigger than even he ever thought possible. I can tell you this though, don't worry too much about Mr. P., something tells me he will be alright. Yes, he will probably lose the team and have to settle many lawsuits but he is a Billionaire. Chris, do not be surprised if Mr. P. does not do any

218

jail time. I know Jessica is saying no deals but at some point a deal may have to be struck."

Chris did not like that one bit but understood what April was saying. He also could not help think that that was the way Jessica was approaching this case a deal would not be eminent. He knew about preparation and its importance on the field but the way Jessica had prepared could be compared to a quarterback preparing for a playoff game. Chris had sat with her for hours over the last couple of weeks. All Jessica could talk about was the case. He never saw her without files or research. When she was not studying or researching, she was on the phone conferring with her colleagues. Chris had watched quarterbacks prepare heavily before games but Jessica brought a new intensity to preparation.   Every time Chris heard Jessica talk about the case the more impressed he was and he knew they were in terrific hands.

Chapter 26

The first day of the trial was a Circus Side Show. There were so many people outside the court house that the trial began late. People simply could not enter the courthouse. In the end, State Troopers had to erect an eight foot steel fence to create a safe walkway to the courthouse. April and company had driven in a large black SUV and were escorted by FBI agents into the courthouse. They each could not believe the throng of people gathered for this event. Except for Chris everyone was shell shocked by the mass of humanity. Chris felt right at home in this atmosphere. He had experienced this in the South when he was playing college ball and he remembered one game in Texas when the players were escorted by Guardsmen into the stadium.

The courtroom itself was not any different. There seemed to be even more people in this room if at all possible. People also seemed to be literally climbing the walls and sticking out of every crevice. Chris couldn't help but chuckle and yelled to April, "Hey I think they're going to need some Ref's!" April shouted back, "I know, this is like a playoff game, maybe we should do the wave!" When everyone finally took their seats and everyone was instructed to rise as the judge entered it was easy to see him fuming about the delay. Judge Azawa did not ask anyone to be seated but instead began with a rant about the sanctity of the court. He made it known that if anyone caused this case to be heard late again he would close the case to the public and take all media credentials away. Chris understood this much, like a huge game the referee had to set the tone. Yes, the judge set the tone, when everyone finally sat down there was dead silence.

That first day except for the chaos, getting started was relatively calm and uneventful. The prosecution and defense respectively led with their opening remarks. Jessica opened her statement drawing attention to the fact that the defendant had willingly destroyed his players civil and human rights. She alluded to the players being human beings not test tube experiments. Chris thought that was great way to get people to start to think about the clone's plight without actually mentioning them. She further added that, Mr. P. had compromised the game irrevocably by his actions and therefore the games could not possibly be on the level bringing this case a racketeering charge as well. She finished with the argument that Mr. P.'s empire was built on lies and unknowing participant's backs, which will cause harm to this generation and others to come altering their passion for sports forever. When Jessica had finished there was not a smile in the room, just stern looks directed right at Mr. P. As if burnt by the looks, Mr. P. shrank back into his chair, his usual confident demeanor smashed. As Jessica went to sit back down Chris stood and applauded. The room broke out into thunderous applause and went on for a few minutes despite the Judge's attempts to calm everyone with the gavel. Once brought back under control the defense began its opening statements.

The Defense went immediately to work to create a picture of Mr. P. as the architect of a team and therefore an entire community. They reminded the jury that the economic downturn had devastated most communities while Mr. P. had kept people working creating a more stable financial environment for everyone. Chris looked around the courtroom, paying close attention to the jury. He was very much aware of the financial hardships faced by those of this area. Chris' own father had been let go by his company after forty years of loyal service. His father had been lucky. He had received a fair buy out and was given early retirement. Chris could see the jury member's faces as George described the stable financial situation and they were nodding their heads. Chris knew these blue collar workers appreciated the team and the support it provided the community. He also thought it was brilliant to play on people's emotions and money with a steady job were always close to people's hearts. This was exactly why Mr. P. was so successful; he used his public relations people to perfection.

They all listened as George went on to illustrate a picture of disgruntled employees hoping to discredit Mr. P. He went on to say that this was nothing more than a clear cut case of corporate sabotage and that the prosecutors witnesses were nothing but vengeful employees looking to ruin a whole communities' economic stability. He further went on to illustrate the fact that Mr. P. was not just an owner but an active member of the community. A member of the community that constantly gave of his time and resources for the good of others. George stated that he would prove beyond a reasonable doubt that his client Mr. P. has always acted in the best interests of his community, his team, and his league. He kept hammering the fact that Mr. P. had kept the community fiscally strong and that as an upstanding member of the community he had a spotless record.

The atmosphere in the courtroom changed considerably after the defenses opening remarks. The initial feeling of elation and excitement seemed to weigh the whole courtroom down. It almost seemed as if all the air had left the room and people were struggling to breath. The judge sensed this as well and looked at his watch. The trial had been scheduled to begin at 9am but with the fiasco to get people in the building the proceedings had not begun until nearly 11am. The judge had given each side their instructions and allowed for a short recess. Returning from lunch the Judge got right to the opening remarks. It was now 3:00pm and the judge, feeling nothing new should begin right now, dismissed everyone for a fresh day tomorrow. A day the judge said better start promptly at 9:00am.

Leaving the courtroom April and company felt the sun on their faces and immediately felt energized. The trial had only just begun but they felt drained and the sun seemed to bring them back to the now. On the way home in the SUV, April spoke first, "Jessica that opening statement was amazing, you had that place rocking!" Pausing a moment she began again, "George went after people's heart strings and he also made a great impact!" Jessica responded, "Yes, we really had them on the ropes but he countered very well. Now we can see what his strategy is going to be, they want to paint Mr. P. as the victim and shift blame. It is a great strategy, only one problem, the mountain of evidence we have is overwhelming and I intend to bury Mr. P. in it. They are going to try and discredit you all but our evidence is as solid as it gets, almost too good. Their opening remarks were good but they do not have enough to sustain this case. Trust me, when what you all know comes out, that courtroom will quickly become ours once more!"

The next day it seemed there were even more people surrounding the courtroom if that were possible. State Troopers were stationed all along the walkway to the courtroom. The steel fence bent with the weight of excited onlookers, so much so, the fence looked as though it might fall in at any moment. Today, however, everyone made it into the courtroom on time and the proceedings began much more smoothly. Judge Azawa informed Jessica that she could begin by calling her first witness. During their initial discussions in the restaurant, it had been decided as a group that the testimony would begin with April. Jessica felt April would be an excellent way to begin considering her close work with both the doctor and the players alike. She had told the group that April would be the tone setter and she would be a powerful witness. The councilor also had chosen April first because there was very little damage the defense could do to her during cross examination. April's life up to this point had been the American Dream. She had been a great student in high school and college. To April, becoming a nurse was a natural as the grass growing in the springtime. She maintained a very straightforward normal life and focused on her career. A few men over the years had interested her but nothing serious and she had dated very conservative men. All in all April was quite the catch for Chris but for George she was a nightmare, a witness with a spotless reputation and no dirt.

April walked confidently to the stand and was sworn in at the bench. Jessica began quickly, "April you are an employee of the Boston Marauders, would you please describe for us how long you have worked for the team and what your responsibilities entail." April did not hesitate, "I have worked for the team for the past seven years. In terms of what I do for the team, I have all the typical duties of a regular nurse. Some examples of these duties include, taking vitals, performing physicals, passing out medication, and assisting with physical therapy. On a daily basis I can perform those duties but most of my time over the last four years has been spent as Dr. Chase's assistant. Most of my day consists of studying research and development. Dr. Chase has been spending a great deal of time lately incorporating different types of proteins into already existing DNA strands. Dr. Chase told me he felt the key to curing many human ailments is going to be protein and gene therapy rather than current medicine. I have to say working as closely with Dr. Chase as I have, I would agree with the doctor. Our findings have been amazing. We have used both animal and plant DNA as well as human to expand our research. Our work with living organisms has shown the most promise. We have worked with the proteins to manipulate cells with many disabilities and ailments with great success. The most advancement we have shown has been our work with cognitive and memory loss challenges. Test subjects that had horrific damage to the brain were able to recoup significant motor development as well as memory recall as a result of treatment. Every moment I have spent with Dr. Chase has been about helping others and bettering lives!"

As Jessica thanked April and headed to her seat she did not smile or show any emotion. Her approach was to keep April's testimony short, sweet, and to the point. Her hope was to make the jurors view Mr. P in a negative manner while building up Dr. Chase's image in their eyes. April had done just as instructed and stayed to the script. Jessica's hope was that April would not be caught off guard by George and slip up.

George popped out of his seat like a spring and strode right to the stand, never taking his eyes off April. George wasted little time trying to cut her testimony down. "You stated that you have worked closely with Dr. Chase for the past four years, is the correct?" April replied simply, "Yes." George pressed on, "well could you explain to the court how working that closely with Dr. Chase, when have you worked on anything remotely connected to human cloning?" April had expected this, "As I stated my work with Dr. Chase primarily concerned genetic research. Dr. Chase would come in early in the morning and brief us on what he expected that day and then leave. He would periodically check in with us throughout the day but really I did not spend a great deal of time right next to him, unless we came across a major breakthrough. The research we worked on would directly however would relate to the cloning of humans." George continued, "That may be so but at no time during your testimony do you mention any direct involvement with human cloning research. Are we to surmise that you did not actually witness any human cloning taking place?" April pressed her lips together, even though she had expected this it was as if she had received a punch to the stomach and answered, "No, I did not directly witness any human cloning." George smiled a cunning smile, "Thank you, that will be all!"

When the judge advised her to return to her seat she hesitated just a moment and looked to Jessica for help. Jessica immediately came to her rescue, "Your Honor, might I request a short redirect?" The judge granted her request but told her to be brief. Jessica stood in front of April and asked, "April you say you did not see any direct human cloning, would you describe for the court what you did see in your experience during this ordeal?" April went on to summarize briefly her ordeal with Chris and company. She did offer detail about what Dr. Chase had explained to her what he had done with their research and how it directly related to his cloning of human beings. She also elaborated on her encounter with Steve, Mr. P., and the security at the Stadium, all of which had confirmed their part in cloning humans. At this point George stood and asked that statement be struck from the record because it was here say.

The judge denied his request and allowed April's explanation of her direct contact with the various versions of research her colleagues worked on next to her on a daily basis, all of which directly connected to human cloning.

The judge went on to tell George to be careful trying to besmirch the reputation of someone with such a spotless record and track record of helping others. George then asked if he might ask one final question. The judge said, "Be quick," and scowled at the councilor. George stood and not moving from his seat, "You claim all of these people told you about the human cloning but for the record, did you or did you not have any direct experience in your position and interaction with the team with regard to human cloning?" April looked at George with seething eyes that would have burned a hole through him, "No, I did not!" George smiled again, "Thank you, no further questions your honor!"

George then did something totally unexpected, "Your Honor, I would ask for a short recess to confer with my client, new information has come to my attention that I need to make my client aware of." Everyone including Mr. P. had a look of utter surprise of their face. The judge even did a double take before answering, "I will allow it. We will break for lunch and return at 1:00. Please be ready then and councilor this better not be a stalling tactic. Time is very precious in this courtroom!" George bowed slightly, "Thank you your Honor and no, this information is of the utmost importance!" The judge dismissed him with a wave of the hand rose and went to his chambers.

Chapter 27

Mr. P. just put both hands up as George entered the small room furnished for them to meet. George raising his hand to say stop and listen, "Listen Mr. P., we are up against it here, all the people Jessica has lined up against us is daunting. These witnesses including Steve, are high character people which makes it extremely difficult for me to break them down and expose any weaknesses. I will give you credit though, you do hire good people. The problem is for our purposes though, they may be too good! Please tell me you or your people have found something that we can use to discredit any of these people. Mr. P. April is such a straight arrow, I guarantee you the jury sided with her despite her not actually seeing the cloning take place or any direct contact." Mr. P. winced and shrugged his shoulders as an elementary school student would do when answering a question. "Honestly George we have files on everyone and believe me we have some suspect characters working for us but the only thing I could always count on is Steve covering up certain loose ends. Even that we do not want to bring up because it could incriminate me more!" George put his head down, "keep digging, we have to find something. I mean come on, Dr. Chase is your head of research, you must have something on him?" Mr. P. put his hands up, "George, I am sorry, his whole life has been devoted to helping others and he is so focused on that, after he lost his brother he swore he never wanted to lose anyone else. Honestly to this day I still do not understand how we ended up with the doctor on board with our program. His integrity is unquestioned and I still think he only did this so no one else would have to go through what he and his family had gone through."

George sat there stunned. "He is the key, we have to find something on him before he gets to the stand. Mr. P. we are already on thin ice, if we do not come up with something soon, you may lose everything!" Mr. P. looked at him, George you have to believe me I am good at finding dirt and sweeping it up, if I had anything I would certainly use it to our benefit. I know we are really in it now but honestly, I only ever wanted to make sure our beautiful game was safe for the upcoming generations. Imagine this, "No football on Sunday's, because that was where we were headed." George knew this, even agreeing with Mr. P. on the reasoning, "Mr. P., that right there may be our only saving grace. We have to keep you as the beloved owner in everyone's eyes, not a monster that has cloned humans for monetary gain."

Upon return from lunch, Jessica chose to put Chris on the stand. She already discussed with the group that she was going for quality and not quantity and she wanted to strike while the pan was still hot. Chris was sworn in and looked like a sardine squirting out of the metal can. The stand was not made for large human beings and his knees were scrunched up toward his stomach. Not only his physical comfort was evident however, his attire was perfect. He cut quite the picture in his dark blue athletic cut suit. His hair was trim and his scruff was gone leaving quite a dashing young man on the stand. There was quite the ruckus by the ladies in the audience as Chris made his way to the stand. April's face went bright red and went into full defense mode, staring down a young lady sitting near her swooning over Chris.

As Chris squeezed into the little box to be questioned it was quite apparent that he was uncomfortable with wearing a tie and kept adjusting his neckline. His broad shoulders spread out far beyond the little box and he had to put his elbows out on top of the box to fit. Chris tried to sit up straight but his head hit the lamp on the wall right in back of him. This brought a few chuckles from the crowd. Chris seemed to be even more uncomfortable after this and his face turned crimson. As he composed himself, he looked right at Mr. P. Even though the box was lower than the judge, Chris's height made him almost on par with the judge. All in all Chris made for an Intimidating sight.

Jessica took him in and smiled inwardly. She knew her little plan would work and Chris was the perfect witness to use. Chris having dealt with so much to get here was going to do all he could to keep his good name and get back to the field. He would not be shaken by the defense but Jessica was sure he would make the defense shake and falter. Jessica secretly wondered if this was what it was always like for Chris, being swooned over and adored by everyone. She thought to herself, that it must be quite the feeling. She advanced to the stand and went on the side of Chris so everyone could keep an eye on him.

Jessica began, "Chris would you tell the court your affiliation with Mr. P..." Chris sat up in his chair and said with pride, "I was Mr. P.'s number one draft pick this past year and was ready to play my first season as a middle linebacker for the Marauders." Jessica continued, "Chris would you tell us a little of what it was like to be selected as Mr. P.'s number one pick?" Chris perked up, "It was a dream come true. I had dreamed of playing for the Marauders my whole life. When that phone call came that I had been selected I felt everyone and everything had helped me reach my dream had been drafted with me. When I showed up at camp I could not believe I had my own locker. I was going to get to play with some of my boyhood idols with my hometown team. It was as if I was living someone else's life." At that statement Chris seemed to choke up for a moment, "It was the happiest I had ever been in my life!" Jessica looked at him with sympathy, "Chris what changed, what brought you here before us today?"

Chris cleared his throat, "The truth! Everything I thought about Mr. P. and the Marauders has been a lie!" George nearly toppled his chair jumping up yelling, "Objection!" Almost as soon as he said it Judge Azawa smashed his gavel and told George, "Over ruled! Now sit down!" George too stunned to say anything sat down with a dazed look on his face. Jessica just motioned to Chris to continue, "I made it through my first training camp and felt ready to take on the world. As opening day approached I threw myself into my playbook determined I would not let Mr. P. and Coach Riley down for the faith they had shown in me." Chris then got a haunted look in his eyes but went on. "I had breakfast with the team and we went over some last minute defensive calls. We then headed to the locker room to prepare for the game."

Chris went on to give an extremely detailed account of what happened, starting with the hyperbaric chamber and waking up in the middle of the game. He described his harrowing escape in vivid detail. The courtroom was mesmerized as he continued his tale, not leaving out a thing. When he got to finding Christopher and escaping with him the audience looked genuinely upset. There was shocked awe when he described the scene of seeing all the clones in row after row in stasis. George tried futilely to stem the tide with objections but was thoroughly beaten down by the judge's gavel.

Jessica could tell she had everyone right where she wanted them and pressed her advantage, stopping Chris and making him repeat certain aspects of his story. She asked Chris to describe Steve's pursuit of the group a few times. During this part of his testimony the jury was clearly disturbed by the graphic nature of Steve's attempts to capture the group. The tactics Steve used especially raised eyebrows and many turned heads to glare at the head of the Marauders security. The key Jessica felt was going to be Christopher, the clones, and especially Mr. P. himself. This proved to be true, as Chris continued with his detainment by Mr. P. and Mr. P.'s subsequent confession of everything to him, the courtroom went from a feeling of upset to one of wrath. Looking at George you could tell he was exasperated but maintained himself waiting for his turn with Chris.

Chris did a great job of telling the tale about alerting the media without divulging Gus' name. He told of Agent Bradley's involvement and how the agent himself had been in mortal danger as a result. The agent's part in this tale raised more than one set of eyebrows from both the audience and Mr. P.'s camp. Mr. P., all along had assumed the FBI was in the bag but he soon found out that was not the case. Chris wrapped up with their flight and the finding of the doctor. As he finished the courtroom remained deadly silent. Jessica thanked him and sat down waiting to see what George would do next.

George had been ready and he approached Chris cautiously. He began, "Chris that is quite the tale! That would make for a wonderful work of SCI-FI fiction!" At this it was Jessica's turn to object. The judge told her to sit but turned to George and told him he would not stand for any badgering of witnesses. George continued, "Chris is it possible that as you

232

stated about this being your dream that you continued to dream this whole thing up? I mean really, football players in sleep cubes and rows of clones in a sports stadium. Chris, this is a lot to take in and have people believe it!" Chris was ready for this attack, "Yes, it is quite a bit and I would have questioned myself had it been just myself that had gone through this ordeal but I have five others that have gone through every excruciating moment as well!" George, if stung did not show it and went on, "Chris we are in an era of brain injuries caused by head trauma in contact sports, are you quite sure we are not seeing the result of this trauma before us right now?" Chris had been prepared well and expected this as well, "I might if I had shown symptoms before this. I have never even lost consciousness or blacked out on my feet. I also have a fantastic memory and have never forgotten anything!" George looked right at him, "Just one more question, what would happen if one of the veterans earned the starting job over you a rookie?" Chris could not understand the question at first but remembered Jessica telling him that George would try to fish for anything to make him look bad. He answered, "I have always earned everything and have never had anything given to me. If a deserving player beats me out then I would work my behind off to make sure I got more playing time. I also understand at the pro level a coach sometimes has more trust and confidence in a veteran player. I am not beyond learning from someone with the experience, that I one day hope to have myself and pass on to another younger player. I have always been willing to learn and what a better way to learn than from those who have come before me and been in the trenches." George had not expected this answer; he had always been told athletes were spoiled brats who thought about nothing but themselves. Today that stereotype was shattered, he had run into the complete team player and had everything starting to go against him in this case. All George could do is look at him and say, "Thank you, no further questions your honor."

When George returned to his seat, Mr. P. was livid, "That's it! You didn't even go after him!" The owners face was contorted and blotched with red. He looked as though he would launch himself like a missile at his lawyer. As if he realized where he was he calmed himself right down and still glaring at the lawyer with hands raised as if to ask, "what next?" George leaned toward the owner and whispered forcefully, "With what! You would have me break down a blue collar kid who turned himself into a hero. If this kid never plays another down for this or any other league he is already a legend. I warned you about this before we even began! If I continue to delve they are just going to have more ammunition against you. All I can do at this point is damage control!"

Jessica stood and asked the court if she might call her next witness. The Judge looked at his watch and said, "If it will not take too long we are pressed for time as it is the end of the session for today." Jessica assured the court it would only take a short time. Mr. P. leaned in and asked George, "What has she got up her sleeve?" George just said, "At this point anything!" Jessica called her next witness, "I would like to call Chris to the stand." Everyone in the entire courtroom had a confused look on their face. Even more so when who walked into the courtroom, none other than the young man who still had not left the stand. Almost as if on cue, Chris got up from the stand and walked over to his mirror image and shook his hand with a hug. The two then turned right in front of the jury so they could get a good long look at them both. The only difference was the Chris that was just questioned wore a blue suit and the new Chris wore a black suit.

The courtroom erupted with individual discussions and people typing on their laptops. The noise reached a fever pitch in seconds. Judge Azawa, smashed his gavel several times until everything came to order. The judge turned to Jessica and wanted to know what the meaning of all this was. She responded in kind, "Your Honor, if you will indulge me for a moment I will clear all this up very quickly." The judge told her to get it over with. Jessica had the new Chris sworn in but the Chris in the blue suit stood fast right next to him. George did not know what to do. Jessica turned to the new Chris, "would you state your name and tell me how you know Mr. P." The Chris in the black suit went on to tell the court he was in fact Chris and the first round pick of this year's Boston Marauders. The judge then stopped the testimony, "Please explain this to the court, is this young man the others brother?" Jessica continued, "no your honor, just give me one more moment to clarify." She turned to the Chris in the black suit, "Tell them!" Chris looked at the jury, "I am Chris of the Marauders, the young man next to me in the blue suit is my clone!"

The courtroom exploded all at once. People were now everywhere and it was utter chaos. By this time the judge had literally broken his gavel and was screaming for order. Cameras were not allowed in the classroom but everyone with a phone had already captured images and video of the two Chris' posting them to the web. More State Police came streaming in and put people back in their seats. It took a good fifteen minutes to calm everyone down and return the courtroom to some semblance of normalcy. Both Chris' maintained their vigil near the stand. When the judge finally had order restored he looked at Jessica, "can you prove this?' Jessica turned to the real Chris in black, "Well?" Chris began to unbuckle his belt and there were gasps. He lifted his shirt up and pulled his trousers down just enough to reveal a scar on his abdomen. Jessica submitted Chris' medical records as evidence. While in college he had a sports hernia repaired. The other Chris did so and revealed no scar in the same spot. Judge Azawa looked at the medical records and said she could submit it as evidence.

George immediately asked to see the records and was allowed but handed it back without comment after reviewing it. Jessica also submitted birth records proving Chris had been a single birth and there was no twin. The judge then surprised everyone by announcing he would have to consider whether or not the testimony of Christopher in the blue suit should be allowed. He said he would have to confer with his colleagues on the matter and render a decision tomorrow. After being dismissed everyone streamed out of the courtroom resembling the running of the bulls.

George followed Mr. P. to his small holding cell, "Mr. P., we seriously need to consider making a deal, you are going to lose the team!" "George," he said, "calm down, that may already be a foregone conclusion. What we need to do is keep me out of jail and if I am going to lose the team I want to have a hand in who takes over." He paused, "But I am not cooked just yet. Sit down; there are some things I need to tell you." George sat and Mr. P. went on to fill him in on his new strategy. When finished George stood staring at Mr. P. and his face was deathly white. Mr. P. told him to calm down, this all depended on which way the judge ruled tomorrow. If the judge ruled in favor of Jessica it would actually help with the new strategy. George could just shake his head and leave for the night.

Chapter 28

Day broke and once again there was a mob scene at the courthouse. If it was possible there were more people than usual. As they looked around there seemed to be people on top of light poles. The barricades were almost bent to the ground. Chris and his friends were escorted by FBI Agents and State Troopers. In spite of the extra security their small group threatened to be trampled by the sheer volume of onlookers hoping to talk to Chris or get a glimpse of Christopher, The Clone. They made their way thru the myriad of people very slowly. Jessica kept looking at her watch. She did not want to be late; the trial had been going so well she did not want to stall the momentum.

The courtroom was another matter; it was eerily quiet when they entered. Come to find out the occupants were warned already about acting out and the courtroom would be cleared today if the judge deemed it necessary. For the first time all trial they were able to make it to their seats on time. When Judge Azawa walked in and saw the courtroom in order, he smiled. The judge asked the councilors to stand while he rendered his decision. Jessica and George stood stone faced as they viewed the judge. Judge Azawa looked around his courtroom and took it all in before speaking. The gravity of this moment was not lost on him and he understood the impact and importance of this far reaching ruling.

The judge cleared his throat and began, "We stand at a great precipice. One wrong move and we could fall into the Abyss. However, we could potentially climb to the pinnacle of

238

human civilization. He paused, "The balance of justice is always a delicate dance and as a judge I would like to think I work in the best interests of man. That being said, what are the interests of man in this case? On one hand we have a young man at the beginning of a promising career and on the other we have a young man that would like to know where he fits into society. In terms of what Chris has gone through, there is no doubt that laws have been broken and we must find justice in this matter. He turned to Christopher, "I have been up all night speaking with my colleagues and there is no doubt that Christopher is a human being and is subject to all human rights, the issue before us is can his testimony is used in this court. In order for his testimony to be heard he would have to be an American citizen or have a legal right to work in the country. In Christopher's case, it is not that easy to establish citizenship. The question becomes, was Christopher born in this country making him a naturalized citizen. Paternity is not easy to establish in this case. The dictionary defines born as to be brought forth by birth. This itself makes things extremely difficult, so I had to look at precedents to compare. In the case of Invetro fertilization and test tube babies an embryo and an egg are brought together in the lab for the purpose of conception. Much of this conception takes place outside the womb but in most cases a women's womb is still used for a natural birth. However, there are cases where the conception has been brought to term without natural birth. In those cases the babies were granted citizenship as a result of a naturalized citizens DNA and being born in the United States. I believe that Christopher fits this definition and after discussing this with immigration officials as well as members of the state department, Christopher is deemed to be indeed an American Citizen. His testimony stands!"

A collective sigh of relief went up in the courtroom. The judge then turned to Jessica, "Is the prosecution ready to call its next witness?" Jessica rose, "Yes, your Honor I would like to call Agent Bradley to the stand." Agent Bradley made his way to the stand and was sworn in. Jessica did not even move from her seat but stood and asked her questions. Agent Bradley went on to corroborate April's and Chris' stories which brought nods to the heads of the jury. Agent Bradley brought a new perspective to the case however and went on the elaborate on law enforcements involvement in this case. Agent Bradley was not kind and implicated many local and Federal Officials in his testimony. This he said was the tip of the iceberg and many others would be under indightment soon as a result of this case.

This was quite a shock to many in the courtroom; they were beginning to understand the many layers of this case. Jessica wanted Agent Bradley to describe the danger he and the group had felt during this ordeal. Agent Bradley obliged the court with the harrowing tale which ended up with Bradley near death and literally nursed back to the living by Doctor Chase and April. He also described in detail their constant need to hide and living in fear for their lives. This part of the testimony was powerful and the jury had extremely serious looks on their faces. Seeing this Jessica decided to go no further. George attacked right away, "Agent Bradley, as you so eloquently described the FBI is also under suspicion! So are we to believe you are on the level. How are we to know you are not working with someone right now just to promote your own agenda?"

Agent Bradley responded quickly, "Sir, the only agenda I have right now is to see those folks right there," he pointed at April and company, "safe and sound with their life back! My job is to ensure the safety of all people no matter who they are of where they come from." George continued, "That is all well and good but if the FBI is compromised, how can you be trusted?" Bradley turned to him and looked him square in the eye, "I took an oath to defend this nation and my word is my bond. I am a decorated agent with a spotless record. If anyone here can be trusted it is me. Besides I have put my own career and life on the line to be here. I think that is proof enough!" At this George seemed stunned but recovered quickly, "Agent Bradley you have testified to what has happened to you and this small group but what of the cloning? Do you have any direct knowledge of Mr. P. involved in cloning?" At this Bradley was noticeably perturbed but answered anyway, "No, I have not personally seen Mr. P. clone anyone!" George looked up, "No further questions your honor."

Jessica stood right away; she had allowed George his little fun, now it was time to put him in his place. "Your honor may I have a moment for redirect? The judge allowed it and Jessica went right to work, "Agent Bradley, you have just stated that you have not personally seen Mr. P. involved in cloning. What have you seen?" Agent Bradley looked right at the jury, "In the process of my investigation I was able to obtain a warrant for the Stadium and Mr. P.'s private residence. While executing the warrant we were able to corroborate many of the witness's statements. We investigated the hyperbaric chambers and indeed did find that they are more than they appear. The chambers from what our investigators have gathered put the player into an induced trance in which they believe they are playing in the game.

When we further investigated the Stadium, we did find the chambers filled with human clones. There are thousands of them!" At this Jessica asked if she could submit photo and

241

video documentation to illustrate the point. It was allowed and the jury stood in awe of row after row of their favorite player as if they were nothing more than a freeze pop in a glass case. The eyes in the courtroom could not believe what they were seeing. George tried to stand to object but at this point the energy would be wasted. Agent Bradley went on to describe interviews with lab technicians that also corroborated previous statements. Yes, the agent's testimony was extremely solid and damaging. In the end however as damaging as it did look they still did not find any direct link to Mr. P. being involved other than owning the team. The court then broke for lunch.

Needless to say not everyone was thrilled about the idea of human cloning and there were plenty of detractors. Such a controversial scientific discovery came with it's own huge moral dilemma. The political and religious implications were so far reaching, people were just beginning to digest the reprecussions of cloning. Each day there would be a large contingent of protestors as the group entered the courtroom. Of course the most venom was directed at Dr. Chase and had been spit on more than once. The Doctor and company were used to this treatment by now and had learned to ignore it. Today's group of protestors seemed extra-large after lunch. The crowds themselves that had been there each day resembled those at a sporting event.

The small group walked into the courtroom together, once again oblivious to their surroundings. That is when the shots rang out and everything turned to pandemonium. April was standing closest to Doctor Chase when she heard the shots. Two rounds struck Dr. Chase, one in the shoulder and one in the forearm. April felt the warm spray of blood on her face and saw Dr. Chase go down in a heap. The State Troopers that were with them already had their weapons drawn and were shielding the fallen doctor and company. People around them were rushing everywhere trying to get away. Out of the pack came a young woman with a crazed look in her eye and a gun pointed at Dr. Chase. She was rushing toward them screaming, "You can't play God, you bastard!" The troopers yelled for her to stop and put her weapon down. She still had the gun pointed at them but stopped and looked at the troopers. In that moment someone smashed into her back, not looking and she squeezed the trigger releasing another bullet striking a trooper. The remaining troopers tackled her to the ground and wrestled the gun from her hand. By that time other law enforcement agents were on the scene including a medical team.

The young woman was taken into custody without further incident and Doctor Chase was tended to. His wounds were not life threatening but he was surrounded by human armor and brought safely to the hospital. The rest of the group was herded into a secure room in the basement of the courthouse and the grounds were cleared and swept for anything else dangerous. The judge had closed proceedings and stated the case would resume when everything was deemed safe. It was well into the night when the group was given the all clear and were escorted to a government SUV. They were driven to the hospital to visit the doctor. He sat propped up by pillows and was laughing with a nurse when they entered. As they walked in Dr. Chase immediately stopped what he was doing and his eyes searched for April. When he spotted her his face showed great relief, "I am glad you are alright! The nurse here has been taking very good care of me but I do not think I need this small army of troopers protecting me here!"

April rushed forward, "Dr. Chase, you just had an attempt on your life! How can you be so calm about it?" Dr. Chase answered, "Honestly April, I am so glad you are okay, really to me nothing else matters!" April and everyone in the group just turned to look at Dr. Chase. Agent Bradley worked his way to the doctor's bedside, "Dr. Chase, they have the young lady in custody and no one else was seriously hurt. I just go off the phone with the lead investigator and all indications point to this being just a case of a crazy fanatic with a cause. The only thing that concerns me is what if that is all it was meant to look like to throw us off? Dr. Chase, my feeling on this is that Mr. P. does not want you on that stand. So far George has done a good job of trying to distance Mr. P. from the actual cloning but the doctor can easily implicate Mr. P. directly. This case has moved quickly and the defense is reeling, this may have been their Hail Mary play."

April moved toward Agent Bradley, "You mean to say Mr. P. was trying to assassinate the Dr?" "April," he said, "I would put nothing past Mr. P. at this point." Chris then chimed in, "No, I don't think Mr. P. would do that. I honestly don't think he would really go that far. He was literally beside himself with the idea of erasing my memory. I really thought he did not know what to do with us and I almost thought he was going to let us go." He looked over at Steve, "Steve, on the other hand might like to rough people up." Steve just shrugged his shoulders, "He would always just ask me to take care of things but he would get furious with me if ever I hurt anyone. Chris, I think you're right, I do not think it was him!" Agent Bradley did not look convinced, "It might not be him but I really think it was definitely someone trying to send a message. It might even be the government trying to make sure Mr. P. goes down and there is nothing linking him to them. We might not have enough clout right now to look that big but if this case finishes strong someone is going to be able to make a strong case against the government." Dr. Chase smiled, "Then we have to finish what we started! Jessica, what do you want me to do?"

Jessica had remained quiet during that whole exchange. Normally, she was quite composed but having been in the middle of the group and seeing the woman come toward them with the gun had shaken her quite a bit. She came to attention, "Oh sorry, just thinking. I am going to ask the judge to have you give your testimony on video chat due to security reasons. The judge could not possibly refuse that request at this time. It will also not allow George direct access to you." Dr. Chase felt very good about things when to group was leaving. As April left the room through he had an overwhelming urge to hug her but refrained. For the first time since being shot he realized how important each of those people that just walked out of the room where to his life.

They were given the next day off to tighten security protocol in and around the courthouse. Barricades were set up around the courthouse and everyone would arrive in bullet proof SUV's. The close access the public had enjoyed to this point was now gone and in its place, a courthouse resembling a bunker on a military base. Troopers were replaced by National Guardsmen and cars replaced by Humvees. The grounds around the courtroom were swept and deemed safe to allow people back into the building. Along with being swept the courtroom now had a one hundred foot perimeter around in which was a no man's land. The trial had quickly gone from a celebrities' a dream to a barren nightmare.

Chapter 29

When they arrived back to the restaurant, which still thankfully to this point was not compromised, they sat right down to discuss today's events. The discussion of course centered around Dr. Chase and how this would now affect the case. The prevailing thought was, that this only strengthened their case. Jessica jumped in and cautioned everyone to think like a juror. She went onto to explain that right now the jury was not thinking about clones and justice, they were thinking of family and safety. Jessica told them she needed to bring them back to that feeling they all had had when they found out Chris' clone had testified in his place. Tomorrow we will focus on Steve and his heavy handedness on Mr. P.'s behalf. Steve just raised an eyebrow but thought better than to comment. Jessica told them to get some rest; she was going to go over Steve's testimony again. They were all exhausted and in spite of the day's events they had little trouble falling asleep. Jessica and Steve on the other hand worked into the night perfecting the big man's testimony. When finished the review of testimony Steve turned in and Jessica readied her own bed in the restaurant. It had been decided that for safety sake Jessica would remain with the group, where they felt they could protect one another.

When they pulled up to the courthouse the next morning they were surprised to see so many security measures in place. Steve was the only one to make a verbal comment, "Where are we going, to Guantanamo Bay to be interrogated? I thought we were the good guys!" Everyone glanced at Steve, surprised that he had said anything, since he was not one to say much at all. Everyone had to agree with Steve's assessment and the mood grew very serious as they continued to make their way to the courtroom. When they were approached by the National Guardsmen to escort them into the courtroom, they all felt very nervous. They all knew it was for their own safety but still being surrounded by barricades and machine guns was a very unnerving place to be. They all had been used to dodging all of the onlookers but today it was a ghost town. Looking around they noticed the nearest people were across the street. The crowd, besides being further away, was much smaller as many people stayed home for safety.

Once inside the courtroom things looked much the way they had always looked. The media was everywhere and if possible more people were stuffed into this small building. So much so, the building seemed to be ready to burst at the seams. They all found their seats without incident and looked forward to getting the ball rolling. George came in with Mr. P. and sat down quickly. Mr. P. did not look worse for wear but George looked very tired and haggard. His hair though combed looked like straw and his eyes had dark circles as well as bags under them. A second glance noticed that George's lips were so chapped that they were split and bleeding. Just looking at George one could easily tell, though this trial was not that old, that the trial had worn him down aging him significantly.

Judge Azawa also showed signs of distress, as the lines in his skin were much more prevalent. Also, the judge's temperament had become more curt and short. He did not greet everyone in his usual fashion, starting the proceedings right away. He directed Jessica to call her next witness and went back to back to reading some of his notes. The tension in the room could have been cut with a knife.

Jessica rose, straightened her suit coat, and walked briskly to the stand. She called for Steve, who walked to the stand. Even though Jessica was a tall woman, she seemed dwarfed by Steve's size. As Chris and Christopher before Steve found it quite difficult to squeeze himself into the seat. Jessica had to chuckle inside, she was used to dealing with what seemed to be small time and small stature criminals. Now she was dealing with what amounted to a bunch of behemoths. Even stuffed into the chair Steve had a military bearing about him as if demanding a salute. He was ready and almost looked as if he would ask himself the questions.

Jessica stood before him and asked him to describe for the court who he was and in what capacity did he know Mr. P. Steve responded that he had been working for Mr. P. for a great many years and was his head of security. This response brought a murmur among the media. Jessica looked at Steve with a very serious look on her face, "Is it true that you worked very closely with Mr. P. and were privy to much of what happened in Mr. P.'s inner circle?" Steve said, "I did spend a great deal of time with Mr. P.," he thought a moment, "I really do not recall a time when we were not together during my time on the clock. That is Mr. P. really values loyalty and before all this had taken place I would have considered myself Mr. P.'s most loyal employee. I considered him a father figure in my life and respected him a great deal. I must say, I am ashamed of many of the things I did in Mr. P.'s name because of loyalty!"

Jessica pressed him on this, "Yes, please describe for us the various duties you performed for Mr. P. while employed by the Marauders." Steve did just that, he went on to describe the numerous times he had fixed things for Mr. P. One especially interesting assignment given to Steve was one that had made

248

many news outlets. One of Mr. P's ball players had been accused of sexual assault and Steve had to make it go away. Steve described for the court how he had intimidated the young lady and her family into not pressing charges. The media had found out but by that time the young lady and her family were not talking. Along with intimidation, Mr. P. had offered the young lady a quite substantial settlement to clam up. Another incident had a player intoxicated and in police custody. Steve walked right into the police station and demanded the player's release on Mr. P.'s orders. The police did not even blink an eye in spite of the destruction of the player's car along with million dollars damage to infrastructure. The damage was then blamed on a hit and run and was paid for by the taxpayers.

There were numerous examples of these types of cover ups by Steve and though none of which were actually illegal but terribly damaging to Mr. P.'s squeaky clean image. So many in fact that they had to recess for lunch and Steve was still going strong, Jessica had prepared him for this, her intention was to saturate the court with as much witnessed atrocities as possible. At lunch Jessica informed Steve that he was doing fantastic but they were going to really focus on things that would put the cloning into an even worse light.

Returning from lunch Steve continued to take Mr. P.'s world apart piece by piece. Jessica had asked him for more specific evidence with regard to cloning. Steve obliged, he recalled a time when Mr. P. had brought him to the lab to handle an unruly lab technician, who threatened to blow the whistle. Steve had once again worked his intimidation magic and scared the young man so profusely that he took off in his car losing control of it while rolling over into a ditch. When the ambulance arrived the young man was already dead. Once again, Mr. P. used his clout to deny any involvement. It was later found in the young man's apartment computer files incriminating Mr. P. that Jessica now submitted as evidence. The files clearly showed the technicians detailed lab experiments with proteins and gene therapy for the sole purpose of cloning. George objected on the grounds of not having time to review the files under discovery. Judge Azawa allowed it as evidence but did take a short recess to allow George to review the files. The review revealed a much detailed account of the labs inner workings and George had to tell Mr. P. more bad news. That there was no way to counter this damning testimony. Mr. P. seemed little fazed by this news. George was baffled but continued to plead with Mr. P. to take a plea deal.

Upon return Jessica had Steve move on to Steve's encounter with April and company. Steve's account of what happened to Chris and Christopher was very frightening to most in the courtroom and terribly damaging. On a number of different occasions the jurors turned away too disgusted to continue. Mr. P. after hearing the full report of Steve's treatment of Chris and company even made him flinch as this was the first time he had heard the uncensored version. Mr. P. just continued to shake his head as if he could not believe how far things had gone. He now just seemed to realize what Steve had done on his behalf over the years. It was the first time he had actually heard it put into words. Prior to this Steve had just reported that things had been taken care. To actually hear in detail what had transpired was quite another thing for Mr. P. Steve took them up to Chris' saving Steve's life and his own subsequent capture.

Jessica stopped here, "Steve please tell the court, why the change of heart? You are a pretty ruthless and brutal man, how can we be made to understand why you are now using this information against Mr. P. when you have spent a career protecting him?" Steve's usually stone face changed, "During my time with Mr. P. I felt as though I was continuing my military missions. I also felt like I was a vital member of a very important organization. I also really felt insulated as to what many of these missions really were harming the team. It wasn't until my encounter with Chris proved to me that this was real life. When Chris would not leave me behind I definitely had a wakeup call. Even then I was a little skeptical until watching Christopher fight for the right to have his own life. It just wasn't his own life, it was fighting for family. He fought for Chris, April, and company as though they were his family that secured it in my mind. In the military we had to fight for each other and our families. It really hit home for me!" Jessica held up her hand, "Thank you so much, no further questions at this time."

George tried as he may to debunk many things Steve said but he really had little ammo on Steve either. Steve had been an excellent employee and as he had stated, he did not spend much time away from Mr. P. His life up to this point had been one of a devoted member of Mr. P.'s organization. Steve had done his job with great distinction. He had covered for Mr. P. so much that it came out of him like flood gates.

The day finally ended with the judge informing everyone that the court would be listening to Doctor Chase's testimony via video tomorrow. The hospital had informed the judge that the doctor was stable enough to answer questions. This seemed to please the judge who could also see the light at the end of the tunnel. The judge had sat through some very high profile cases in his career. This case had proven to be more than just high profile. Even a rock star would have had a difficult time during this trial. The trial itself had quite a few twists and turns but it was the overwhelming interest that had turned it on it's head. The amount of coverage received by this trial had not only caught the judge off guard but obviously the stark resentment toward those participating in cloning brought it to a whole new level. The judge was so used to total control in his court, quite frequently found things now out of control. He found himself wondering how others would view this trial after it's completion. Everyone was dismissed and escorted to their SUV's without incident. The ride home was very quiet and everyone just leaned their heads on the head rests.

On arrival to the restaurant they immediately called Dr. Chase to update him on their progress. The doctor was quite animated in his discussion about what Steve had said during his testimony. Dr. Chase asked quite a few questions about Mr. P.'s response to Steve. The doctor could not wait to have his day in court. Which was interesting because Dr. Chase had spent so much time looking for a way out. Jessica asked the doctor if he was feeling up to going over his testimony over the phone. The doctor informed Jessica that he did not need to actually stay in the hospital any longer. The only reason they were keeping him there is because it was a safe and secure location. Also it would be easy to set up for his video testimony having all the technology right there in the hospital. He told them as soon as his testimony was over he would be released.

After discussing things with Dr. Chase Jessica hung up and walked to her own booth sitting without speaking to anyone. Chris had seen that look before in many athletes' eyes before; many would call it getting into the zone. He watched as

Jessica peered at her notes from the day oblivious to anything else around her. Chris admired her focus and had felt extremely comfortable with her at the helm. It was easy to see in Chris' eyes why Jessica had been chosen for this case. To think when he first met Jessica, he just saw what most people saw, a stunning blond. Chris laughed to himself, boy had he been wrong, someone who might be interested in wooing Jessica would be in for a big surprise. After a few minutes Jessica peered up as if feeling the eyes on her and glanced at Chris offering a warm smile.

Jessica sat with her notes thinking how lucky she had been to this point in the case. She had kept waiting for the other shoe to drop and something to go dreadfully wrong. She really had not felt much pressure during the trial. That all changed when Dr. Chase had been shot. The enormity of the case hit her hard after that, especially approaching the doctor's testimony. Jessica did not want anything to go wrong while Dr. Chase was on the stand. Out of all the witness' Dr. Chase's testimony would be the nail in the coffin. The other witness' had built a strong case as she had described to Chris and company. Now was the time to slam the door shut, leaving no doubt in the jury's mind that Mr. P. was the master mind and guilty of all charges. Jessica planned to leave no stone unturned while trying not to leave herself open to George's attack which was sure to come furiously. When finally she felt comfortable with her strategy and line of questioning it was well into the night. Stretching her arms above her head and arching her back she looked around her surroundings only to see everything was darkened. Everyone had long since fallen asleep. She took a deep breath placing both hands on the chair pushing herself upward. While standing she took one last look around and

turning out the light, she made for her own bed feeling
exhaustion sweep over her.

Chapter 30

The next morning came much too early for everyone and they all appeared at the large table looking quite haggard. Jessica laughed, "What a crew we make! It will soon be over and life will return to normal." At this comment Chris looked at her, "Jessica, you do not know how much we would like that to happen!" Jessica smiled, "I know Chris, I know." In spite of her obvious confidence nervousness hung in the air throughout breakfast. It was not until they were in the SUV making their way to the courthouse did the mood lighten. Thanks in part, to of all people, Steve, who out of the blue remarked, "Hey, you think Judge Azawa wears a wig?" They all turned with shocked looks. He continued, "I mean really his hair looks way too perfect. It has to be a hair piece right!" They all stared at one another and started laughing, not really due to the comment but more because that was probably the longest Steve had spoken to them at one time. During his captivity if it could be called that he had done little talking except with Jessica about his testimony. The mood changed considerably in that moment and they were all smiles walking into the courtroom. A welcome change to the solemn nature of the circumstances surrounding them and this case.

The proceedings were ready to begin but during the Judges introduction George was nowhere to be seen. Mr. P. sat there turning this way and that trying to locate George to no avail. Judge Azawa noticed right away and responded, "Mr. P. is there something wrong with your councilor? I do not see him anywhere in this courtroom." Mr.P. stood, "Your honor, I really have no idea! When last we spoke, he was ready to go and had everything prepared, he said nervously." The judge took Mr. P. in and stated, "He has five minutes, after which you are on your own!" The owner of the Marauders looked desperate, "Yes, your honor." As if on que, the defense attorney came stumbling into the courtroom hurrying to the table. "Your honor please excuse my lateness, new information literally just became available to me as I was walking in this morning. The judge looked at him sternly, "Councilor, you know how I feel about promptness!" George frowned, " Yes, your honor, I am deeply sorry." The judge just waved, "Let us proceed please. Is the Prosecution ready to continue?" Jessica rose, "Yes, your honor we are ready." The judge responded, "Then let us not waste anymore of the courts precious time please."

Taking the hint Jessica walked to the stand, which today had a large computer monitor set up with a camera for Dr. Chase's testimony. Jessica pressed the button and the screen jumped to life. In a moments time the courtroom could easily make out Dr. Chase on the screen. The doctor in spite of his injuries looked in great spirits and his skin color was rosy. A quick glance in back of the doctor revealed several officers in the room keeping an eye on the doctor. Clearly the doctor was still in his hospital room but things were moved around and flowers were put close to the doctor as to not offer such a sterile environment. The doctor looked comfortable and ready to begin.

Jessica began by asking the doctor to explain to the court why he had chosen to become a doctor in the first place. Dr. Chase looked down for a moment and began, "I never really thought about it much until this whole ordeal happened. For me, it was more out of need; I needed to become a doctor to save my Brother's life! Sure I had the ability, the knowhow, and the calling but ultimately it was the love of my brother. My brother had become extremely ill. He had multiple ailments, all genetically based including the most devastating, end stage Alzheimer's. Sure the doctors tried everything in their power to save him and at times it looked as if they might succeed. In the end, in spite of many of my colleagues and my own work becoming a doctor, my brother succumbed to the disease passing away. I watched him wither away to nothing both physically and mentally. It was truly horrifying to watch someone you love disintegrate before your very eyes. I swore I would never have that feeling again, I was helpless. I swore I would do everything in my power to never let another family feel that pain. From that moment on I have devoted my life to genetic research.

Though the doctor was just an image on the screen, the impact of his statement was profound and felt throughout the courtroom. The jury once again could be seen seriously contemplating the doctor's words. Mr. P. could not hide the fact that it was emotional for him to hear the doctor's story as well. He had known Dr. Chase for a long time and knew the doctor's pain well. George was rifling through his notes to see if he could counter anything the doctor offered as testimony today. Jessica even held up a moment to let everyone digest what the doctor had shared with them this day. She wanted everyone to think of their own families and what lengths people would go to in order to save a loved one.

Jessica then turned back to the doctor, "Dr. Chase would you please tell us in what capacity you know Mr. P." Dr. Chase smiled, "I have known Mr. P. for more than twenty years. It was he that offered me the chance to work on the research I so dearly wished to work on." Jessica continued, "Mr. P. has been very important to you personally and your research? How is it you are here testifying against the man that offered you the opportunity of a lifetime?" Dr. Chase actually laughed, "That is the Billion dollar question! Just my being here has put my life in danger." He offered his audience a look at his injured shoulder and arm, "I also may have destroyed any chance of continuing my research to honor my brother! Mr. P. offered me an unbelievable opportunity and I will be ever eternally grateful. There came a time however that my research became larger than saving lives and money became the driving force behind what we did in the league. Oh sure, initially the idea sounded interesting, having the faces of the franchises stay healthy. I think we all became blinded by the possibilities of what we could do with the research and how it would benefit the league."

Jessica asked away, "Doctor Chase would you please tell the court what your research actually led to with regard to the Marauders and Mr. P." The doctor thought a moment, "As previously stated the nature of my research is curing genetic diseases. The major body of my research deals with the genetic code or DNA. That is why Mr. P. approached me, the league was on the verge of collapse based on the impact head injuries were having on the game. Everyone loves football, when Mr. P. initially spoke to me however; it was to see if I could develop some proteins and supplements that would do the job of PED's but naturally. He had really struggled keeping his players on the field because almost every supplement showed up on the banned list. I did just that and every player on our team uses the regiment prescribed for them and we have no problems with PED's because it is league approved and monitored."

"After seeing the success we had with the supplements more and more people came to us looking to benefit from our research. One of our players suffered a serious spinal cord injury and Mr. P. was beside himself. He came to me right away to see what could be done. He genuinely loves his players as much or in some cases more than his family and he was devastated to see this player hurt so grievously. We have been doing a lot of research with nitrogen therapy, keeping the spinal cord from swelling and have had much success with that and stem cell regeneration. It was the stem cell research that intrigued Mr. P. and he came to me one night pitching the idea of cloning players. At first I thought he had gone off the deep end, however after a bit of time thinking about it, I thought, what an opportunity to expand my research. I have to admit I became blinded by the possibilities. I saw only the chance to honor my brother's memory and save lives."

"I threw myself into the work. Between what we already knew about proteins, stem cells, and genetic codes, cloning was the next evolution. The work went very quickly producing stunning results. Within a few years we had cloned our first human. The subject was one of our lab technicians who had been a chain smoker and had developed lung cancer. The cloning was successful but we had to find a way to grow the clone to full grown and not just an infant of the subject. By using a chamber similar to the hyperbaric chambers we were able to accelerate the growth rate just enough to bring the subject to full growth within month's rather than years. The research has progressed to the point where a full grown clone can be ready in a few weeks instead of months. Once we were able to achieve this, the idea of using clones as football players became feasible. Again using the Chambers we conditioned the subjects mind to simulate years of practice and playing games."

"We have a separate practice facility underground on which our clones practice until they are at a proficient level to perform. Then we augment their memories to believe they are actual players. When a clone hits that field they are literally a mirror image on and off the field of the actual player. So anyone worried about the legitimacy of the games be rest assured these players are the real deal. Mr. P. would not have it any other way and he wanted not to damage the game in any way."

There was an eerie hush in the court room as the doctor finished his sentence. Jessica asked another question quickly, "Dr. Chase, although this research has allowed the game to continue, how do you respond to those who would say, you are playing God. What about the lives of these clones, do they not deserve every bit of life that we all do?" The doctor swallowed deeply before responding, "As I have already admitted, I had tunnel vision when it came to my research. My drive was that of many of the athletes I work with, one with a chip on their shoulders, one that would not be denied! I just saw it as a way to help all mankind. So much of my research will be able to help everyone; currently my team is working on ways to slow the aging process. We are close! I am always looking for ways to help others. As for a life, the way I understand the process is the clones when their service to us is complete they have their memory erased and then they are enlisted into the military. It is at that point that my research ends because they now belong to the government."

Jessica turned to the judge, "Judge Azawa, we have repeatedly requested access to these soldiers themselves as well as their records and programs. The government has requested and was granted an injunction on the grounds that any information used in this trial would put the Nation at risk. The defense is aware of this and we cannot offer any further information on what happens to these men when they go into the military. She turned once more to the doctor, "One final question, Dr. Chase how would your brother feel about what you have done, in his memory? Would he feel you have honored him the way you said you always wanted?"

The usually very stoic Doctor choked back his emotions at this question and was visibly shaken, being on the verge of tears. It took several moments and throat clears for the doctor to respond. "He would understand," as if questioning himself, "He would understand. If what I have done saves even one life, then I will have honored my brother greatly. He lived everyday as if it were his last long before he ever knew he was sick. He inspired me every day and continues to do so today! What I will say is I am not proud of how everything has turned out. What I thought was a great opportunity has turned out to be my ultimate shame. I will never be able to view my work the same or another human being for that matter. That is if I am even allowed to continue my work. My brother always told me I would be famous. I just did not think he meant infamous. All the work I have done to help others has been the cause of so much pain. The last thing I wanted was any of this to happen!" Jessica smiled sympathetically, "Thank you Doctor Chase, no further questions."

The Judge turned to the defense, "Your witness councilor." George, with an extremely determined look on his face strode toward the doctor. "Dr. Chase, your story is rather touching, however you would have us believe that Mr. P. is the mastermind behind everything, but is it not true, that you are the real ring leader. After all it is all your research is it not? It is

261

the reason we are all here is it not?" Jessica stood quickly, raising an objection for badgering the witness. The Judge was not swayed, allowing the question to stand and waited for the Doctor to respond. The doctor looked at George, "I am responsible for myself and my staff. I have neither funded nor done any research that was not requested, no pleaded by Mr. P. for me to perform to save his precious team! If I am the ring leader, then he is the Puppet Master!"

George was taken back by this response and quite unprepared for this, he always remembered the doctor as a meek and polite man in his previous dealings. He was caught off guard by the strength of conviction the doctor had before him. Regrouping he continued, "Doctor, we have seen the success of your cloning before our eyes but is it not true that there have been epic failures as well!" The doctor had anticipated this question and was ready with a response, "With any research on any living organism there is failure. In nature there is always a struggle to adapt in order to survive." George cut in, "Pardon me doctor but we are not dealing with nature here are we? You have all but forgotten that step! We are really dealing with science and if you want to go a little further, Science Fiction comes to life!" The doctor retorted, "Yes, science, science that studies nature. Over the centuries man has changed, adapted to survive in his environment. For example, once man had teeth much like that of a wolf or even a large cat with which he could rip and tear food. These teeth we still have, they are still called K-9's, but today they are less sharp and not quite so large. That if you will is natural science. Even today with all our modern medicine not every child is born perfect, are we to say that these children are failures!"

There was rage in his eyes looking at George and just as he was to continue, George countered. "Dr. Chase, funny you should mention children. You are not married, correct?" Dr. Chase gritted his teeth, "No, I am not married!" George smiled, "Do you have any children?" At this the doctor turned ghostly white and beads of perspiration appeared on his forehead, "No, I do not have any children." George seemed to move on, "Yes, I could see where a man in your position would have little time for love or a family." The doctor looked at him with hatred. George smirked, "Now doctor with all that time spent on research and working on other humans, I am surprised you never tried to create your own." The doctor could be seen on the screen in a full sweat now. George pressed his advantage, "But wait, doctor my sources tell me that you did just that! Did you or did you not create another human being using your own DNA!" At this the doctor's eyes rolled back in his head and before their eyes he passed out, falling to the floor.

The entire courtroom could see doctors and nurses rushing to help Dr. Chase. A doctor came on the screen and apologized, saying the stress must have been too much for him this soon. They moved the doctor back to his bed. On the screen, it was easy to see the doctor looked ghastly white. The doctors moved in around him working to revive him. As this was going on the judge noticed the entire courtroom was to the point of tears. The Judge called for a short recess so he could check on the status of the witness.

George returned to Mr. P. with a bright smile. Mr. P. chuckled, "Well George, and here I thought you were a pussy cat. It is about time I started getting my money's worth out of you!" George looked genuinely hurt. Mr. P. smiled, "George, you have worked for me for a long time and I have never seen

263

you go bulldog on someone until now. It is rather impressive. It is great to see that out of you, I wish we had seen it sooner, that is all." George defended himself, "Mr. P. with all due respect, you threw me into a case where all of your own people are lined up to testify against you. Not only that, they all have great cause to see you brought to justice!" Mr. P. winced, "George, I know but let's finish with Dr. Chase and then focus on me." George just shook his head vigorously, "Mr. P., I am telling you, this is a bad idea! You may survive the trial but then what? Won't the government themselves come after you?" Mr. P. looked weakly at George, "That is a chance I am going have to take. I have ways of moving around and disappearing more than most."

When court returned, the atmosphere was solemn. Many immediately looked to the monitor to see how the doctor was faring. The doctor was resting comfortably in his bed and seemed to have his color back. The judge announced that the doctor would answer the final question asked by the defense but that would be the extent of his testimony due to medical considerations. George walked to the monitor, "Doctor Chase, would you please tell the court, did you use your own DNA to create a human being?" A definite look of panic struck the doctor's face, "I had always thought I would be married by now. In my tunnel vision focus to continue my research there just never seemed to be any time to find someone. As I was getting older and the likelihood of me finding a wife faded the thirst for a child never did! Women can use their eggs and still give birth without a man, but a man wishing to have a child; well that is another matter entirely in our society!"

"As my research progressed to the point that cloning a human being became reality, I also ventured into the possibility of having my own child. When one of my dear colleagues got sick and was beyond help, she too had always wanted a family so she donated an egg to me and asked that I fulfill both our dreams with a child. I debated with myself untold times about the consequences of having a child in this manner. In the end I simply wanted a child so badly nothing else mattered and I would let nothing stand in my way. I used both natural and genetic engineering to create a human being, yes."

The air seemed to be let out of the courtroom. No one breathed for several seconds. A look around the room by George revealed the opposite reaction he had hoped for, one of anger. In its place, every face George viewed had a genuine look of sympathy and compassion for the man who wanted a family. Many of the people sitting in the courtroom that day had been in the doctor's very shoes struggling to have a family and children. George almost choked himself as he asked his next question, "Doctor Chase, is that person in this courtroom today?" The doctor's face blushed but had a proud look to it but yet he still seemed to stave off the faintness, "Yes," he stammered, "That person is in the courtroom today." There was a collective gasp by the members of the media, jury, and other family members in the courtroom. George continued, "Dr. Chase would you please identify that person for the court, the person here that is your dependent!"

Jessica shot up to object but the doctor saw her and raised her hand to ask her to sit. With an embarrassed but prideful face the doctor answered, "I have wanted so much to tell my child everything but could never face them. As hard as this is, I am glad I finally get to tell her about her father." As soon as Dr. Chase said this everyone in the courtroom turned in unison to look at Jessica. Jessica laughed slightly, "Not me folks, my mom and dad were from Boston!" Dr. Chase looked to the bench toward Chris and April, with a look of immeasurable pride the doctor's eyes came to rest on April. April as though having an electrical shock, her eyes almost popped out of her head. "I remember my mom and dad; I know they passed away when I was young." Dr. Chase answered, "April, those are memory implants, I am sorry!" There were tears streaming down the doctor's cheeks and he couldn't look at the monitor anymore. The head doctor appeared on the screen and announced that the doctor needed rest.

George tried to get April's testimony thrown out with various arguments concerning her paternity as well as her personal closeness to the case. None of which flew and the Judge would not hear of it putting the councilor in his place. Having his arguments put right back in his face once again left George with nothing. George knew that he was throwing the long ball but really had no choice at this point in the case. With that settled George went back to report to Mr. P. how things now stood.

George sat with Mr. P. after the court session ended for the day. "Mr. P., we are really up against it here. Our strategy to break down Dr. Chase has backfired. The whole court just wanted to give the doctor a hug instead of putting him in jail." Mr. P. said, "George, we have been fish swimming upstream this whole trial. All we could hope to do is discredit and hope the jury saw things our way. We have one last trick up our sleeve; let's see how it plays out."

Chapter 31

After the day's events, April practically ran out of the courtroom. She had not said anything else after the doctor had finished his testimony. Chris raced after her and slipped his hand in hers. She turned slightly, smiling she continued toward the SUV. April did not say a word but clasped his hand warmly and led him to the car. The ride to the restaurant was quite uneventful and everyone walked in very subdued. Once inside, April asked if the group would come visit Dr. Chase with her. Everyone just looked at one another as if to see who would say, yes or no. There was nervousness in the air; no one seemed to want to answer wrong. April looked at her friends, "Guys, listen, I am totally freaked out by this and I have no idea what I am supposed to think or do about any of this at this point! The one thing I do know is, I cannot do this by myself and I do not even want to try. I would appreciate as many of you as will go with me as may."

Christopher came up to her and put a sympathetic hand on her shoulder, "We are here, whatever you need! I am so glad for you, that you know the truth and you have a father." A pang of sorrow shot through April. She had grown up surrounded by people who loved he or so she thought. Christopher, on the other hand had no one, no family, no home, and no history. She immediately hugged Christopher tight and when she finally broke away she just looked into his eyes telling him she understood everything. Christopher just held her at arm's length for a moment. When they broke there seemed to be a growing bond between them as a brother and a sister would have. The type of bond once forged no one; no one would be ever able to put a rift between these two.

Doctor Chase was sitting up comfortably in his hospital bed when they arrived. As they walked in the room a look of panic was on the doctor's face until he saw April. His eyes let up at the sight of her. The rest of the group offered a cordial greeting and moved swiftly to the side, allowing April total access to the Doctor. April moved with uncertainty toward Dr. Chase, "What am I to call you? Should I call you father?" Dr. Chase smiled a warm smile, "you may call me what you wish. I am honored to know you at all and to see you become the woman you are has been more than any father could hope for!"

At this, April leaned over the doctor and engulfed him in a smothering embrace. The doctor at once let out a wail and tears flowed as he embraced her back. The two held on to each other for what seemed a moment frozen in time forever. When they let each other go, they just sat looking at each other through watery eyes. April sat in a chair right next to the doctor's bed and continued to look longingly at Dr. Chase. Chris came up behind April and said nothing but yet stood for moral support. Dr. Chase began, "April I cannot begin to tell you how excited I am that you now know. I have spent many long years thinking about this day and what I would say to you. I practiced a long speech in front of the mirror thousands of times and all I can do now is stare, smiling at you!"

April sat there smiling and took his hand in hers. "All those years working together, how could you keep everything secret? I have to tell you I am having mixed feelings right now but I have to tell you, I always had this feeling that you were more to me than a colleague. I should have known, you have always been there for me at every turn." Dr. Chase looked into her eyes, "I thought it better to support you through actions rather than a title. I felt if you go to know me then when I eventually got up the courage to tell you that you might not hate me." April responded, "I could never hate you, but truthfully I am still in shock. I have no idea how I am going to feel tomorrow or even the next day." Dr. Chase shook his head, "I know, I am just so glad to see you!"

April just sat looking at her father, just the notion causing overwhelming thoughts, she just held his hand. Chris motioned everyone to go and they followed him into the hallway. Chris started, "I just want to give them some time alone. This has been a huge shock to everyone. I can't imagine how April is feeling right now. If you all want to go back to the restaurant, I will catch up to you later. I just want to be here in case she might need me. Jessica led the others back down the hall toward the car. She turned briefly to look at Chris one more time and winked as she turned the corner and disappeared.

Chris sat in the chair outside Dr. Chase's room and picked up a copy of the latest, "Sporting Life." He opened the magazine right to an article of all things, about himself! He laughed but continued to read, imagining how the story would be written now with all that had taken place. He had always just considered himself an ordinary American kid. His life to this point had been a living dream turned to nightmare overnight. Chris sat for a moment, he was going to have to talk to Gus and have a him continue to tell his story. He knew from his experience with the media that he would never be left alone now. Trusting Gus to write his story would be the only way to control anything that was put out in the media.

Would he ever make it on the field again? This was his last thought until he felt a hand on his shoulder. Realizing he had dozed off, he looked up to see April's beautiful face. Chris stood, "Is everything alright?" April smiled, "Better than you might imagine. You would think I would be more upset but truly I am somewhat relieved to know the truth. He is resting now. The day's events have exhausted him as might be expected. I stayed for a while but I really need to take a walk to clear my head. Would you walk with me?" Chris stood to his full height, "It would be my distinct pleasure, where to?" April touched her stomach, "Can we start at the Cafe, I am starving." Chris smiled, "Lead on, the quickest way to a man's heart is through his stomach. So I have been told." April laughed, "It's that easy huh, then how come it took me this long to meet you?"

April took him by the hand and led them to the Café. It was late at night and the guests in the café were sparse. The couple chose a secluded booth and sat down to eat. They were both so hungry that they said very little to one another until they had finished. April broke the silence, "Chris, everything has changed. What are we going to do? Mr. P. most certainly is going to be found guilty, then what do we do? Are we going to be able to go back to work for the team? Will it be sold, Mr. P has no heirs!" Chris had been thinking much the same as the trial continued to progress and it looked more like things would go their way. Chris said, "April, I have no idea what is going to happen. By the time everything is said and done. I am going to miss most of my rookie season. That does not bode well for a football player. The one thing I am sure of is You! I know one thing, if none of this happened, I would not have found you!" He reached over the table softly cupping her face with his hands. "I like that you have learned some amazing things about my friends and myself. Things I never would have thought possible. Whatever happens from this moment on, I am with you. We will figure it out together!" He took her hand in his and kissed it gently. They sat for what seemed to be an eternity starring into each other's eyes like teenagers on their first date.

The mood was broken by an alarm going off, bringing the couple back to reality. They stood looking at one another and at the same time shouted, "The Doctor!" The couple raced to the doctor's room and saw security crawling all over the place. A tall security guard came over and informed them that the doctor had gone missing. He further went on to explain that security footage shows him leaving the room in a coat and not returning. The security guard apologized telling them the doctor was not a prisoner and occasionally had taken walks but always returned. April thanked the man and turned to Chris, "What does he think he is doing! He is no condition to be going anywhere!" Chris just shrugged his shoulders, "April honey, I am still trying to figure that guy out. Is he friend or foe, villain or hero, I just don't know!"

Agent Bradley returned to pick them up, "Listen you guys, I have no idea what Dr. Chase is up to. I do know however, he is more afraid of what the government might do to him than the law. He might be trying to go underground. He is a grown man that can take care of himself. We have to concern ourselves with Mr. P. and what he is going to say tomorrow." April got very close to Agent Bradley, "After this is over, we are going to find Dr. Chase and I'm going to kill him!" Agent Bradley patted her arm, "It would be my pleasure to help you with that. Now let's get back and get ready for tomorrow."

Everyone was extremely anxious as they walked into the courtroom. They all simply had no idea what Mr. P. had up his sleeve. To this point in the case he had offered little resistance. Everyone knew Mr. P. as a fighter, so they could not understand why they had not seen much fight out of him to this point. He had not become a billionaire by playing patty cake with people. The owner of the Marauders had forged a true path in his league and others had turned to him for guidance. Almost at every turn Mr. P. had always covered his back and come out swinging. During this entire trial, it seemed as though he had been resigned to his fate. This made everyone come to the conclusion that something big was coming quickly. What could he possibly have in his back pocket that they did not know about? Jessica had been amazing in her preparations for the case. Her attention to detail was staggering and she had stoned George at each turn.

Jessica addressed them quickly, "Whatever happens today, realize the jury is in your corner. When Mr. P. comes out, he is going to try something major, but at this point it will seem to the jury as just a desperate act. Just keep calm and focused so we can finish him off. They all marveled at her confidence. This calmed them all down and they took their seats ready for action. Everyone looked around the room to see by chance if Dr. Chase had made his way back. When they could not make him out in the crowd, they all turned to focus on the trial.

Judge Azawa came in much like he did every day and the trial got underway promptly. The judge did something out of character and requested the councilors come to the bench. As Jessica and George walked to the bench and looked at each other as if to ask, "why is the judge asking this of us?" The judge's purpose as it turned out was to inform Jessica that the defense only had one witness. This of course was highly irregular; usually the defense would try to rebut each of the prosecution's witnesses. Also the defense usually had a doctor of their own to refute evidence brought about by the prosecution. In this case George, had one witness, Mr. P. and that was it.

The judge eyed George, "Councilor, Mr. P. is fighting for his life! Are you sure you do not need a brief stay to invite some more witnesses?" At this, Jessica raised her eyebrows but chose not to say anything. George looked at the judge with genuine gratitude, "Judge Azawa, normally I would take you up on that offer and I would have multiple witnesses lined up. In this case however, no amount of witnesses is going to change the outcome of this trial!" The judge understood and dismissed them.

Jessica was still in shock when she sat down. She informed everyone what was happening but could not explain why Mr. P. had chosen this strategy. They were just as surprised as Jessica but smiled at each other at their continued good fortune. The entire group watched as George called his lone witness, Mr. P. to the stand. Mr. P. stood and pulled his suit jacket down straight while making sure his tie was correct. He walked slowly and with purpose to the stand and sat down calmly. George followed Mr. P. and looked at him questioning eyes. Mr.P. returned a gaze to urge his councilor to continue.

George stood up straight, "Mr. P. much has been said during this trial about your involvement in cloning human beings. How do you respond to the accusation that you are directly responsible for the cloning of human beings?" Mr. P. with steel in his eyes looked up at George, "How do I respond, well that is an interesting question. I have listened for weeks as people sat up here and degraded me. My team has been dragged through the mud. Every tabloid and media outlet in the world have taken their turn destroying me! There is only one thing that these people are missing; I am not guilty of any of these accusations!" George nervously asked his next question, "Mr. P., you say you are not guilty but as the trial has progressed even I would find it hard to believe that you were not guilty. How can you prove to this court that you are beyond a doubt, not guilty?"

Mr. P. Looked straight at the jury through bright brilliant eyes, "Because, I am not Mr. P.!" He let that soak in for a minute. Everyone in the courtroom had a look of complete befuddlement on their faces. Mr. P. had a sly smile on his face, "I mean, I am Mr. P. but not in the way you think! I am a replica or a clone of Mr. P." There was dead silence in the courtroom. Even Judge Azawa, who was always in complete control looked baffled. He sat at the bench staring into space with a blank look on his face. Then the courtroom became a beacon on activity of hushed tones and whispers. No one seemed to know how to proceed. Christopher had been one thing to take in but had been a non-descript person. Here, before everyone however was the owner of a professional football team claiming to be a clone.

The judge scanned the room and saw almost everyone on some type of electronic device trying to get the information out to the public. This was definitely something he had not foreseen. Judge Azawa was all about control and in this case it seemed he had never really had a firm grip. He had exerted his will time and time again keeping things from flying apart. This time however, this might be one bombshell too many and his ruling would be twice as important. The judge raised his hands up waiting for people to quiet down and then began to speak, "Councilors in my chambers, NOW!"

The crowd hushed as people do when others are in trouble. George and Jessica followed the judge to his chambers. Usually the judge handled everything with a calm demeanor but the councilors sat before him and they immediately sensed the rage rising from the judge. The judge spoke, "I do not like being made a fool of! You two have done everything in your power to create this Kangaroo Court!" He turned to George burning wholes through him with his eyes, "You! You have total disregard for procedure and protocol! This is in my eyes the ultimate in Grand Standing! As if there was not enough shock and awe to this case, you go and add more! You know very well this information should be inadmissible due to the prosecution not being given proper discovery time. This information was purposefully withheld and you know damn well that could cause a mistrial!"

George sheepishly looked at the judge, "I had no idea that was what he was going to do! Honestly, I am just as shocked as anyone! I have offered strategy after strategy to Mr. P. and he would not follow any of my advice. I am just a mouthpiece. He wouldn't tell me anything and all he kept telling me is that he was not sunk just yet." George sat in his chair and the judge took him in. George looked a wreck; he was pale and drawn with his hair straw like. His suit usually pressed was disheveled and wrinkled with stains on his tie. One look at George told the judge all he needed to know. The truth was this version of Mr. P. had been playing games with them all. He dismissed the lawyers and sat back in his chair contemplating his next move.

Chapter 32

Emerging from his chambers the judge strode to the bench and remained standing to address the courtroom. "I am going to allow the testimony to stand based on the outline already described in this trial previously. There does however remain the matter at hand and that is what to do with Mr. P., "You have the right to be a witness, it remains to be seen if these charges will ultimately apply to you!" Mr. P. bowed his head with sheer gratitude, he could not have asked for more. He had added to the element of doubt to the case and hopefully it was enough to save him. George continued his line of questioning, "Mr. P. would you please tell the court how you came to be in this position as owner of the Marauders?"

Mr. P. began, "Most of what I know may very well be memory implants but I will tell you what I know and the things I definitely remember. My first memories that I am sure are my own, is working with a medical team as they put me through rigorous testing. After my tests, I was introduced to the real Mr. P.. Mr. P. informed me that he had a terminal form of lung cancer. He had sought every possible treatment but because of the fragile nature of lung tissue there was nothing that reversed his condition. He went on to describe how this was the only way to ensure his legacy and make sure the team survived intact. At first I had no idea what he was talking about until I walked by a mirror and noticed my reflection. It was Mr. P.'s reflection and during my testing I realized I had never viewed myself in a mirror. The shock was overwhelming but after talking more with Mr. P. I began to understand."

"It was quite a bit to handle, being told you are going to take over day to day operations of a professional sports franchise. I had just found out whom I was supposed to be. Mr. P. seemed so sure this would work seamlessly but as I spoke to him I was not so confident. Not only that, when he told me, I had no frame of reference to run the team. The only business sense I had was how to present a credit card to someone to pay for a suit. How could I be expected to run a professional team. The medical team continued to work on me to update my memories to meet those of Mr. P.'s himself. I may not be the original but, I am him in every way possible. I can tell you anything you would like to know about Mr. P's life before me."

"Although I understand the question before this court stands, Did I have direct involvement in Human Cloning? The answer simply is, No, I did not. Now I was privy to the fact that this was taking place under my watch." He paused, "That my friends is the ultimate question. According to my memories, I knew everything that was going on; however, this is where things are a little hazy for me. I truly cannot tell you whether I actually saw this taking place or they are simply memories. The only actual physical contact if you will was when we were trying to bring Chris and company in to contain everything!"

George's eyes were like those of a deer in the headlights look, "Mr. P. when did the real Mr. P. pass away and how was this kept quiet?" Mr. P. thought a moment, "According to what I remember, it was about a year ago when he finally succumbed. I have been running the team since." George raised his hand, "Again, how was this kept quiet and did Dr. Chase have anything to do with this?" Mr. P. had a puzzled look, "Well I really do not know what actually happened to Mr. P. The actual day he passed I was with the medical team and no

278

as far as I know Dr. Chase had nothing to do with me. That is he was my employee and led the research, but he never once mentioned anything about my situation. The only thing I remember that was odd or out of the ordinary was a man in a military uniform that came to speak to my medical team. When I asked, the team quickly changed the subject."

George ended his questions, which in most eyes left more questions to be answered. Even George at this point did not know where to go and finished looking for more. Jessica then rose to cross examine, which once again was new territory, because of the whole revelation before her. Jessica glanced at Christopher and walked with purpose toward Mr. P., "Sir," she began, "You state that you are a clone but yet what proof can you offer that this is not some attempt on your part to skirt blame for your crimes!"

At this a surprised look came across Mr. P.'s face. He quite clearly had not expected this line of questioning. He recovered enough to answer, "In terms of being able to provide evidence, my Medical Team, they disappeared shortly after I took over day to day operations of the team. The only substantial proof I can offer is the microchip attached behind the ear of each clone. This chip from what I understand allows the medical staff to adjust memories and cognitive thinking." Mr. P. then stood and turned a quarter turn lifting his ear lobe to reveal a small metallic device attached to his skull right behind the right ear. Jessica viewed this and made him walk to the jury so they might see.

Jessica did not look convinced, "That is interesting but anyone could put a fake chip in that area easily. What further proof can you offer?" Mr. P. shrugged his shoulders, "The only other thing I can think of is something the medical teams mentioned briefly and that is a special sequence of proteins used on all clones to accelerate their growth to a certain point. I am sure you could test for that. Dr. Chase can confirm all this I am sure as well." This seemed to Jessica to be a dead end. She asked one final question, "Sir, why did you have Steve use any physical means necessary to capture Chris and his friends, but yet when it came right down to it you couldn't finish the job!"

A question like this threw everyone for a loop. This was the type of question the defense would ask. George even looked up with renewed hope in his eyes. For the first time all trial it seemed Jessica had stumbled. Mr. P. was even caught off guard, "My dear, whatever Mr. P. may have been or what I may be, we are certainly not killers. I have really come to value life, probably more than most others and my players are part of my family. Everyone from time to time becomes mad with a family member and Chris is no different in that regard needing to be put in his place. Even with all these life memories, every day I find myself learning what it means to be more human, if you will. As the case progressed I became less Mr. P. and more myself putting Chris in my own shoes. I know it was and still is a lot to handle finding out about cloned human beings and our impact on people's daily lives."

Jessica did not expect this answer but pushed on, "Sir, then it would devastate you to find that the military uses the clones in highly dangerous training exercises only to kill those who survive!" This shocked everyone in the room. Mr. P. looked helpless, "If that is true, that is deplorable and despicable!" Jessica smiled, "Yes, it is! Now imagine that you yourself have provided the military the clones for these killer exercises for the last year. I wonder how many that could actually be, hundreds! You Sir, are quite possibly responsible for the murder of hundreds of people!" Before George could object or Mr. P. could even answer Jessica walked away saying, "No further questions."

The shocking news of the military's involvement to this point had meant nothing. Jessica and company had not been able to find much hard evidence beyond the training exercises in the military's role. Unlike Mr. P, the military had covered their tracks. For Jessica however, she was laying the groundwork for going after the government next. Whether Mr. P. was a clone or not would not change the fact that he was responsible for supplying hundreds of clones to the military. Jessica, if she could prove what was being done to the clones she would go down in the annals of law as a legend.

All attempts to contact the government in order to obtain cooperation had failed. With no further witnesses, Jessica had no choice but to wrap up her case. She spent the night rifling through her notes trying to produce the perfect closing argument. Jessica wrote and re-wrote her statement at least fifty times. She kept reading it to herself over and over without feeling it was good enough. In the end, she decided that the case really spoke for itself and all she would have to do is keep her statement straight to the point. After going over her statement for one final time she rose from her desk and went to the kitchen for a drink of water. Walking past her sleeping friends, for the first time she noticed that Doctor Chase's belongings were no longer where they had always been. Even though she thought this odd, she retrieved a glass of water and returned to her notes. She reviewed her statement one more time turned in for the night.

At breakfast everyone was anxious with tempered enthusiasm. Jessica could sense this but told them they needed to keep an even keel until the verdict came back. She described how many times she had seen a case look as if it were going one way only to have it implode when handed to the jury. This put things into perspective for everyone and they all entered the courtroom with their best poker faces showing. Even George who throughout the entire case had seemed on the verge of falling apart seemed quite composed and confident. This did not sit well with Jessica.

The entire courtroom was dripping with anticipation and an anxious tension roamed the air. For most of the trial the courtroom had been a chaotic, circuslike atmosphere, but today it had an air of professionalism. The courtroom was once again overflowing with people, all in anticipation of what the prosecution and defense would say to surmise their cases. When Judge Azawa entered, he was all business and asked that they get right to closing arguments.

George as defense went first and walked confidently to the jury. He was dressed in a stylish, pin striped athletic cut suit. Jessica thought for the first time all trial that he looked the part of a power, high priced lawyer. George had wanted to convey this impression upon the jury for his final statement. As he began, he stood tall, confident and strong. He began by thanking the jury for allowing him the chance to address them. He stated how important it was to have the people working together to deal with cases of this magnitude. Then he unloaded, "Ladies and gentlemen of the jury, the defense would have you believe that my client is the master mind behind an illegal cloning ring. This could not be farther from the truth. My client is just as much a victim as everyone else in this case! He was created and tossed into an impossible situation with no regard for him as an individual. The real perpetrator here, unfortunately is no longer here to defend himself, but this does not absolve him of the atrocities he has committed. Left in his wake are all the victims in this courtroom. I would ask that each of you put yourself in my client's shoes. Imagine the world you thought was yours all along turns out to be nothing but an illusion. My client has done just that, his entire world had been destroyed. He has been left with no life of his own and accusations that do not belong to him. I ask, ladies and gentlemen that you consider this strongly while making your decision in this case. My client is beyond a shadow of a doubt not guilty of all charges. Please give him the chance at the life we all deserve. Thank you for your consideration." George, when finished walked slowly to his seat and sat with his face unreadable.

Jessica rose and walked with purpose toward the jury. She put her hands on the railing with conviction and began her oration, "Ladies and gentlemen of the jury, this case has proven to be anything but simple. You have before you many things to weigh when making your decision. The decision you make today will affect many trials and laws in the wake of this case. You as a jury will be the measuring stick for many cases yet to come. Your work here will ensure justice for those yet to come as well as those who are here today. Ladies and gentlemen, we have shown to great conclusion that Mr. P. was in fact as the owner of the Marauders, has indeed directly been responsible for the illegal cloning of human beings. Through Mr. P's direct actions the lives of natural born and clone alike have been irrevocably harmed. His unwillingness to accept any responsibility for the ruin of life now and yet to come says all we need to know about this case. Mr. P. is guilty of all charges and deserves to be punished to the fullest extent of the law! There is no doubt that Mr. P. needs to be accountable for his actions, therefore I ask that a verdict of guilty be brought back! A guilty verdict will speak volumes to those who would treat human beings in this way that you will be punished swiftly and justly! Thank you for your consideration. Jessica turned and returned to her seat.

She, like George had kept her statement short and to the point. They both wanted the jury to focus on the last thing they heard. Yes, much had been given to the jury during the trial but short focused facts now could be the difference between winning and losing at this point. Both attorneys' sat contemplating the effectiveness of their closing arguments. The jury and judge alike were also digesting the statements, while the media was waiting for the judge's reaction.

They did not have to wait long for the judge to respond. The Judge raised his hands and asked for silence. When the courtroom was silent he began, "Ladies and gentlemen, I know that this is the time in which I would give the jury their final instructions but today that will not be necessary." There was a collective gasp among the onlookers. Judge Azawa continued, "There are many elements of this case that are fully in my power to rule on, which I will. However, there are also elements that have no precedent and no law to allow for a proper ruling. Therefore, I have little choice but to take the case out of the hands of the jury and rule myself.

At this all eyes went wide in the courtroom. Everyone seemed to look around the room at one another as to question this stance. Even the veteran media had known from the outset that the judge would have his hands full with this case. For the judge, he was used to control, having the full force of the law to back his decisions. In this case he would have to interpret much as he ruled in order to dispense justice. What had played out in the media is that Judge Azawa had done a masterful job up to this point of handling the twists and turns of an immense case such as was before him. The judge had always been aware of the enormity of the case and he worked admirably to conduct the case in a professional manner.

Judge Azawa folded his hands and furrowed his brow, "Being aware of the intricate facets of this case, I have decided to rule without the use of the jury. As one who has to rule on laws and interpret laws, I am the most qualified in this case to do so. That does not in any way take away from the importance of the jury in this case or any case going forward. This case however has brought forth questions that will have to be addressed for many years to come by law makers and Juries alike. I am not a law maker and can therefore only judge the laws that are provided to me. In this case the laws I have to work with leave us all open to great scrutiny. This is something as an official of the law I try extremely hard not to allow considering the importance of the cases brought before me on behalf of the American people. With this in mind, I have chosen to rule on what the law allows to this point."

The judge thought for a moment, "In the matter at hand, whether or not Mr. P. is guilty of directly manufacturing clones, to this charge, I rule he is guilty. However this ruling being posthumous does little to dispense justice to his living victims. That leaves how to help those affected by these tragic events." He looked at Mr. P's clone, "Sir, would you please rise." Mr. P. did as instructed. He looked at the judge in a panic. "Sir, you I have to say, may be as much a victim as anyone in this case. With that said, you are still an accomplice to terrible reaching events. Due to your uncertain status with regard to the law, I cannot charge you as of yet. What I will do in the interest of justice is place the Boston Marauders in trust until such time as an owner can be found to purchase the team. The team will be held responsible for the wellbeing and acclamation of all current clones into society. The clones will be provided sufficient monetary and counseling support to enhance their transition. You sir will be held in protective custody until such time as the law can judge you properly."

"To the victims: you will also be given monetary awards commensurate with the amount of damage caused by the team's actions. I know this in no way makes up for the pain and suffering you have been through. The actual cash value will have to be settled upon before sale of the team takes place. My hope however, is that we will all have a chance to heal and move forward in our lives. My intent here is also is not to destroy an institution such as the Marauders, which provides so much joy to an entire community. The economic value to the community by the team cannot be understated as well and to punish those employees further would harm said community beyond repair."

Judge Azawa turned to Jessica, "To the prosecution, thank you for your courageousness in tackling this case." At this he laughed a bit. "You have opened doors for many others to walk through because of your work here. You have laid a great deal of groundwork for the law to follow for years to come. I cannot thank you enough for your thorough preparation and execution of your case from beginning to end. I hope this in some small way will help everyone return to some kind of normalcy. I wish you all the best. This case is now concluded,

Thank You!" The judge and the entire courtroom stood and watched the judge walkout into his chambers.

Chapter 33

For weeks following the trial all every media outlet could talk about was what would become of the clones and how people would react to them in society. There were pros and cons to be sure, yeys and neys but one thing was certain, the clones were now part of everyday life. They were living, breathing human beings in search of their own american dream. The same support people showed of the clones during the trial allowed many to assimilate into various neighborhoods with little or no fanfare. Most people were struggling to keep their own life together to get in the way of another human being searching for their own life. Only time would tell if the public would truly accept these engineered humans or would this be the beginning of a larger issue to come.

Chris and company had much healing to do in order to move on and put their own life back together. Although vindicated in most regards they still had so many unanswered questions. With their slates cleared they were able to try and work their way back into the rhythm of their own lives again. The Spector of what happened to them hung over their heads but yet galvanized them together in a way that was indescribable in words. This group would remain close friends for the rest of their lives.

Chris returned to play in the playoffs that year for his team. Even among all the distraction Coach Ridel had steadfastly maintained over his team guiding them forward through all the noise. Although personally playing well, Chris' team bowed out during the conference championship. Even despite the disappointment of no championship that year, the team was extremely proud of the way it had responded in the face of terrible adversity. Chris himself was amazed at how easily he was able to transition back into the game he loved. In spite of missing much of the season Chris' statistics were good enough to have him in the conversation for rookie of the year. The league then ruled that in light of Chris' circumstances he was allowed to be considered. His peers then voted unanimously for him to be a candidate and therefore he went on to win the Rookie of the Year Award.

Steve continued to work for the team as their head of security. He had been granted immunity from prosecution in exchange for his testimony as was Dr. Chase. It was decided by the team that Steve's knowledge of the team's inner workings would be an invaluable resource in the team's time of need. Steve helped dismantle the clone labs at the stadium and reorganized the nurses and lab technicians to work with the regular training and medical staff. He even seemed less rigid and one of the nurses who had a secret affection for him finally approached him. Things settled in nicely for Steve and he remained very close with the others.

April, out of the whole company but Christopher had the most questions. She was still coming to terms with being someone's engineered child and not of natural birth. Chris was very supportive and helped where he might. She spent a lot of time with the clones helping them assimilate to their new environments. Such unselfish acts as these made her even more of a celebrity than she already was. This new found fame for all her and her cohorts was both a blessing and a curse. She used her celebrity to help even more people but found that everyone wanted more and more of her time, media wise.

Her favorite thing to do of course was spend time with Chris. Of course this seemed less and less as more and more people wanted the couple's time. They made it a point however to see each other as often as possible. It seemed to be years instead of months when April had first taken Chris' vitals and become smitten during his team physical.

April's greatest question at this point had to do with Dr. Chase and his whereabouts. No one had seen or heard from Dr. Chase since his disappearance at the trial. Not so much as a text or email, it was as almost as if he had fallen off the face of the earth. Agent Bradley spent much of his time using his considerable resources to locate the doctor to no avail. This really bothered April, she just found out who her real father was, only to have him disappear. She was confused enough about the situation without having to try and wrap her mind around him no longer being in her life period. There had always been a certain comfort level with the doctor in her life which now was gone causing a vacant feeling.

Christopher with the knowledge of his new life and new found opportunity, spent much of his time trying to adjust. Coach Ridel had offered him a place on the practice squad for the time being so he could still be on the team. The coach let him know he only had so many slots available under league rules on the active roster so he might have to wait for a roster spot to become available. Christopher was just grateful to continue to practice with the team and he spent a lot of time with Chris. Jessica had offered to help Christopher with different aspects of assimilation, mainly taking him to dinner or the movies. The two had become fast friends and were quickly becoming inseparable.

Jessica continued to work on her case against the government and she had actually made some headway. She had found two former lab techs that were let go by the government. They did not want to cooperate but once they were subpoenaed and promised protection they began to give her a great deal of missing information she had been looking for. She continued to hunt down leads and information with Gus' and Agent Bradley's assistance. During her investigation she had noticed some inconsistencies in some emails she had run across. April worked tirelessly to make things right.

As the months began to pass, Jessica found that her work in Chris' case caused many people to open their eyes to the uses of technology. People began to take a stand and no longer watch technology just pass them by. By nature technology is like a huge wave that continues to pick up steam as it crashes into shore, disrupting everything in its path. Jessica's office became swamped with phone calls and inquiries asking for her help in cases involving technology based healthcare. Jessica was faced with the reality that technology, though fantastic in many ways, needs to be kept in check.

Jessica was forced to open several more offices and focus just on technology based healthcare cases. Her team was just as committed as she to see justice prevail. The largest issue they faced with the law is creating and enforcing laws took a great deal of time in most cases. Technology on the other hand waited for no one. The speed with which technology upgraded itself continued to be cause for great frustration among law makers. As soon as a law was passed and instituted it quickly became out of date due to new technology taking its place. The good news for Jessica and company was the fact that they all were forced to keep up to date with the very latest laws and technology. Jessica became the foremost lawyer in this regard and people from around the world sought her out to handle their cases.

Jessica kept in touch with everyone and they all became fast friends. The ordeal they had all endured had forged a bond that not many outside their group would understand. To Chris' group their experience through this whole situation had left an unbreakable mark on their lives which allowed them to turn their attention to help others. Each member of their companionship had volunteered without being asked to help Jessica in her fight for justice. The courage they all showed continued to be remarkable and people for generations to come would benefit from the work the all signed up for.

Chapter 34

One day Jessica called them all together at the restaurant. The restaurant was no longer a hide out. Agent Bradley's family had chosen to open it again and it was thriving in light of its new found celebrity because of its use during the trial. It became a hub for lawyer and justice seekers alike. Jessica greeted her friends warmly at the door. "It is wonderful to see you all, thank you for coming." April said, "Jessica it sounded urgent on the phone is everything alright?" Jessica smiled, "Fine April, I have some interesting news for you." They stared at her and all at once said, "Well?" Jessica continued, "I was looking through various emails and research the doctor had given to me to prepare for the next case. I was logged into one of his old accounts when I saw someone remotely logging into his account. Agent Bradley helped me triangulate the position where the log in occurred. It is about a half an hour away would you like to go with me to check it out?"

Even before answering April was on the move toward the door. They piled into Agent Bradley's vehicle and sped toward the newly discovered location. After driving for about twenty minutes, April announced she recognized the area. The area was a place for recreation along a lake. April had been here once with Doctor Chase for a cookout and a day of fun with some co-workers. Chris looked out the window admiring the serene location. He thought to himself what a great place this would be to get away from it all and still not be far away from civilization. Within a few minutes the lake itself came into view. Through the trees they could make out the sunlight glistening like diamond droplets on the water.

Then all at once the lake opened up before them and Agent Bradley stopped for everyone to take it in. The majesty of the lake was awe inspiring and everyone in the SUV sat dumbstruck. After everything they had been through, to see such beauty before them made the stress just melt away. Agent Bradley continued along a dirt road until they pulled up to large log cabin. The cabin itself looked rustic which included an old fashioned water pump. The grounds around the cabin were immaculately taken care of along with a path leading directly to the edge of the lake. They made their way up onto the porch and turned for a moment to look once again at the beautiful surreal panoramic view available to them. The lake itself seemed to rise up to greet them and they could see people in canoes further out in the water.

April reached for the handle of the door but before she had a chance to grab it, the door opened. To their shock, standing in the doorway was Doctor Chase. The doctor stood looking at them for a moment, "Well, it took you long enough! I did after all leave you a trail of bread crumbs!" The inside of the cabin was rustic but homey and they immediately felt comfortable. Dr. Chase strode over to April and engulfed her in an embrace. While holding each other, tears came streaming out of their eyes. After breaking the embrace, they noticed another man standing behind Dr. Chase. April viewed the man speculatively with some recognition. Dr. Chase turned to put his hand on the man's shoulder, smiling from ear to ear, "Everyone, I would like for you to meet my brother!"

Epilogue

A small wispy four year old girl sits on the ground with two dolls in her hands. Her beautiful curls bouncing gently in the wind, she peers out between the slats from underneath the bench. She is scanning the field for her brother. Seeing her brother tackle another boy on the football field she squeals with delight. As young as she is she is no stranger to football and is a regular in the practice huddles bringing the boys water. Although a soccer player herself, she has come to enjoy watching her brother play. She hears her mother's voice searching for her and with a sneaky smirk she reaches out and grabs her mother's ankle causing a surprised squeak from her mother.

Still laughing she emerges from her bunker and jumps up each of the stairs until she plows into her mother's arms. Her mother just engulfs her in a hug laughing at the little tomboy struggling to be a little girl. She is covered in dirt from head to toe with jeans that seem to have more holes than fabric. Her sneakers are so worn and filthy that one cannot tell what color the shoes once were. Mom sets her on the bench beside her and tells her they are going to have to hose her down before she comes in the house today. She just looks at her mom and asks when the game will be over. Her mother assures her there are just few minutes left and they will be driving home shortly. The little girl not even listening to the response is already scrambling down the bleachers toward the field.

Two booming laughs ring out together. The two men who to the stranger's eyes would just look like identical twins are looking at one another with their hands on each other's shoulder. Chris and Christopher watch the little girl run straight to the coach. Chris turns, "One of these days she is going to run straight on the field and clobber someone!" Christopher laughs again, "I want some of her energy. She is a little tornado!" Chris responds, "It is definitely hard to keep up with her!"

With the game ending the two giant men lumber down the bleachers and reach the sidelines in no time to meet the players as they come off the field. The little girl already has her brother's helmet in her hands and walking in front of her brother. Chris and Christopher join the small girl and the sweat smeared boy who is also joined by another game weary boy in the same uniform. Both boys high five Chris and Christopher, Chris chimes in, "You guys played a great game today, how was it out there?" Both boys looked at Chris and together said, "We rocked it out there today!"

The boys went on to describe their epic battle against the other team and the referee's. Their tale wove together an intricate battle of deception and power that in the end won them the game. Even though the boys were just finishing their elementary school career, to listen to them describe the game in such detail was impressive to the two former professional football players. Both fathers looked at their respective sons with a look of unquenchable pride.

The small group was soon met by two stunning women. April and Jessica came walking up to the group with snacks and drinks. April began, "Perks of working the snack bar, anyone hungry?" Everyone's face lit up and eagerly grabbed a snack with a drink. They then found a picnic table and each found a comfortable spot. On this crisp fall afternoon, the sun still had that warming quality.

This merry gathering was in full swing when they were joined by two more men. Doctor Chase and his brother made their way to the table. They were warmly greeted and quickly fit into the festivities. Anyone viewing this scene would automatically think of one of those surreal pictures in a magazine. This celebration however was real. Anyone who knew these people knew how genuine their love for one another was and how strong a bond there was between these folks.

Chris and April walked off a short distance to throw the trash anyway and just stood there starring at their brood. April started, "They go to junior high next year! Can you believe it! Pretty soon we will be looking for high schools and colleges! That is crazy! Where did the time go?" Chris looked lovingly at her, "We are so lucky! I can't believe we have such beautiful children!" With their hands held tight they walked back to their group as the rays of the late sunlit fall afternoon fell on their shoulders almost creating a force field around them.

47788431R00167

Made in the USA
Middletown, DE
02 September 2017